The Mapmaker's Eye

"I examined it
very carefully, and
made a map of it,
along with the rest." (Champlain, *Voyages*)

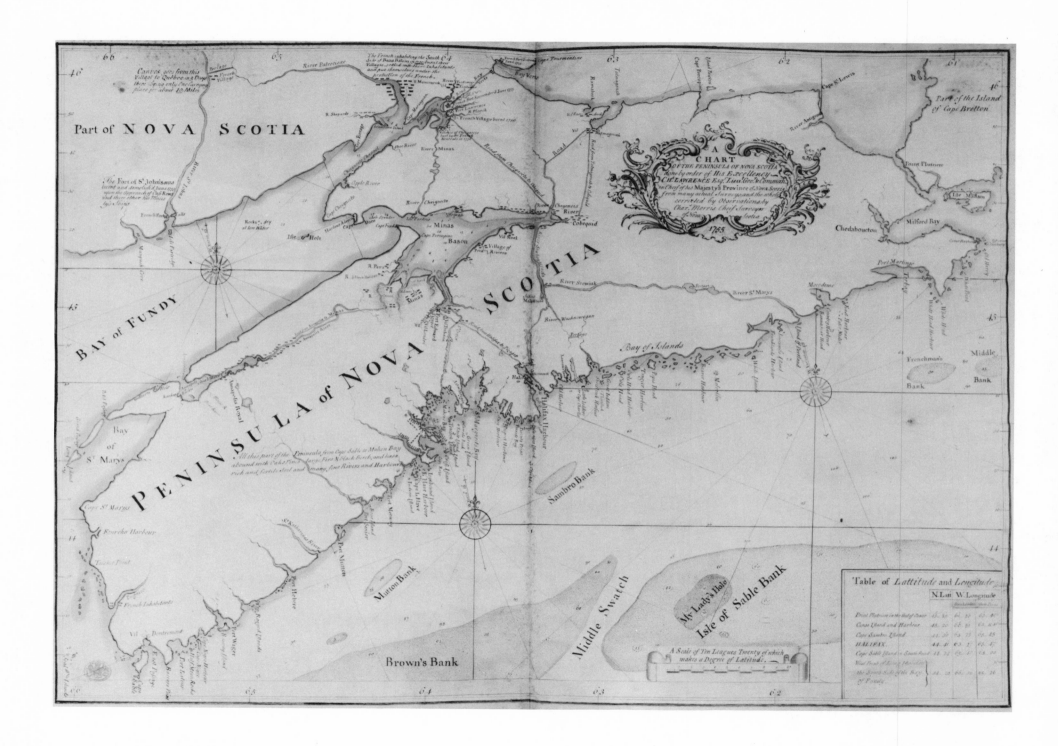

The Mapmaker's Eye

Nova Scotia Through Early Maps

Joan Dawson

co-published by
Nimbus Publishing Limited
and
The Nova Scotia Museum

Halifax, Nova Scotia
1988

© Crown copyright, The Province of Nova Scotia, 1988

The Department of Education

Nova Scotia Museum
All rights reserved.

Co-published by Nimbus Publishing Limited and the Nova Scotia
Museum as part of the Education Resource Services Program of the
Department of Education, Province of Nova Scotia

Minister: The Hon. Ronald C. Giffin
Deputy Minister: Blenis J. Nicholson

A product of the Nova Scotia Government Co-publishing Program.

Printed in Nova Scotia, Canada
Design: Kathy Kaulbach, Halifax, N.S.

Typesetting: Braemar Publishing Limited, Halifax, N.S.
Printing and Binding: McCurdy Printing & Typesetting Limited, Halifax, N.S.

Canadian Cataloguing in Publication Data

Canadian Cataloguing in Publication Data

Dawson, Joan, 1932–

   Mapmaker's eye

   Co-published by Nova Scotia Museum.
   Includes index.
   ISBN 0-921054-12-2

1. Cartography—Nova Scotia—History.   2. Nova Scotia—Maps—
To 1800.   I. Nova Scotia Museum.   II. Title.

GA475.N68D38 1988   912'.716   C88-098623-9

This book is dedicated, with love,
to my long suffering family —
Bob, Bobby and Peter;
and to David, for auld lang syne.

Contents

Maps and Illustrations

Acknowledgements

The maps in this book are reproduced by courtesy of the following institutions which hold the originals:

Canada

National Archives of Canada, Ottawa. Cartographic and Architectural Archives Division. Maps 1:1, 1:2, 2:4, 2:5, 2:7, 4:2, 4:3, 7:4, cover map.

National Library of Canada, Ottawa. Maps 2:1, 5:1, 7:1, 7:2, 7:3.

Dalhousie University, Halifax. Special Collections, Dalhousie University Library. Map 2:2a. (This acquisition has been made possible by a contribution from the Government of Canada under the terms of the Cultural Property Export and Import Act.)

Department of Lands and Forests, Nova Scotia. Map 7:1a.

Department of Lands and Forests, Nova Scotia. Research Section, Provincial Crown Records Centre. Map 7:9.

These maps are based on information taken from © Her Majesty the Queen in Right of Canada with permission of Energy, Mines and Resources Canada. Maps 2:1a, 3:2a, 3:5a, 5:1a, 5:2a, 7:3a.

Maritime Resource Management Service Inc., Amherst. Map 2:3a.

Nova Scotia Museum, Halifax. Map 7:8.

France

Bibliothèque Nationale, Paris. Département des Cartes et Plans. Maps 1:3, 2:2, 2:4a, b, c, d and e, 3:1, 3:2, 4:5, 7:5, 8:1 (Phot. Bibl. Nat. Paris), 8:6. (Transcript from National Archives of Canada.)

Archives d'Outre-mer, Aix-en-Provence. Maps 6:1, 6:2, 6:4, 6:9.

Archives Nationales, Paris. Map 6:8. (Transcript from National Archives of Canada.)

United Kingdom

Public Record Office, Kew. Maps 2:6, 2:8, 3:3, 4:4, 5:2, 5:5, 5:6, 6:3, 6:5, 6:6, 6:7, 7:10, 7:11, 7:12, 7:13, 8:4, 8:5 (Crown Copyright photos), 7:6. (Transcript from National Archives of Canada.)

British Library, London. Frontispiece; Maps 4:1, 5:3, 7:7.

Bodleian Library, Oxford. Map 3:4.

Ministry of Defence, Hydrographer of the Navy, Taunton. Map 8:3.

Hydrographic Section, National Maritime Museum, Greenwich. Map 8:2.

United States

Newberry Library, Chicago. Maps 2:3, 3:5.

William L. Clements Library, Ann Arbor. Map 5:4.

Preface

Cartography has been recognized for many hundreds of years as a way of representing the surface of the earth, both in its natural form and with the modifications brought about by human activity. The many purposes for which maps have been made throughout the ages include descriptions of topography, or what a place looks like physically; descriptions of location, or how to get to a place; descriptions of territorial demarcation, or who owns what, and many subdivisions of these themes.

The study of maps is traditionally associated with the discipline of geography. But when we look at maps made in the past, we find that the questions of "what?," "where?," and "whose?," when answered for a particular moment in time, also give us valuable historical information. For this reason, the selection of maps in this volume represents a cartographical approach to the history of Nova Scotia.

The majority of these maps were hand-drawn, usually on the spot, by French and English surveyors, military officers or local officials, during the seventeenth and eighteenth centuries. A small proportion of them were engraved in London, Paris or Boston. Many of the maps ended up in the files of departments of the British or French governments and most have since come to rest in national collections such as the Bibliothèque Nationale's Département des Cartes et Plans (Paris), the Public Record Office (London), or the British Library's Map Library (London). Others have found their way into private collections on both sides of the Atlantic. Still others are in Canadian public collections, which, as well as preserving original maps from early periods of our history, have also acquired photographs of some of the material kept elsewhere. A number of these photographic reproductions are available at the Public Archives of Nova Scotia, along with original maps of the region. But the most extensive collection of Nova Scotian maps and of material relating to other regions of Canada is that of the Cartographic and Architectural Archives Division of the National Archives of Canada in Ottawa, which supplied photographic copies of most of the maps in this book.

Working with photographic reproductions, however good, cannot equal the pleasure nor provide the sense of direct contact with the mapmaker that an original map offers, and I have been fortunate to be able to examine a number of such originals. But for practical purposes of research, the easy access to hundreds of maps from many different collections provided by reproductions in the Cartographic and Architectural Archives is of great value. I am most grateful to Ed Dahl, the Early Cartography Specialist, and to the staff of the Archives for their assistance while I was assembling material for this study.

My thanks are also due to Fred Scott of the Nova Scotia Museum for his encouragement to pursue this project, and for his advice and comments while the work was in progress. Thanks also to Walter Morrison, Cartographer Emeritus, Nova Scotia College of Geographic Sciences, for sharing with me his expertise and valuable knowledge of early Nova Scotian mapmakers, and to Gary Shutlak, map curator of the Public Archives of Nova Scotia, for his help. Special thanks to Geraldine Beech of the Public Record Office for her patience in tracking down the originals of some of the maps.

I am particularly grateful to Ed Dahl, Walter Morrison, Scott Robson of the Nova Scotia Museum and M. Brook Taylor of Mount Saint Vincent University for taking the time from their already busy lives to read the manuscript and offer valuable suggestions for changes and additions. To Barbara Robertson of the Nova Scotia Museum, who first encouraged me to write about maps, and who commented on parts of this text, a further debt of gratitude. To Bruce Erskine, my thanks for his sympathetic editing of the text. And to John Hennigar-Shuh, who patiently coordinated all of this on behalf of the Nova Scotia Museum, my most sincere thanks. Many other individuals have assisted in one way or another during the researching, writing and production of this book; their kindness and courtesy are much appreciated.

A source of inspiration throughout this work has been the late Andrew Hill Clark's *Acadia: The Geography of Early Nova Scotia to 1760* (Madison, 1968). This very detailed study of the interaction of geography with history in the development of the province has formed a valuable background to my investigations, and kept me from many errors of judgement in interpreting the maps.

It has obviously not been possible, within the scope of this study, to include maps of every community in Nova Scotia. Some areas have a long recorded history, and successive mapmakers have marked significant stages in the development of these areas that seemed worth examining. In other cases, where a number of communities have an essentially similar background, representative maps have been selected as examples of settlement patterns or other recurrent themes. Readers will be aware of many areas in which they have a particular interest that have been omitted. It is hoped that this glimpse of some of the mapping which took place during the first 200 years of European occupation of Nova Scotia will encourage them to seek out examples of maps of their own communities or fields of interest.

Joan Dawson
Halifax, 1988

Introduction

Maps are familiar objects to most people. We see them used on television to locate places in the news, we consult highway maps to plan our vacation routes and we use street maps to find our way around unfamiliar cities. Specialized maps can tell us about anything from population density to tomorrow's weather.

Modern general maps bring together information on many aspects of the regions they represent. The large scale topographical maps produced by the federal Department of Energy, Mines and Resources are most useful in this respect. The range of information they provide can be seen from the key to the conventional symbols found on the backs of the current series of maps. Among them are symbols representing land forms, water resources, vegetation, transportation routes and political boundaries, as well as "miscellaneous culture." This category includes areas of settlement and other man-made modifications to the landscape—dams, power lines, lighthouses, mines, wrecks, historic sites and other items. From such a map, with a little practice in interpretation, it is possible to obtain a clear picture of the area represented, and of man's impact on it up to the time the map was made.

The maps of Nova Scotia made during the first 200 years of European settlement do not begin to approach the sophistication of these modern maps, yet the information they convey is, in many cases, remarkably similar. They provide valuable documentation about how the region appeared to those people—chiefly French and English—who explored and settled it. The mapmakers' work enables us to see the territory through their eyes. From Champlain's earliest harbour maps, which show Indians standing on wooded shores, to the plans drawn up in the 1790s for the construction of the Shubenacadie Canal, the maps are a record of the way the land was perceived and the manner in which its natural resources were exploited.

In general, the maps reflect a growing awareness of the geography of Nova Scotia as it was settled and developed. They also reflect an increasing ability on the part of the mapmakers to represent accurately what they saw. These two factors combined to allow cartographers of the late eighteenth century to produce a much clearer picture of the region than their predecessors could.

The data needed to construct an accurate map include latitude and longitude, which pinpoint places on the earth's surface, and distance and direction, which establish their location in relation to each other. While latitude could be determined with some accuracy by Champlain's time by measuring the height of the sun and stars, longitude was harder to establish, and until well into the seventeenth century mapping was based essentially on compass bearings and estimated distances between principal landmarks. As well as the compass, the instruments used were the astrolabe, quadrant and cross staff, which were nautical instruments suitable for making and using mariners' charts. Early maps of North America therefore tended to represent only the outline of the newly discovered—and largely unexplored—territory, with vague hints of relief and vegetation as they appeared from the shore or from verbal accounts. The coastlines themselves were often out of proportion because of the navigators' problems of estimating longitude. These difficulties were gradually overcome in the latter part of the seventeenth century as scientists achieved a better understanding of compass declination and variation. Another important development was the invention, in 1735, of a chronometer which would measure time accurately.

As the interior of the region became more familiar, surveying chains and poles were used to measure the surface of the land as it was divided into grants to settlers or laid out into towns. Use of the telescope and plane table, and the development of the theodolite, allowed surveyors to observe and record the features of these newly developed areas with greater accuracy. By the end of the eighteenth century a number of such surveyors, many of them military officers trained in mathematics and in the use of these instruments, had mapped significant areas of the province, while more scientific coastal surveys resulted in charts that defined the shoreline in detail and provided reliable aids to navigation.

One of the essentials of the discipline of geography is the observation of the relationship between the physical characteristics of a region and the activities of the people who, over the centuries, have left their impression on its surface. This relationship is a dual one: just as human endeavours are influenced by our physical environment, so we in turn modify and shape the environment to suit our purposes.

This interaction is particularly apparent in the cartographic records of the early European settlement of Eastern Canada. In the seventeenth and eighteenth centuries, expeditions from France and England came with varied commercial, political, religious and social motives to establish settlements in the New World. They found an aboriginal population living in these regions whose essentially stone age culture depended on a symbiotic relationship with the virtually untouched natural resources of their surroundings. The new arrivals, with their relatively sophisticated technical knowledge, were at a disadvantage in the short term, because of their dependence on man-made goods for survival. But in the long term they were able to exploit the resources they found in order to live at a less primitive level than the native inhabitants. In order to do so, however, they immediately began to make changes to the environment. These changes are reflected in the maps which were made throughout the period of settlement.

Only a relatively small number of these maps were intended for publication. These were engraved and printed as illustrations for books on travel and exploration, used in atlases, or sold as individual items to satisfy public curiosity about the New World. The majority are manuscript maps, made with varying degrees of skill and accuracy. Many of these hand-drawn maps were made to accompany reports sent back to colonial authorities, civilian or military, in England or France. Maps were a way of conveying information to governments about territory which most of their officials had never seen. The maps frequently accompanied requests for funding, and sometimes outlined projects that were never realized because funds were not forthcoming. Some maps reflected military strategy, while others consisted of records of land allotments and other aspects of settlement.

Early maps are important documents for students of local history. They provide vivid contemporary records of specific places, shown from the point of view of explorers, military and naval surveyors, visiting administrative officials and others. Large scape maps of relatively small areas can provide valuable information about early stages of settlement or economic development. They often contain a fascinating mixture of well-known elements, such as familiar landmarks or the unchanged street plan of a town, with long-forgotten, unfulfilled projects and vanished buildings. Features or names on a map that are half-remembered in local tradition or merely mentioned in history books may come to life again as we see them in the context of a contemporary map.

The maps presented here vary in accuracy depending on the technology available to the mapmakers, their personal skills and the degree of their knowledge of the areas portrayed. But they all contain features which will be recognizable to people familiar with these areas, or to those who wish to compare them with modern maps. Readers should note, and make allowances for, the undisciplined spelling in both French and English that was current among cartographers and even administrators and their clerks in the seventeenth and eighteenth centuries. With a little imagination, these "spelling mistakes" should present no difficulties in identification.

Although considerable use has been made of the 1:250 000 and 1:50 000 maps of the federal Department of Energy, Mines and Resources in the preparation of this material, readers will find that the Nova Scotia Official Highways Map will enable them to locate most of the features mentioned in the commentaries. Modern roads are identified by their provincial Department of Transportation numbers, and modern landmarks are identified where appropriate. In cases where modern place-names differ significantly from those used in the original maps, the modern form is given alongside the early name. Additional information on the development of many of these names may be found in C.B. Fergusson's *Place-Names and Places of Nova Scotia* (Halifax, 1963). The *Nova Scotia Resource Atlas* (Halifax, 1986) provides an up-to-date picture of the province's natural resources and their development. A comprehensive account of surveying and mapmaking in Canada during the period under consideration can be found in the first volume of Don W. Thomson's *Men and Meridians* (Ottawa, 1966, reprinted 1975 and 1984).

Chapter 1 Prologue:
First Impressions

The earliest maps representing that part of the east coast of North America now known as Nova Scotia bear little resemblance to today's maps. Early North Atlantic navigational charts, made chiefly by and for seamen, were intended as guides to the fishing banks and to nearby harbours; they were not much concerned with the land beyond. Interest in actual exploration was stimulated by John Cabot's voyages of 1497 and 1498. From the early 1500s, the emerging picture of a great landmass at the western edge of the ocean led other explorers to build on Cabot's discoveries, and to make territorial claims on behalf of their sponsors, the monarchs of western Europe. The voyages of Giovanni da Verrazźano in 1524 and of Jacques Cartier 10 years later resulted in the appearance of the name "New France" on a number of sixteenth century maps.

Maps of this time offered little more than a picture of the coastline, and that very inaccurately. Areas of the interior were roughly allocated names derived from the claims of the discoverers, and mountain ranges appeared randomly scattered across the continent. But apart from the fishermen who came to work on the banks, going ashore only for necessities, and those who used the harbours as bases for the seasonal inshore fishery, there was no European presence established here. It was not until the early 1600s that French colonizing expeditions founded settlements in the area which would be known as Acadia. This activity was followed shortly by English settlement further south. The mapping of these territories would form an integral part of the colonization process that took place during the next two centuries.

Before considering the maps made during the period of settlement, it is worth looking at a few examples of earlier maps from which the prospective colonists derived their information about the New World.[1] Based on the observations of navigators who had sailed along the coast and up the Saint Lawrence, maps that showed the travellers' destinations were often extremely sketchy, sometimes even imaginary in part. By modern standards they were hopelessly unreliable, yet they provided those with the courage to set sail with some knowledge of where they were going.

Two early maps showing New France were made by Italian cartographers working in Venice. Giacomo Gastaldi's mapping of the North American coast was based on Verrazzano's written account of his explorations, rather than on new maps.[2] Although made after Cartier's voyages, Gastaldi's maps do not reflect the discovery of the Saint Lawrence. His portrayal of *La Nuova Franzia* (Map 1:1) is more interesting for its pictorial elements than for its accuracy of outline. Bolognino Zaltieri's career as a mapmaker began at about the time Gastaldi's ended; he followed his predecessor in much of his representation of North America (Map 1:2). This included the indication of "Arcadia" on the much elongated east coast.[3] Although Zaltieri's map looks more workmanlike than Gastaldi's, it is still badly distorted. Both maps show Newfoundland as a fragmented group of islands.

The third example, an extract from a larger map by Guillaume Levasseur of France, shows a more realistic picture of the northeast coast of North America (Map 1:3). Cartier's discovery of the Saint Lawrence is clearly represented, and Newfoundland has become a recognizable island. The outline of what is now Nova Scotia lacks the distinguishing orientation of the Bay of Fundy, but its other features are beginning to take form, and the map exhibits a notable increase in knowledge.

The name Arcadia which appears on Zaltieri's map had been given by Verrazzano in the 1520s to an area of the coast of America in what is now Virginia or Maryland.[4] Its location migrated northeastward on later maps until it appears on Levasseur's map in the New England area as the more familiar *Coste de Cadie*, which is written on other seventeenth century maps as *La Cadie* or *L'Acadie*. By the mid-1600s the name would be firmly attached to the area now comprising all of Nova Scotia and much of New Brunswick.

Within a few years Champlain was to survey and map New France, including both Acadia and the Saint Lawrence area, in considerable detail, as the French established a precarious foothold in the New World. Until that time, however, the coast of North America remained only a rough outline with a hinterland yet to be explored.

Gastaldi's New France

This map is one of the illustrations in Ramusio's *Voyages*, a collection of accounts of explorers and their discoveries. Gastaldi was an established cartographer working in Venice, where he held the post of Cosmographer to the Republic. Because his mapping of North America was dependent on written accounts and out-of-date information, Gastaldi's map of New France does not reflect the actual state of knowledge in the mid-1500s, long after Cartier's voyage to the Saint Lawrence. But its pictorial imagery includes a range of subjects which give us some idea of how Europeans thought of eastern North America before the seventeenth century period of colonization.

Apart from the few voyages made specifically for the purpose of exploration, most of the traffic off the shores of North America consisted of fishing expeditions. On this map, the most recognizable illustrations are of the sailing vessels in which sixteenth century

fishermen crossed the Atlantic, and the smaller boats in which they can be seen hauling cod on lines or seining with nets. The cause of all this activity was, of course, the rich fishing banks of the eastern North American continental shelf. The banks are shown here as a ribbon-like formation curving along the eastern and southern edges of the map (the conventional orientation is indicated by the words *Tramontano, Ostro, Levante* and *Ponente*). The square *Isola della Rena* (Sable Island) stands out clearly from the rest.

Beside the fishing boats are canoes manned by the native Micmac whose primitive shelters are shown on the land. The Micmac themselves are shown engaged in various activities, particularly hunting with bows and arrows. Their quarry consists of birds (including waterfowl), bears, a rabbit and a member of the deer family that is being carried back to camp by two hunters. These representations were apparently based on observations made by explorers and fishermen, and suggest some awareness of the way of life of the native people of the area. On the other hand, there seems to be little attempt at precise location of any of the activities depicted, or of any particular species of wildlife. "This," the cartographer appears to be saying, "is what life is like in *La Nuova Francia*, and it is much the same wherever you go." The one exception is the *Isola de Demoni*, or Isle of Demons, where the demons can be seen, with horns, tails and wings, at the northern end of the island.

On a more practical level, the sea is shown as full of fish, including a spouting whale and a dolphin, with various species scattered along the bank. Because of the well known economic value of the area, the depiction of the banks as the habitat of numerous varieties of fish is clearly a matter of serious representation rather than a decorative filling of space. Even the appearance of two dog-like creatures with ears and paws fighting with or over a large fish seems to be based on factual information, though the result is fictitious. The cartographer may have been attempting to represent dogfish (small shark) or perhaps "sea wolves," otherwise known as bass. But the term *loup marin* was also used for seals, which may be what the illustration is intended to depict.

The place names in eastern North America during the sixteenth century were frequently attached to rather vaguely defined areas of land. *La Nuova Francia* or New France, shown here, appears to extend as far as the *Parte Incognita*, the unknown territory which occupies the northeastern section of the map. The term *Terra de Nurumbega* clearly applies to the coastal region south of New France, but again is ill-defined. *Terra de Labrador* and *Terra Nova* have survived as Labrador and Newfoundland, but the name "Isle of Demons" no longer appears on maps to the north of Newfoundland, which is shown here as an archipelago. The proportions of all the land areas are arbitrary and confusing, and the rivers quite unrecognizable. Names of individual islands and harbours known to fishermen help to bring some order to the confusion, but need to be used with caution; Cape Breton appears twice, once plausibly located on an appropriately placed island, but a second time on the mainland, while the *Isola de Bretoni* or Bretons' Island lies some distance offshore.

The fact that many of the names on this map appear in somewhat different locations on other sixteenth century maps emphasizes the lack of knowledge that hampered cartographers attempting to represent North America. The claim of the French to a considerable area is clearly established by this map, while the Portuguese explorations are reflected in the name *Labrador*, which they applied to the area they visited. A few other names are established, some of which have survived, particularly in Newfoundland. But except at a very general level, the map can have done little to enhance European knowledge of the region's geography. Its pictorial imagery, on the other hand, suggests a better awareness of the inhabitants and of the wildlife, and of the commercial advantages of the fishing banks, than do the more accurate maps made by other cartographers.

"Arcadia"
appears on the map

Zaltieri's "Drawing of the discovery of New France" brings together much of the information derived from the explorations of the first half of the sixteenth century, including those of Verrazzano and Cartier on behalf of France. Although, like Gastaldi, he still shows an archipelago in the place of Newfoundland, he attempts to represent the Saint Lawrence, which Cartier had explored some 30 years previously, as well as the coast from Florida to Cape Breton along which Verrazzano had sailed in search of a passage to Cathay in 1524. The exaggerated length of the northeast coastline of North America, placing Newfoundland due north of the Azores, is perhaps the result of juxtaposing, rather than overlapping, previous pieces of information. Thus the map shows a great unnamed river, recognizably the Saint Lawrence, running due east, with the *Terra Dellaborador* (Labrador) to the north of the Gulf, while the name *R.S. Lorēzo* is attached to a shorter river which runs southeast out of

a large lake, further down the coast. Offshore, between the two, lies a much enlarged *Y Darena* (Sable Island).

La Nova Franza (New France) is shown well inland behind the mountains, while *Terra Norumbega, Larcadia* with *Canada Pro [vinzia]* beyond, and *Terra de Baccalos* (whose name is preserved in Newfoundland as Bacalieu Island and perhaps in Nova Scotia as Baccaro) are names given to the coastal regions. These names begin to appear regularly on maps of the late 1500s and were applied rather haphazardly to various areas of what are now the eastern American states and the Atlantic provinces. It was at this time that the name *Acardie* (Acadia), first attributed by Verrazzano to an area of Virginia or Maryland, became familiar. It would be some time before this name came firmly to rest in the present Maritime region.[5] Norumbega, for its part, has vanished without a trace.

Both the title of the map and its toponymy (place names) — including the term *Mare della Nova Franza* given to the coastal waters from Arcadia to Baccalos — attest to Zaltieri's acceptance of the French claim to a considerable area of North America. The inland location of New France itself, however, is only roughly established, and it is not clear whether it was considered to include neighbouring Norumbega and Arcadia, nor indeed whether the French were conceded jurisdiction over Canada. But the publication of this map clearly

Map 1:2 Bolognino Zaltieri. *Il Disegno del discoperto della nova Franza...*, 1566. Engraved.

supports French claims to the right to establish colonies in North America.

A map such as this was clearly not intended as an aid to navigation. Mariners' charts could provide travellers with a more reasonable chance of arriving safely at their destination. The title claims that the map represents the most recent French voyages of discovery, showing "all the islands, ports, capes, and places inland. . . ." It is these inland areas which are the most arbitrarily named and located. The depiction of mountains and the indications of vegetation in the interior are equally vague. European knowledge of much of North America was still limited to what could be observed from a ship, and the cartographer depended on a mixture of travellers' tales and political propaganda for information about what lay beyond the horizon. Zaltieri's map, like others of the same period, was made to satisfy people's curiosity about the New World, and encourage their interest in its potential development.

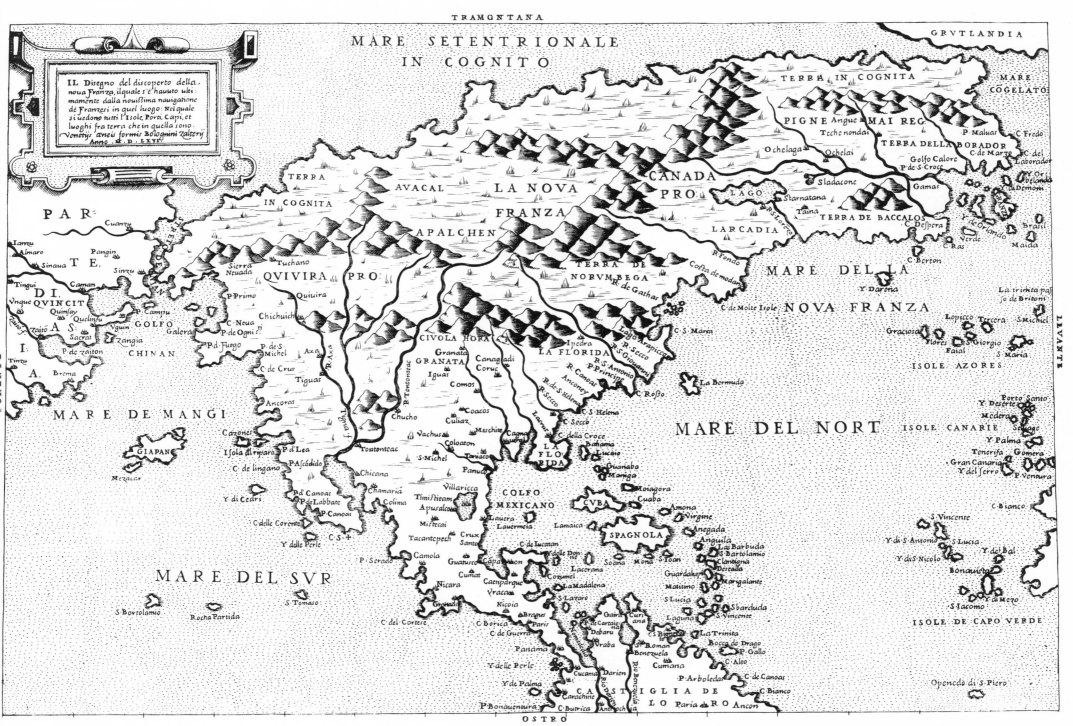

the Atlantic Provinces take shape

A quick glance at this portion of Levasseur's map shows us how European knowledge of the northeast coastline of North America had developed by the early 1600s. Comparison with the previous map shows a number of important features that had been recognized during the previous century and were now incorporated in this representation of the region. Although the Great Lakes had still not been mapped, the more accurately depicted Saint Lawrence is shown in detail as far as the Montreal area (*Mont*

Royal). Newfoundland now appears as a single island, generally recognizable in outline. Anticosti, the Gaspé coast and the Bay of Chaleur stand out clearly. *I[le] S[aint] Jean* (Prince Edward Island) is located and named, and what are now the Magdalen Islands are also shown. Cape Breton Island is clearly distinguishable, and the cape itself named though the island is not. Sable Island and some of the banks are also shown. Although the Nova Scotia and New England coastlines are less immediately recognizable because of the unusual orientation of the Bay of Fundy, the proportions of the Atlantic coast are beginning to be established.

The interior is still generally unknown, but as in previous maps, some names are attributed to broad regions. Canada lies just south of the great river, *Nouvelle France* between it and the Atlantic Ocean, and the *Coste de Cadie*, another manifestation of Arcadia/Acadia, has moved up into the New England area, closer to its final destination. A coat of arms bearing the *fleur de lys* emphasizes French territorial claims in the region.

Place names abound along the coast, reflecting the voyages and reports of a number of sixteenth century explorers.[6] Many of these names were to be replaced by Champlain and his companions within a few years; some have survived. Their very number reflects the increasing frequency of visits from Europeans and the resultant growing familiarity with the coast and its harbours. The naming of a haven suggests the likelihood of a subsequent return there.

This map, though probably not itself intended for practical use as an aid to navigation, includes the compass stars and rhumbs (lines) of a nautical chart. These lines establish a spatial relationship between the different areas of the map, enabling travellers to draft a route and plan their landfall with some degree of accuracy. By the time Pierre Du Gua de Monts set sail for Acadia, Frenchmen were sufficiently familiar with the coast towards which they were heading that Champlain could later describe the beginning of the journey as follows: *We set out from Havre de Grace on the seventh of April, one thousand six hundred and four, and Pont-Gravé on the tenth, with a rendez-vous at Canso, twenty leagues from Cape Breton. But when we were on the high sea, the Sieur de Monts changed his mind, and set his course towards Port Mouton, because it is farther to the south and also a more convenient place for making land than Canso.* (*The Works of Samuel de Champlain*, ed. H.P. Biggar, Vol. 1, p. 234)
Maps such as this still did not give a complete picture of either Acadia or New France, but they enabled men like de Monts and Champlain to put their finger on a spot and say "This is where we are going."

Map 1:3 Guillaume Levasseur. Northeastern North America, 1601. Manuscript.

Chapter 2 *the Maps and the Mapmakers*

Many cartographers, some very well-known and some obscure or even anonymous, contributed to the surveying and mapping of Nova Scotia during the seventeenth and eighteenth centuries. Their work was a way of providing information both to government officials and to the general public in France and England about the progress of the colonization and development of territories in the New World. In this chapter we shall look at some of their maps, to see how they reflected increasing European knowledge of different parts of the province, and how they recorded the process of settlement.

There were many reasons for making maps of hitherto unexplored territory. Like any scientific discovery, knowledge of a place had to be documented in order to be understood and accepted by those who had not seen it personally. Territorial claims were more likely to be respected, or at least negotiated, if they were laid out clearly on a map for consideration by the parties involved. Colonial government depended on an orderly division of the new territory into administrative areas and the recording of lands allotted to settlers. Even when the actual development of an area lagged behind the indications on the map, the very fact that a plan had been committed to paper gave it a credibility it might otherwise have lacked. A good map could both record the progress of colonization and enable an official seated at his desk many hundreds of miles away to make intelligent plans for future development of its potential. Even a rough map, inaccurate by today's standards, could convey spatial information more quickly, and often more clearly, than a detailed verbal description. The act of making a map implied in itself an understanding, even if incomplete, of the area depicted, and thereby furnished a measure of control over that area. Some of these aspects of mapmaking will become apparent as we examine individual examples.

The technology of surveying and scientific mapmaking was still in a fairly primitive state in the early seventeenth century. Champlain and his contemporaries could determine latitude fairly accurately by measuring the height of the sun or stars with an astrolabe or a cross staff. Direction could be established with a compass, though the problem of declination, or the variation of magnetic north from true north, caused some confusion in calculations. This same problem, combined with the lack of an accurate means of measuring time, made the precise calculation of longitude almost impossible.[1] Champlain appended a treatise on navigation[2] to his *Voyages* of 1632, setting forth what was, for that period, a practical and scientific approach to the subject. His careful application of these theories, within the limits of the instruments available to him, resulted in an enormous increase in the accuracy of the representation of New France, but considerable distortion is still apparent in some of his maps. By the end of the eighteenth century, technological advances enabled surveyors to produce much more accurate mapping. Many later maps of Nova Scotia were made by military officers whose training had included surveying and drafting with up-to-date instruments, and who

were increasingly capable of producing work of high quality.

The initial mapping of Acadia was essentially the work of one individual, Samuel de Champlain. Rough charts had existed for many years showing the east coast of North America and identifying the capes and harbours with which fishermen had become familiar. But it was not until 1604, when Pierre du Gua de Monts set out with an expedition to found a French colony, that Europeans became more fully aware of the outline of the coast between Cape Breton and Cape Cod. Champlain, a member of the expedition, spent a good part of the next three years examining the area and mapping it more accurately than any previous visitor.

The French were nominally in control of the region for much of the seventeenth century, and, after Champlain's surveys, there was a long lull in the mapping of Acadia. Very few large scale maps have survived from this period, although the 1680s saw a revival of interest in the area and some maps of settlements were produced. English cartographers, in the meantime, produced coastal charts but were not concerned with the communities along the shores.

In the eighteenth century, the situation was to a great extent reversed. Up until 1710, French mapping of the Port Royal area continued, chiefly with the work of Jean Delabat. But with the British capture of the fort, control of the colony passed into their hands and it was the turn of British cartographers based in New England to map the inhabited areas of Nova Scotia. The French turned their attention to coastal surveying and the detailed mapping of settlements in Cape Breton. The establishment, in 1749, of Halifax as the administrative centre of the province, the encouragement of settlement and the appointment of Charles Morris as Surveyor General for Nova Scotia resulted in a period of systematic mapping of potential settlement sites. This detailed surveying continued under Morris's son Charles, so that by the end of the century the province had been extensively and intensively mapped.

In the meantime, J.F.W. DesBarres had undertaken an equally ambitious coastal survey, with the assistance of a team of naval officers. His *Atlantic Neptune*, first published in 1776, is an atlas which includes detailed charts of most of the harbours of Nova Scotia.

The cartographers whose work is reproduced in this chapter worked under many different circumstances. Some did their own fieldwork and surveying, while others collected and collated information gathered by others, in order to publish maps in London or Paris. There is a clear progression in accuracy from Champlain's maps of the ports of Acadia to DesBarres' series of coastal charts, and from Franquelin's maps of settlements to the surveys of townships made by the younger Charles Morris in the 1780s. All these men, and many more, made maps which reflected contemporary impressions of different parts of Nova Scotia. The information they gave to their countrymen at the time is still of interest today as we try to reconstruct aspects of the history of these communities.

Champlain comes to Acadia

This map is the first of a number made during Champlain's three-year (1604–1607) sojourn in Acadia, which resulted in an enormous increase in European knowledge of this region. In 1613 he published his *Voyages*, which included not only a detailed account of his exploration up to that date, but also reproductions of the maps that he had made as he journeyed.[3] The expedition's first anchorage was in a bay at a place which they named La Heve (LaHave) and Champlain's "Port de La heve" is the earliest known large scale map of any part of the province.

The map is explained by a legend describing the main features. The soundings, and the place "A" where "the [expedition's] ships dropped anchor" show that the "port" which Champlain drew was what is now known as Green Bay, and that he had not explored the present harbour area within the river mouth. The *Petite Rivière*, "B", "a little river which is dry at low water," retains its name today; at low tide, now as then, much of the estuary gives way to sand flats. The letter "C", representing "the places where the Indians camp" and omitted by the engraver, clearly refers to the areas west of the Petite and east of the LaHave where Micmac encampments are indicated by cabins and wigwams; at the former site, two of the inhabitants are shown. Also omitted was the letter "D", marking a shoal at the entrance to the "port" that is clearly visible on the map. The letter "E" (the one closer to the soundings) marking "a little island covered with woods" represents the western part of Cape LaHave Island, while "F" in the legend (a second "E" on the map) indicates the cape itself. The letter "G" refers to "a bay where there are many islands covered with woods," that is, of course, the mouth of the LaHave. Within it,

---

Map 2:1 Samuel de Champlain. *Port de La heve,* 1613. Engraved.

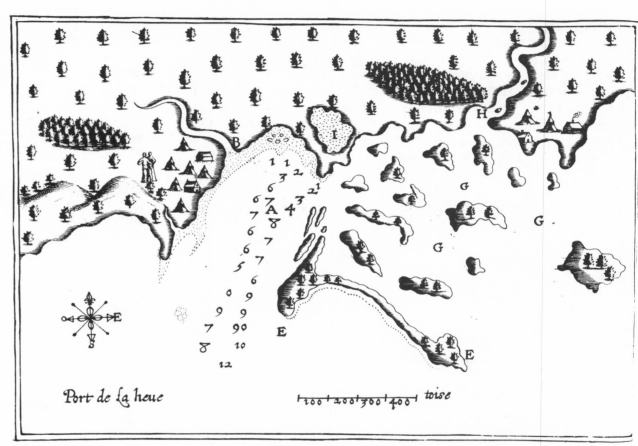

Port de La heue

Les chifres montrent les braſſes d'eau.

A Le lieu où les vaiſſeaux moullent l'ancre.

B Vne petite riuiere qui aſſeche de baſſe mer.

C Les lieux ou les ſauuages cabannent.

D Vne baſſe a l'entree du port

E Vne petite iſle couuerte de bois.

F Le Cap de la Héue.

G Vne baye ou il y a quantité d'iſles couuertes de bois.

H Vne riuiere qui va dans les terres 6, ou 7. lieux. auec peu d'eau.

I Vn eſtang proche de la mer.

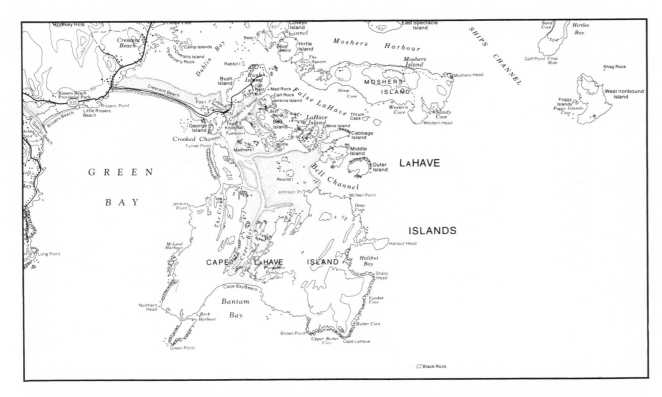

Map 2:1a Green Bay and the LaHave Islands today.

some of the islands can be identified on a modern map, with a little imagination, but they are fairly crudely represented and clearly not thoroughly explored or surveyed. The river, "H", "which goes 6 or 7 leagues inland, with little water" was obviously underestimated by Champlain, who evidently had not sailed up the LaHave. Finally, "I" represents the lagoon behind Crescent Beach, which may have been completely enclosed, particularly at low tide, in Champlain's day.[4]

The compass star and the scale of 400 *toises* (1 *toise* = roughly 2 metres), as well as the carefully recorded soundings, show that this first map is a business-like

effort, despite some inaccuracies. The sands of Crescent Beach, Rissers Beach and Green Bay, as well as the tidal flats of the lagoon, are clearly shown. The dense forest covering the interior, like the trees on the islands, are shown in a stylized form, but the native dwellings are apparently represented as Champlain found them. Nicolas Denys, who visited the same area nearly 30 years later, describes Micmac "cabins" as follows: "If the family is a large one, they make it long enough for two fires; otherwise they make it round, just like military tents."[5] The chimneys on the two easterly long huts are probably an engraver's embel-

lishment, as are the European-style walls. The native dwellings in the map of Port Rossignol (Map 7:1, p. 96) are more realistically reproduced.

The first impression of a country of forest vegetation inhabited by "Indians" was not to change to any great degree as Champlain continued his journey. Further details were added as he saw and recorded new aspects of this unknown territory in subsequent maps. Later, he would record the settlements established by the French, and the first modifications brought about by Europeans to this part of the New World.

Lalanne & the place names of Acadia

The Sieur de Lalanne, about whom very little is known except that he was an officer in the French navy, was sent to Acadia in 1684 as an *écrivain* (clerk, or keeper of accounts), in order to examine and report on the territory's ports and harbours, its forest resources and its ability to supply timber for shipbuilding.[6] The results of the voyage were a report on the available wood, a journal[7] lavishly illustrated with sketch maps of the coastal areas he had observed (see Map 2:2a) and several copies of a manuscript map of Acadia, of which a section is reproduced here.

Unlike many cartographers who were only too willing to fill in the gaps in their first-hand knowledge by copying from other people's maps, Lalanne states in his report that in his map "he marked no place which he had not visited."[8] Having travelled from Port Royal to the Saint John River and back, he omitted the upper part of the Bay of Fundy from his map. The section shown in Map 2:2 includes the coast from LaHave, where his voyage began, to Port Royal. It is unusually oriented, with north to the upper left, and although a scale is given, the South Shore and the Fundy shore are badly out of proportion. His observations were made almost entirely from the ship on which he was travelling; his only glimpses of the interior came when the ship was in port. As a result, only the lower reaches of the LaHave and the Annapolis Rivers appear on this portion of the map. The many other rivers along the South Shore are represented only by the harbours at their mouths.

Lalanne's journal shows that he was familiar with navigational details, as one would expect of a naval officer, but his knowledge of surveying and drafting seems to have been minimal. The sketches in his jour-

---

Map 2:2a   Pages from Lalanne's journal, 1684.

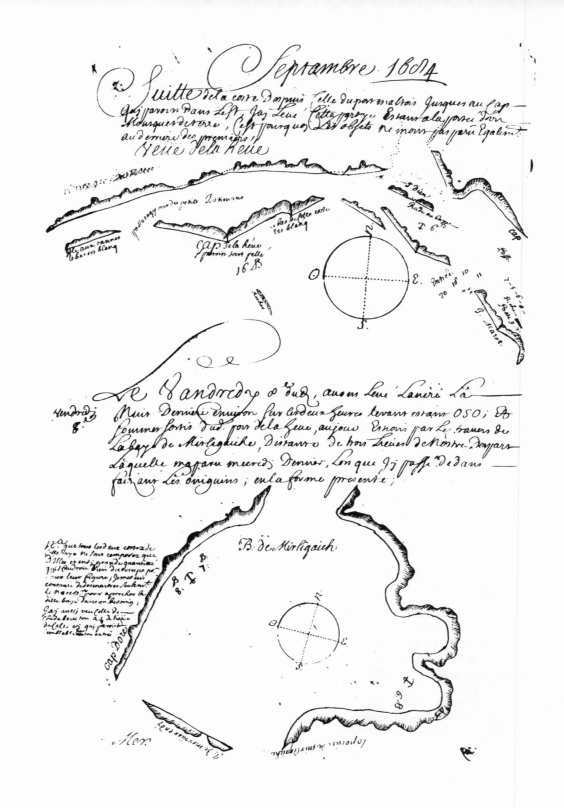

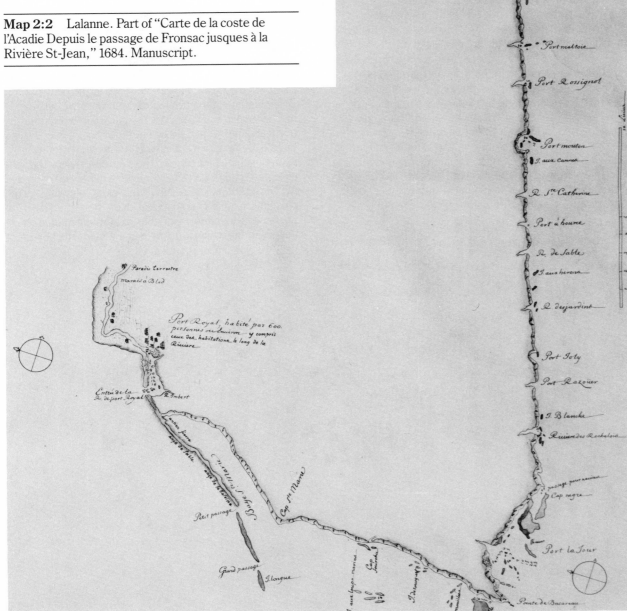

Map 2:2   Lalanne. Part of "Carte de la coste de l'Acadie Depuis le passage de Fronsac jusques à la Rivière St-Jean," 1684. Manuscript.

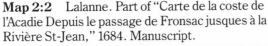

nal, recording roughly the profile of the coastline as it appeared to him, simply indicate the relative location of various features. Compass directions are given in most of the sketchmaps, and estimated distances between places sometimes appear. More details about distance and direction are found in the text of the journal, but they refer to the ship's course and can have provided only general assistance in compiling the map. The result was a recognizable but distorted outline of the coast that, despite its deficiencies, provides a certain amount of useful information.

One of the interesting features of the map is the number of river mouths and harbours identified by name. Lalanne seems to have fulfilled his instructions in this regard meticulously. Some of the ports had been visited and named by de Monts and Champlain 80 years previously; some names may have been bestowed by fishermen who worked along the coast, and others by men like the LaTours, father and son, who had established trading posts earlier in the century. The only place where any significant population is noted is Port Royal.

Among the harbours shown on this section of the map are *Port de la heve* (LaHave), *Port Maltois* (Port Medway), *Port Rossignol* (Liverpool), *Port Mouton*, *R[ivière] Ste. Catherine* (Port Joli: the name St. Catherines River is still found in the area); *Port à Hource* (Port Hebert, by a peculiar linguistic muddle whereby Hource, more usually written *ours*, "bear," became confused with the French name Hébert); *R[ivière] de Sable* (Sable River); *R[ivière] desjardins* (Green Harbour or Jordan River: the latter sounds more appropriate, but this would leave Lalanne's *Port Joly* unaccounted for); *Port Razoüer* (Shelburne Harbour: the name Roseway survives in the area); *Rivière des Rochelois* (Negro Harbour: *Cap Nègre* appears somewhat displaced to the west); and, much exaggerated in size, *Port LaTour*. Rounding the *Pointe de*

Bacareau (Baccaro Point) we find that Barrington Bay and Passage are completely missing, but *Cap du Sable* (Cape Sable Island) thrusts out to sea from a flat coastline. Then come the *I[les] Mouillées* (probably the islands off Shag Harbour), *I. de Tousquet* (Tusket Islands), *I. aux Loups Marins* (Seal Islands, somewhat displaced), and *Cap Fourchu*, with a hint of a river-mouth behind; *Cap Ste Marie* and *Baie Ste Marie* (St. Mary's Cape and Bay), *I. Longue* (Long Island, which seems to have slipped to the location of Brier Island), and finally *Port Róyal*. A number of other capes, coves and islands punctuate this list of familiar and unfamiliar names. Despite this map's topographical shortcomings, it is an invaluable record of the place names of southwest Nova Scotia at the time. It is useful not only for locating places mentioned in contemporary documents, but also in tracing the origin of many of the names in use today.

The shapes, proportions and distances between the places shown are very inaccurate, as might be expected from such an unscientific survey. Lalanne has provided soundings for some of the harbour entrances, but navigators might be unwise to rely on the accuracy of their location. Forts are shown at the mouth of the LaHave and at Port LaTour, as well as at Port Royal itself. The fact that all these were in a state of considerable disrepair at the time is not made clear.

Also shown at Port Royal are a windmill, a church and some houses, both in the main settlement and farther up the river. The position of the windmill and the church are confirmed by Franquelin's map of Port Royal of two years later, but the suggestion of fields along the river seems to indicate a more extensive area under cultivation than actually existed. The estimate of the population as 600, including those in the settlements along the river, is very close to Demeulle's estimate in 1686 of 592 souls, not counting the 30 soldiers of the garrison.[9]

Except for some of the place names, this map adds little information to what had been generally known and more accurately mapped in Champlain's time. The one important new feature, and this may be its earliest cartographical representation, is the relocated settlement of Port Royal, now established at the head of the Basin instead of the original Habitation site. Lalanne had been sent not to survey the coastline but to identify ports and harbours, and he seems to have fulfilled this task to the best of his ability. His journal, with the sketch maps which formed the raw material for the completed map, gives us some idea of how he compiled his information. The result, while clearly hazardous to navigators if used as a nautical chart, nevertheless presents in an understandable, schematic manner, the observations which Lalanne had made for the benefit of desk-bound civil servants in Paris.

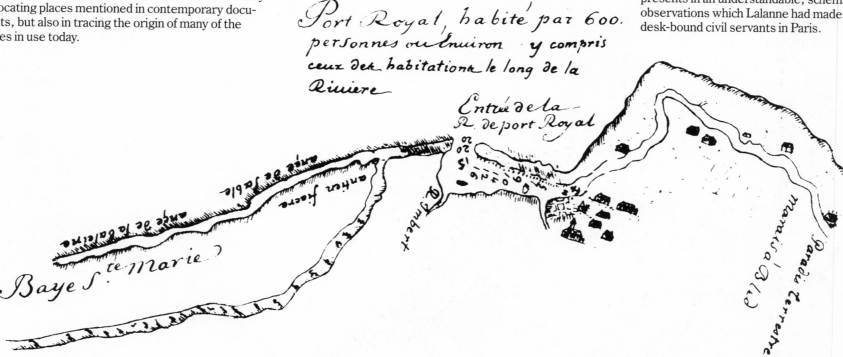

A bird's-eye view of Port Royal

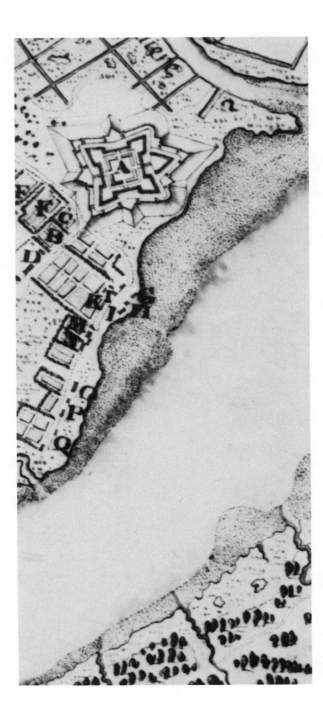

The maps produced by Jean Delabat during the final years of the French occupation of Port Royal are among the most vividly descriptive of any made during the period under consideration. Delabat was a military engineer, sent out from France to supervise the long overdue reconstruction of the fort at Port Royal (now Annapolis Royal). His talents as a cartographer provide a unique record of the community immediately before its final surrender to the British in 1710.

This is one of several of Delabat's maps drawn to an extremely large scale, so that the reader has an impression of a bird's-eye view of the area represented. The extract shown is only a very small section of the area covered by the entire map, which extends from several kilometres above the fort to just below Goat Island, and a short distance back from the river on each side. It is oriented with north to the bottom; it includes a key to the letters which identify features on the map. The information which follows is derived from the key unless otherwise stated.

The section of the map that has been reproduced is centred on the town of Port Royal. We see, as if in an aerial photograph, the site of the settlement on the peninsula between the main (Annapolis) river and the small meanders of its tributary, the *Petite Rivière* (Allain's River). The fort, reconstructed under Delabat's supervision in the first few years of the eighteenth century,[10] dominates the town. The two main streets, one running along the shore and the other along the spine of the peninsula, are bordered by the houses and gardens of the inhabitants. A number of these houses

had been burned during the English attack of June, 1707; they are identified by the key.

The houses closest to the fort, "A", are identified by capital letters, not all of which are very legible. They include the residences of the most prominent inhabitants of Port Royal. Among the group clustered directly against the fort, "B" and "C" represent "the houses and gardens of Mr. de Bonnaventure, presently belonging to Mr. Subercase"; "D" is the King's Barn, "E" the houses and land of Mr. de Falaise, and "F" the houses and land of the Sieur de Coutins, more usually written De Goutin.

These are all familiar names in Acadian history. Simon-Pierre Denys de Bonaventure was a great-nephew of Nicolas Denys. He had been appointed second-in-command to Brouillan, the governor, and left in charge of the settlement while Brouillan returned to France. On Brouillan's death, he hoped for the governorship, but was passed over because of his scandalous relationship with one of the neighbours, Madame de Freneuse (see below). Instead, the governorship, and the governor's house, went to Daniel Auger, Sieur de Subercase, who was in residence when the map was made.[11]

His neighbour, Louis de Gannes de Falaise, was a senior military officer who had been in Port Royal since 1696.[12] Next door to him lived the lieutenant for justice in the colony, Mathieu de Goutin. De Goutin was also the royal *écrivain*, or clerk, with considerable financial and administrative responsibilities.[13] All of these people played important roles in the administration and defence of Port Royal.

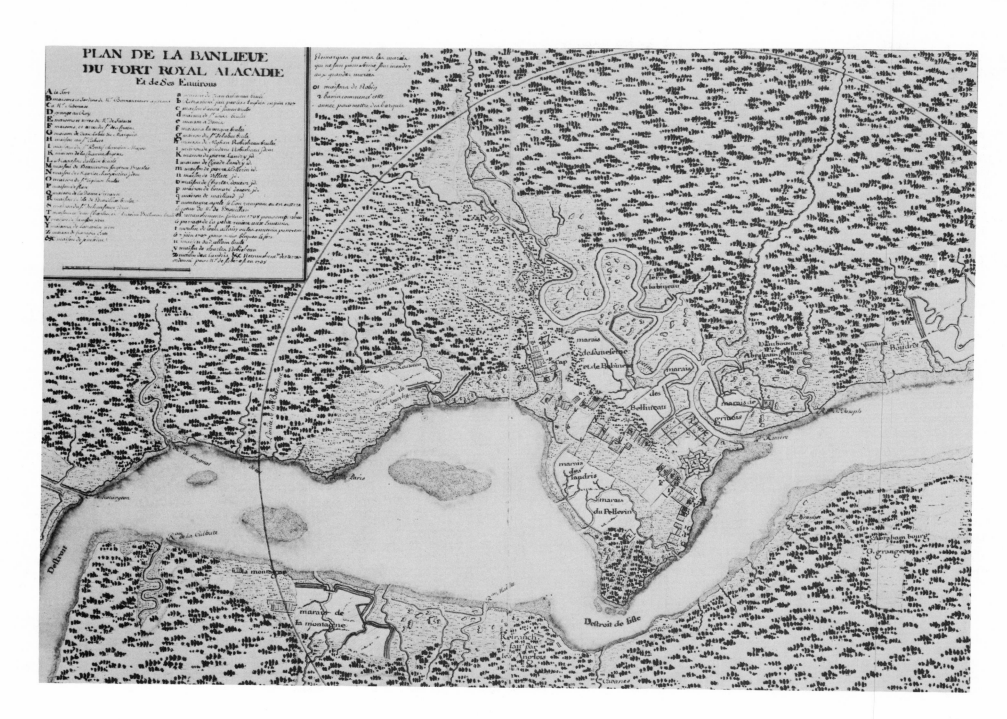

Map 2:3 Jean Delabat. Part of "Plan de la Banlieue du Fort Royal A L'Acadie et de ses Environs," *ca* 1708. Manuscript.

On the street along the waterfront lived another group of prominent citizens. Jean Labat, otherwise known as Marquis, and his business associate "Sieur de Cahoet" lived at "G" and "H" respectively. Labat, by then in his seventies, had once lived and traded at Petite Rivière near LaHave, and owned considerable property at Port Royal.[14] Christophe Cahouet's name appears with Labat's on a document from the minutes of Jean-Chrysostome Loppinot, notary, clerk of the court and King's attorney at Port Royal,[15] whose house "O", stood a short distance along the street. Cahouet's house stood next to the burnt out store of Louis Allain, "L". Allain was a businessman who owned not only the store but also a mill on the river which still bears his name.

Across the street, and apparently undamaged, stood the houses of the surgeon-major, Sieur Pontif, at "I" and of La Chaume, a sergeant (whether in the military or civil sense is not made clear), at "K". "M" and "N" represent the houses of the blacksmith, Beaumont, and the carpenter, Maurice. Both of these houses had been burnt, as had the house of the lawyer Loppinot, though that of his neighbour Flan, whose occupation is unknown, seems to have survived.

The last house on the street, "Q", which also apparently survived the raid, belonged to the notorious Dame Freneuse. Louise Guyon Damours de Freneuse, 34 and twice widowed, came to Port Royal with her sister and brother-in-law in about 1702. Almost immediately she embarked on a relationship with Simon-Pierre Denys de Bonaventure that caused considerable scandal in the community and cost Bonaventure the governorship.[16]

Map 2:3a Aerial view of Annapolis Royal.

The lives of the people who once lived on the street running along the height of land, while probably not blameless, did not attract attention at such a high level. The identifying letters are hard to decipher, but the owners' names on the key read like a roll call of the original Acadian families whose descendants are today scattered all over the Maritime provinces. They include Babineaus, Doucets, Landrys, Pellerins, Robichauds and others. The houses of these families were all burnt during the English raid of June 1707. The letters "b" indicating the entrenchments made by the English at that time show how far the enemy had penetrated into the town. Fortunately for the inhabitants, many families also owned property just outside the town where they could take refuge.

On the peninsula itself, gardens, meadows and cultivated fields are clearly visible. The *marais* or marshlands, which were the areas drained and dyked for farming, are identified according to their owners: Landry, Pellerin, Saintseine, Babineau and Belliveau.

Across the smaller river the Babineaus had another piece of property, the Grivois had drained an extensive area at the river mouth, and farther downstream a Boudrot farm can be seen. Across the main river, the Bourg, Doucet and Granger holdings are only the first of many farms extending down toward Goat Island.

A map such as this is an invaluable historical document. It records many of the essential details about the community: its location and layout, its physical aspects, and its inhabitants. In this case, it also gives information about the results of the enemy attack of the previous year. In conjunction with other historical records, such as censuses, church and legal records, administrative records and correspondence, it provides a vivid backdrop against which an historian can reconstruct many aspects of the settlement. At a more casual level, it allows anyone, familiar with maps or not, to look down on the area as if from an airplane window, and get a glimpse of the surroundings in which the people below lived their daily lives.

Bellin
and his sources

Jacques-Nicolas Bellin is unusual among French mapmakers associated with Nova Scotia in that his maps were compiled at his desk in Paris. Bellin was employed in the *Dépôt des Cartes et Plans de la Marine*,[17] and had not set foot in New France when he produced the major series of maps which were published as illustrations for Charlevoix's *Histoire* in 1744. The maps were based on material stored in the Dépôt, a collection that is now in the map department of the Bibliothèque Nationale.

Among the maps in this collection is a group of four manuscript maps of LaHave (Maps 2:4b–e) that are clearly related to the engraved version (Map 2:4). One bears a note attributing its authorship to Bellin; the others appear to be his source material, perhaps including early drafts by Bellin or an assistant. The original survey was probably carried out before 1713, when British ownership of Nova Scotia was confirmed by the Treaty of Utrecht. All four maps are oriented with north towards the right, as in the engraving, but the manuscript maps are less extensive in scope than the engraved version. They show only the eastern shores of the islands and leave out the coastline of the mainland behind them, giving the impression that the islands form part of the mainland. A fifth map in this same collection is Franquelin's 1686 manuscript map, "Le Port de la Haive" (Map 2:4a). It covers a wider area, including the present Crescent Beach and Petite Rivière, but gives a rather confused picture of the shape and location of the islands.

From this source material, and some unidentified additional information about Dublin Bay, Bellin compiled a surprisingly accurate picture of the lower reaches and mouth of the LaHave River. Comparison most with a modern map (see Map 2:1a) shows that Bellin's most obvious difficulties were in representing the LaHave Islands. It is here that his known sources were particularly inadequate, offering only a partial and simplified

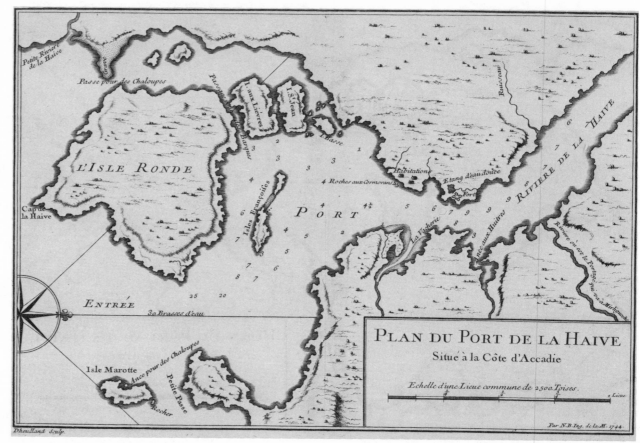

Map 2:4   Jacques-Nicolas Bellin. *Plan du Port de la Haive Situé à la Côte D'Accadie*, 1744.

record of what is indeed a very complex and confusing group of islands. Only the *Isles Françoises* (Spectacles) and the *Isle Marotte* (West Ironbound) are immediately recognizable. The *Isle Ronde* incorporates not only Cape LaHave Island, but also the group of small islands just to the north of it which are separated only by sandflats at low tide. *I[sle] aux Lièvres* seems to be a foreshortened representation of Moshers Island, while *I. St Jean* represents a considerably enlarged version of Hirtles Island, and *I. Basse* is present-day Coveys

Island. Several small islands correspond to Bushen and other islands in the north of Dublin Bay. This tentative identification does not account for the two islands shown in the southern part of Dublin Bay, which seem to be badly displaced. The *Grave*, or beach (Crescent Beach) is much shorter in this map than Franquelin had shown it, but the shape of the mouth of Petite Rivière, with a suggestion of a sand spit across the mouth, corresponds with his representation.

Bellin's delineation of the rest of the area is clearly based on better evidence: here the manuscript maps are much more reliable. The shoreline in most areas is exaggerated, but follows the correct basic directions. On the east side of the river, *La Vacherie* is clearly the

Map 2:4a Jean-Baptiste-Louis Franquelin. "Le Port de La Haive," 1686. The earliest of the LaHave maps in the Dépôt de Cartes et Plans, made at the time of Demeulle's tour of inspection.

inlet at Oxners Beach, despite the enlarged size of the stream running into it. The name is an interesting survivor from the early days of settlement and was still current at the beginning of the eighteenth century, when Simon-Pierre Denys de Bonaventure wrote: *La Vacherie [a place where cattle were kept] is a cove on the other side from the fort in which there is a stream where the tide rises and which is dry at low tide. There are meadows lying on both sides on which thirty head of cattle could be pastured. This was reserved for the governor's animals in the time of the Commander de Razilly.* (Archives des Colonies, CIID v4. 12 Oct. 1701. Mémoire des Costes D'Acadie.) (Author's translation) The *Ance aux Huîtres* is Ritceys Cove, unfortunately no longer noted for its oyster beds, and farther upstream we find Park's Creek, identified as the "River where the portage is which goes to Mirligueche." This ancient route between the LaHave and the Lunenburg area is still commemorated in the name Indian Path.

On the other side of the river, a stream (Pernette's Brook), identified only by the word *Ruisseau*, flows into the river above the *Fort*, and beside the fort site itself is a "freshwater pond" drained by a small stream running northwards. The pond is still visible on Fort Point, though Razilly's fort had been destroyed long before any of these maps were made. Annotations on three of the source maps describe the point where it once stood as "suitable for fortification" and in fact several proposals for rebuilding the fort had been sent back to France during the late seventeenth and early eighteenth centuries. Just below the fort, the *Habitations* along the shore correspond with the northerly

Maps 2:4 b, c, d, e. A series of four manuscript maps which were the chief source material for Map 2:4. Map 2:4d bears a note stating that it was made by Bellin, and lent to Chabert (a fellow cartographer) in 1748.

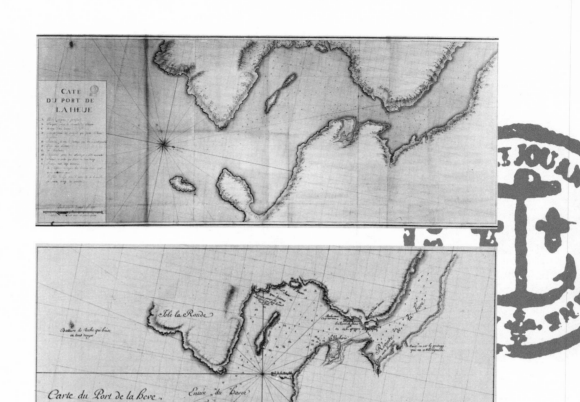

group of houses shown on Franquelin's map, which are not found on the other source maps. The *Roches aux Cormorans* (Cormorant Rock[s]) lying just off this part of the shore will be immediately recognizable to anyone familiar with the area as Bull Rock, where the descendants of the eighteenth century cormorants still congregate.

Other details on the map indicate the channels through which smaller vessels could make thier way through the islands without having to round Cape LaHave to enter the river mouth, and the cove on West Ironbound where fishing boats could shelter. The soundings have been carefully copied from the source maps. Relief seems to have been estimated only roughly, and the suggestion of vegetation is perhaps deliberately noncommittal.

Bellin's plan of the port of LaHave was the first large scale representation of the area to be published since Champlain's *Voyages* appeared some 130 years earlier. A comparison between the two will show how greatly knowledge of the river had increased in the intervening period. The fact that the area had been settled, even if for only a relatively short time, had obviously contributed to the greater accuracy of the mapping. Clearly, however, nobody had undertaken a survey of the LaHave Islands at the time the source material was produced. This task would now fall to the British surveyors, who began to map Nova Scotia in detail toward the middle of the eighteenth century.

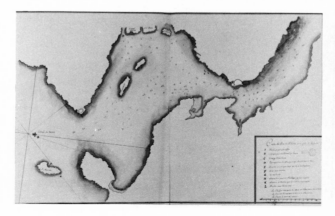

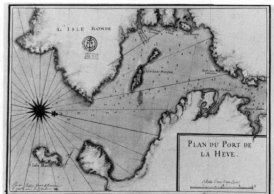

Jefferys' promotional
map of Halifax

Thomas Jefferys was a commercial mapmaker working in London, "at the Corner of St. Martin's Lane, Charing Cross," in the middle of the eighteenth century. He was, by appointment, "Geographer to His Royal Highness the Prince of Wales" (later George III). As well as publishing maps of the English counties, he issued maps of North America to satisfy the demand of the British public for information about their colonies overseas. These publications included a number of maps illustrating British claims in North America in 1755, when the boundary dispute was at its height, and an *American Atlas*, published posthumously in 1776. Among his earlier works were a number of maps of Halifax, put out shortly after Cornwallis's settlement of the town in 1749. These included maps of the town itself, maps of "Chebucto Harbour" (the overall area comprising Halifax Harbour and the Bedford Basin) and general maps of the province.

Jefferys was not an original cartographer. Like Bellin, he stayed in his office and supervised the production of maps based either on manuscripts made on location by more adventurous surveyors or on previously published work. His sources for maps of Nova Scotia included the published works of the French cartographers Bellin and D'Anville, though they were not always acknowledged, and material provided on the spot by English surveyors.

Map 2:5 first appeared in January 1750, only a few months after the establishment of Halifax during the previous summer. The location and layout of the town are thoroughly documented by a series of maps to different scales. An advertisement in the *Gentleman's Magazine* for December 1749 announcing the composite's imminent publication states that the maps of Halifax and of Chebucto Harbour, and the view of Halifax, were "Drawn on the Spot by Moses Harris,"[18]

while the map of Nova Scotia was "by Mons. D'Anville, Geographer to the French King."[19] The map itself is more sparing in its acknowledgements.

In the top left inset we see a very small scale "Map of the South Part of Nova Scotia and Fishing Banks Engraved by T. Jefferys Geographer to His Royal Highness the Prince of Wales." The boundaries of Nova Scotia were yet to be definitively established, but the term generally included present-day New Brunswick. Some versions of Jeffery's map bearing the same date but obviously representing another state of the engraving have a different title for this inset, reading "A New Map of Nova Scotia with Boundaries according to Mr. D'Anville."

The inset at top right consists of a reduced version of a contemporary plan of Halifax, "Survey'd by M. Harris." Harris' map was first published by Edward Ryland in October 1749, and again in the *Gentleman's*

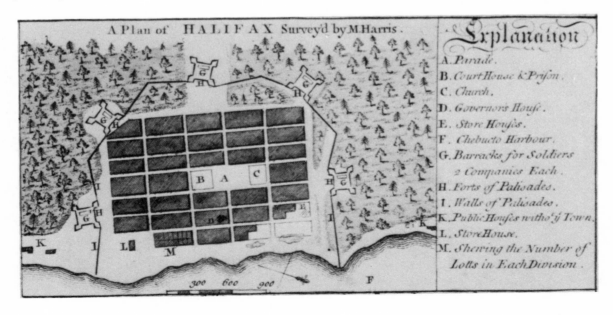

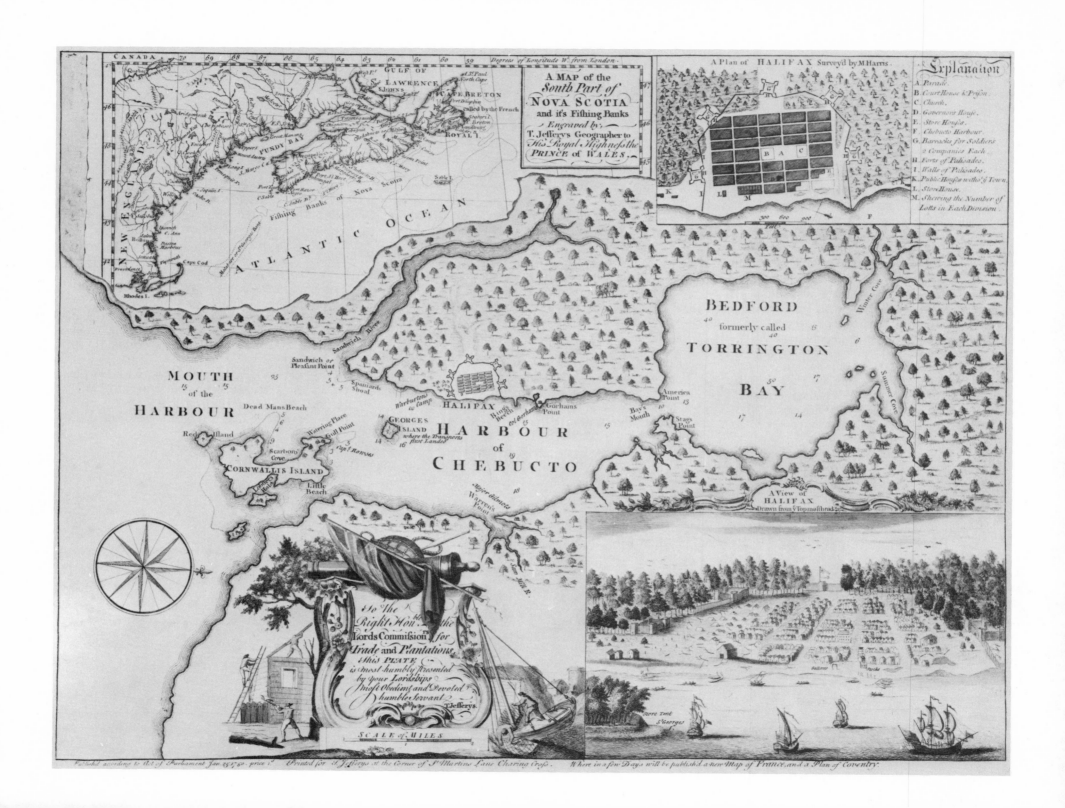

A MAP of the
South Part of
NOVA SCOTIA
and it's Fishing Banks
Engraved by
T. Jefferys Geographer to
His Royal Highnefs the
PRINCE of WALES.

CANADA

Degrees of Longitude W. from London.

NEW ENGLAND

GULF OF St LAWRENCE

S.t JOHNS

C.t BRETON

ROYAL.

PUNDY BAY

ATLANTIC OCEAN

Fishing Banks of Nova Scotia

Cape Cod

Rhodes I.

A Plan of HALIFAX Surveyd by M. Harris

Explanation

A. Parade.
B. Court House & Prison.
C. Church.
D. Governors House.
E. Store House.
F. Chebucto Harbour.
G. Barracks for Soldiers
   2 Companies Each.
H. Forts of Palisades.
I. Walls of Palisades.
K. Public House with 2 Town.
L. Store House.
M. Shewing the Number of
   Lotts in Each Division

BEDFORD
formerly called
TORRINGTON
BAY

Winter Cove

Summer Cove

MOUTH
of the
HARBOUR

Sandwich River

Sandwich or
Pleasant Point

Spaniards Shoal

Dead Mans Beach

Red Island

Watering Place

Gull Point

Scarbory Cove

CORNWALLIS ISLAND

Little Beach

Warburtons camp

Col Gorhams camp

HALIFAX

Blue beech

Gorhams Point

GEORGES ISLAND
where the Transports
first Landed

HARBOUR
of
CHEBUCTO

America Point

Bay's Mouth

Stags Point

A View of
HALIFAX
Drawn from y.e Topmosthead

Major Gilmans
Warren's Point

Sam Mill R.

To the
Right Hon.ble the
Lords Commision for
Trade and Plantations,
this PLATE
is most humbly presented
by your Lordships
Most Obedient and Devoted
humble Servant
T. Jefferys.

SCALE of MILES

Store Tent
S.t Georges

Publish'd according to Act of Parliament Jan. 25. 1750. price 1.º   Printed for T. Jefferys at the Corner of S.t Martins Lane Charing Cross.   Where in a few Days will be publish'd a new Map of France, and a Plan of Coventry.

Map 2:5 Thomas Jefferys. Composite map consisting of an untitled map of Chebucto Harbour; *A Map of the South Part of Nova Scotia and Fishing Banks. . .; A Plan of Halifax Survey'd by M. Harris;* and *A View of Halifax Drawn from y[e] Topmasthead,* 1750. Engraved.

Magazine for the same month. This version, with its Explanation, is essentially similar, though the Explanation has been rearranged.

Although his name is attached only to the inset map, comparison with the manuscript map entitled "A Plan of Chebucto Harbour with the Town of Hallefax by Moses Harris, Surveyor" (Map 7:7, p. 113) confirms Harris' authorship of the central portion of Jefferys' map. His "View of Halifax Drawn from y[e] Topmasthead" is found at the bottom right corner.

The bottom left corner is occupied by a dedicatory cartouche symbolically decorated with a fishing boat, a house building scene, a cannon and an ensign, which reads as follows: "To the Right Hon[ble] the Lords Commission[rs] for Trade and Plantations This PLATE is most humbly presented by your Lordships' Most Obedient and Devoted humble Servant T. Jefferys."

In spite of lingering doubts as to the genuine nature of Jefferys' professed humility, it must be admitted that his composite map offered both the Lords Commissioners and the general public (to whom, according to a note under the bottom margin, he would sell this document for one shilling) a good introduction to the new settlement. The map of Nova Scotia, which in fact extends down to Cape Cod, locates Chebucto Harbour and Halifax within the province. The central portion of the map gives some details about the area surrounding the new town (discussed more fully in Chapter 7), while the upper right plan gives information about the nature of the town itself. This structured and organized presentation was designed to inspire confidence in the new colonial enterprise, both in official circles and among the populace at large. Any disparity between appearance and reality would perhaps be lessened with time.

The "View," whether actually drawn from the topmasthead or not, is interesting when examined in con-

junction with the town plan, where Harris suggests a rather more advanced degree of construction than had actually been achieved. His plan shows the town completely laid out, with church, courthouse and other buildings identified, including a defensive palisade with five forts, each with its own barracks, marking the landward limits. Construction of these defences was, however, nowhere near complete at this time, and at the end of 1749 a rough barricade of felled trees was a makeshift substitute for part of the planned palisade.[20] St. Paul's Church was not built until the following year, and it was located at the south end of the Parade rather than at the north end, as shown here.

The "View" may be a rather more accurate representation of the actual, as opposed to the planned, state of affairs. The palisade appears still incomplete, but a surprising number of houses seem to have been constructed, and the forts look quite impressive. The storehouses ("E" and "L" on the plan) are recognizable in the view, as is the Governor's House, "D", of which Cornwallis had written in July of 1749 ". . .I hope to begin my own house in two days, I have a small frame and planks ready."[21] The Parade, "A", visible as an open space, shows neither church nor courthouse ("C" and "B" respectively on the plan). The store tent on George's Island reminds us that the settlement was still at an early stage of development: the centre map tells us that this is where the transports first landed. Wharves had not yet been built; small boats could pull into shore, but the larger vessels had to remain out in the channel. The first sight to greet a new arrival would be the gallows and the stocks, which appear prominently located on the waterfront, presumably as a deterrent to any immigrants disembarking with evil intent. The tents to the left of the laid out blocks may be temporary accommodation, or part of Warburton's camp which appears in the central map as lying wholly outside the palisade. Also to the south of the town ("K" in Harris' plan) but not shown in the view are a group of "Public Houses witho[t] y[e] Town" which presumably supplied entertainment and refreshment at a safe distance from the more serious work of the settlement.

Part of Jefferys' job as Royal Geographer was to publicize British colonial enterprises. Later, his mandate would include propaganda maps in the Acadian boundary dispute. Clearly an establishment man, he shows considerable skill in promoting British colonial interests and bringing information about them to the attention of the public.

The *Surveyor General maps Canso*

Charles Morris is a familiar, if confusing, name in the history of the mapping of Nova Scotia. The first Charles Morris was Surveyor General of Nova Scotia from 1749 until his death in 1781. He was succeeded as Surveyor General by his eldest son, also Charles, who was succeeded by his son, Charles III, who was in turn succeeded by *his* son, John Spry Morris.[22] It is the first two men whose work dominates the surveying of Nova Scotia in the second half of the eighteenth century.

Charles Morris senior began his mapping of the region in 1748, with a survey of the upper part of the Bay of Fundy (See Map 7:6, p. 110). A New Englander by birth, he was to spend the rest of his life in Nova Scotia. With the selection of Halifax as the provincial capital in 1749, he was given the task of laying out the new town. He was appointed Surveyor General in the same year. His next major task was to survey part of the Atlantic coast and to select a suitable location for the settlement of the Foreign Protestants who had been encouraged to emigrate to Nova Scotia. He examined the area between the present town of Liverpool and Chezzetcook Inlet, and produced a number of maps of this part of the coast during the early 1750s (Map 8:3, p. 137), although unsigned, is almost certainly his work). When a site was chosen, it was Morris' responsibility to lay out the town of Lunenburg, including its garden lots, as well as its farm lots in the surrounding countryside (See Map 7:9, p. 117).

Morris' 1755 "Chart of the Peninsula of Nova Scotia" (Frontispiece) shows clearly the state of development

Map 2:6   Charles Morris. "A Draught of the Harbour of Canso with the Islands circumjacent, Shoals, Soundings &c, taken by order of his Excellency Montagu Wilmot Esq. Governor of the Province of Nova Scotia," 1764. Manuscript.

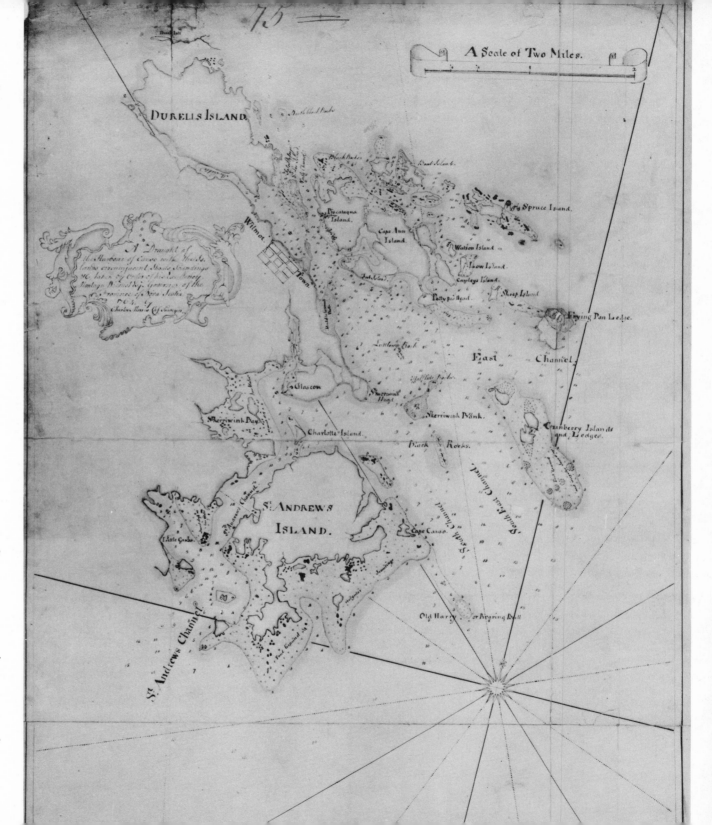

of communities and communications which marked the progress of colonization up to that time. As the population of Nova Scotia continued to grow, the work of surveying and laying out settlements became increasingly important. The 1760s saw the beginnings of the migration of settlers from New England, which was to culminate in the mass exodus of Loyalists after the Revolution. This was a period of considerable land speculation, as well as of serious attempts to settle and develop the province. Morris was kept busy surveying land to be granted out, and choosing suitable town sites on which to centre the new communities.

Canso was already well-known to the British, and particularly to New Englanders who fished in that area. The French also claimed fishing rights there for a number of years after they lost control of mainland Nova Scotia, and sporadic fighting over these rights had discouraged all but minimal settlement. By the 1760s, the fall of Louisbourg and the subsequent capture of Québec had left the British in undisputed possession of the area. With freedom from the threat of French raids, and with the control of the fishery in British hands, the time had come to establish a more permanent settlement on Canso Harbour.

The area had been mapped previously by the French (Map 3:2, p. 38) and by British officers, including Southack in 1720 (Map 3:3, p. 41) and Durrell in 1732.[23] Morris produced a much more detailed picture of the harbour and islands, and added to it the plan of a town that was to be established there. The orientation of his map is with north towards the upper right; characteristic of Morris' work, a scale of two miles is displayed in the scroll.

Because of the long established presence of fishermen in this area, almost every island and many of the rocks already had been given names, which Morris recorded. Some of these are picturesque: Sherriwink Bay, Bank and Head; Old Harry or Roaring Bull (a rock at the harbour entrance); Frying Pan Ledge and Piscataqua Island (from the Latin word for "fish" and "water"). Others are simply descriptive: Cranberry Islands and Ledges, Spruce Island, Low Island, Black Rocks, and Fort Island, which had been the home of a garrison established for the protection of British fishing

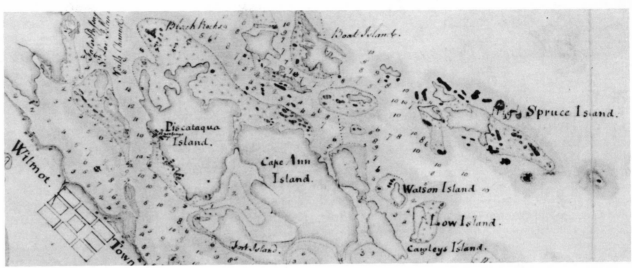

interests in the 1720s. Some islands were clearly named after their proprietors, who had received allotments of land known as "fishery rooms." Durrells Island reminds us that Thomas Durrell was not only a mapmaker, but also a landholder in this area, where both he and Southack had fishery rooms in 1725.[24] Glascow, and St. Andrews Island and Channel, suggest a Scottish presence in the area. A number of these names still survive, sometimes in a slightly modified form.

The map shows that by the 1760s the settlement consisted of a cluster of buildings on Piscataqua (now Piscatiqui) Island, one or two on Fort and Cape Ann Islands and a number along the mainland shore. Along this stretch of shore, Morris proposed to establish a small town to be known as Wilmot in honour of the then Lieutenant Governor, whose name is mentioned in the map's title. It is shown here as a rectangle of nine blocks, with two open spaces, fronting onto Canso Harbour. Despite this reasonable looking scheme and the commercial advantages of the fishery, Morris' expectations for the development of the town of Wilmot were not to be realized. T.C. Haliburton wrote in 1829 that:

The original location extended about half a mile on the shore; but it has in great measure been destroyed, in

consequence of a large portion of it having been subsequently granted, without any regard to the former allotments. This circumstance is much to be regretted, as it has greatly retarded the settlement of the town. (Haliburton, *History of Nova Scotia,* Halifax, 1829. Vol. 2, p. 94.) A contributing factor to the problem of settling Wilmot is evident from the map. No road, existing or planned, is shown; the only contact with the rest of the province was by sea. The distance of the proposed community from other settlements in the province might well have deterred those who were not actively engaged in the fishery from establishing themselves there.

When the town eventually developed, despite delays and alterations to the original plan, it was at least on the site that Morris had chosen. "Wilmot Town" eventually reverted to the old name of Canso, which with variations of spelling had been used in the area since the earliest days of European exploration of the Atlantic coast. It still remains one of the more isolated communities of the province.

None of this detracts from the accuracy of Morris' survey. It compares well with a modern map and is a good example of the work of Nova Scotia's first Surveyor General.

DesBarres' Halifax
in Atlantic Neptune

N o account of mapping in Nova Scotia would be complete without an example of the work of J.F.W. DesBarres. This controversial character, who later became Lieutenant Governor of Cape Breton, is best remembered for his *Atlantic Neptune*, a major atlas of the east coast of North America, first published in 1776.[25] His map of the Harbour of Halifax shows in great detail the growth of the town and suburbs since the foundation in 1749. With a scale, compass star, soundings in the harbour and relief and drainage patterns on land, as well as streets, buildings and fortifications, this map gives a comprehensive picture of the settlement.

The original downtown street plan, as it appeared in earlier maps such as Maps 2:5, p. 26, 6:5, p. 83, 6:6, p. 84, and 7:7, p. 113, can still be seen here. The central feature is the Grand Parade, not named but clearly shown as an open space. St. Paul's Church, also unnamed, stands not as originally planned at the north end of the parade, but to the south where the projected courthouse and prison were shown on maps of 1749. The line of the palisade originally surrounding the town can be traced approximately along the brook running to the south of the central grid of streets, up along the slope of the hill and down the zigzagging road to the harbour. Beyond the old town limits, the streets of the north and south suburbs now extend in each direction, parallel with the shore.

The streets in DesBarres' map, although not named, are easily identifiable with the help of a modern street map. The layout of the central district is little changed; even the wharves, though altered in detail, present a similar aspect. In the north suburb, most of the buildings lie along the waterfront and along Brunswick Street, where at the intersection with Gerrish Street, the Little Dutch Church can be distinguished. In the south suburb, a number of houses can be seen along Morris Street, while another group lies towards the south end of what is now Barrington Street.

Behind the town and suburbs, roads crisscross the peninsula, giving access to the immediate hinterland and also linking up with routes to other parts of the province.

As well as showing something of the state of settlement, DesBarres' map of Halifax gives us an interesting glimpse of the military and naval installations on the waterfront in the early 1770s,[26] before the threat of the American Revolution gave impetus to a new round of defence construction. A notable addition since early days is the Dock Yard, lying on a point to the north of the original town. Despite the strategic importance of its harbour, Halifax did not have a naval yard to repair ships until 10 years after its founding. The nearest naval base where British vessels could be repaired had been in Bermuda.[27] The establishment of a Naval Yard in Halifax in 1759 was a significant development in the town's long history as a naval and military base.

DesBarres shows the Yard in some detail. The Careening Wharf, begun the year before the Yard itself, was the earliest naval repair facility to be constructed in Halifax. It allowed vessels to be tilted in the water to expose the lower part of the hull for repairs or cleaning.[28] In 1759, adjacent land was acquired for further development, and construction of the Yard was undertaken under the supervision of Captain James Cook in 1760–61.[29] Here we can see the Mast Pond, a vital part of the repair facilities in the days of sail, where new masts were stored floating in salt water until needed as replacements, the StoreKeeper's Wharf where supplies were brought in, and a number of other unidentified structures which formed part of the complex in the early 1770s.

In front of the town itself, the batteries established along the waterfront in 1755 were still in service (see

Map 2:7 J.F.W. DesBarres. *The Harbour of Halifax,*
1777. Engraved, from *Atlantic Neptune*.

Chapter 6). The Five Gun and Nine Gun Battery (formerly the South Battery) had been augmented by a
new South Battery built in 1761 on the shore opposite
George's Island.[31] The island itself, with its fortifications protecting the harbour entrance, is clearly
shown.

Commercial interests were clearly flourishing as the
town developed and most of the wharves along the
waterfront were private, commercial wharves. Among
them, though, were a few built for government purposes: the King's Slip, the Wood Yard Wharf, and the
King's Lime Kiln Yard Wharf. All this activity, both
civilian and military, much of it outside the original
town site, contrasts strongly with the isolated community depicted in the earlier maps of Halifax. Clearly,
the inhabitants of Halifax had developed considerable
self-sufficiency and self-confidence over the intervening quarter-century. It is equally clear that much of the
development was due to the level of military and naval
activity apparent from the map. The link between the
presence of the military and local economic growth has
characterized the history of Halifax.

While focusing on the harbour and the waterfront,
the map gives considerable attention to the physical
features on the landward side of the town: the hills and
hollows, and the several now obliterated streams.
Citadel Hill stands out clearly, though in this state of
the engraving Des Barres made no attempt to detail its
defences, which were in any case due to be reconstructed shortly. The map as a whole is a good example
of the kind of precise observation which went into
DesBarres' 10 years of surveying the Atlantic coast of
North America, and which won general acclaim for the
Atlantic Neptune.

Charles Morris II and the Loyalists

This map showing the town and township of Digby exemplifies the planning which took place in Nova Scotia during the 1780s under Governor John Parr. It is one of a series made by Charles Morris II, the son of the first surveyor general of Nova Scotia, who succeeded to his father's post on the latter's death in 1781. Digby was one of a number of townships laid out during this period under Morris' supervision to accommodate the influx of Loyalists. Much of the work on the site was done by deputy surveyors, but the official maps were made by Morris himself.

This portion of the map, in which north is to the bottom left, shows the area between the head of St. Mary's Bay and the Annapolis Basin. The remaining portion not reproduced here depicts the lower part of the bay, the town of New Edinburgh (which was planned on an extremely grand scale) and the lots laid out along the Sissiboo River, backing onto a Crown reserve. An inset plan shows the town of Digby itself.

The main part of the map shows the location of Digby, with its Common behind it, and its Glebe and School lots close at hand. These provisions are typical of the maps of the period; the reservation of a proportion of land for the Crown as also normal.

Like Shelburne and Pictou (see Maps 7:11, p. 123 and 7:12, p. 125), Digby was established on land once granted to that ubiquitous entrepreneur, Alexander McNutt, and a group of his associates.[32] But they had failed to establish any significant population here, so that when the land was divided for the Loyalists, existing settlers' claims did not impede its distribution. The

---

Map 2:8 Charles Morris II. Part of "Plan of the Township of Digby with the Alotments of Land Laid Out & Granted Loyal Emigrants & disbanded Corps done under the Orders & directions of His Excellency Governor Parr," 1784. Manuscript.

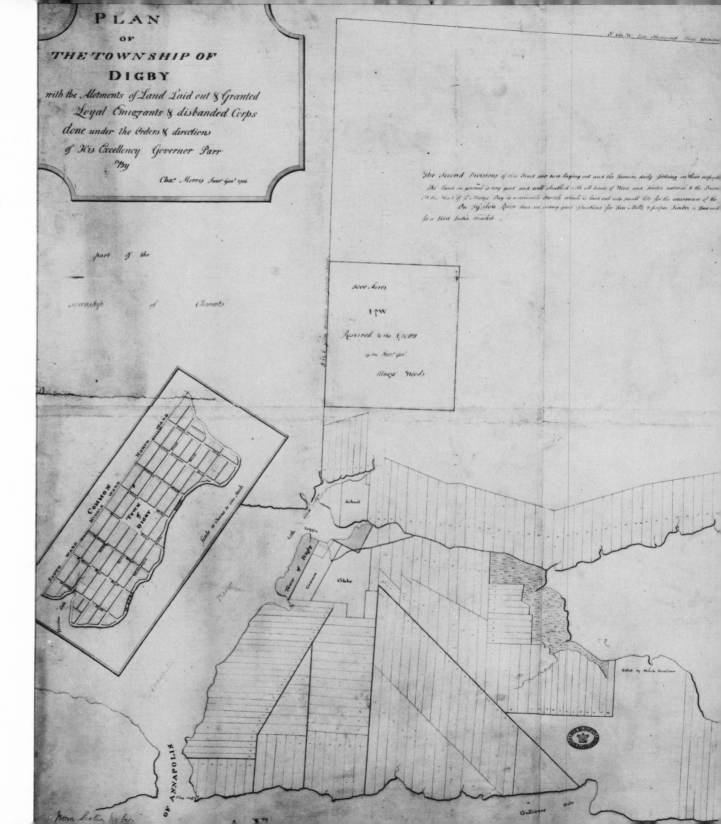

PLAN
OF
THE TOWNSHIP OF
DIGBY
with the Alotments of Land Laid out & Granted
Loyal Emigrants & disbanded Corps
done under the Orders & directions
of His Excellency Governer Parr
By
Chas. Morris Junr. Genl. 1784.

only exception is shown on this map, where at the head of St. Mary's Bay an area is marked as "settled by French Accadians." These, of course, were the Acadians who had returned after the Expulsion and, finding their former farmlands occupied by British settlers, had established themselves in other areas, including the shores of St. Mary's Bay.

The Loyalists began to arrive in the area in June, 1783, in vessels under the command of Admiral Digby, whose name was given to the township. They immediately began to negotiate for land on which to form a settlement, and Deputy Surveyor Thomas Milledge was authorized to survey the area and lay out the Town Plot.[33] The first grants were made early in 1784, and while no names are assigned to the lots marked out on the map, a note states that "the Second Divisions of this Tract are now laying out and the farmers daily settling on their respective Alotments." The long, narrow lots, most with water frontage on either the Bay of Fundy or St. Mary's Bay, are typical of the land grants of this period.

The note goes on to tell us that "the Land in general is very good and well cloathed with all kinds of Wood and Timber natural to the Province. At the Head of St. Mary's Bay is a valuable Marsh, which is laid out in small lots for the convenience of the Setlers." The marsh is clearly marked on the map. A final natural advantage is identified on the Sissiboo River, which runs into the lower part of St. Mary's Bay and is off this section of the map; ". . .there are many good Situations for Saw Mills & proper Timber to Saw into Boards &c for a West India Market." Clearly the new settlement was considered to have a sound economic base, and was expected to prosper.

The town itself, seen in the inset, was laid out in the standard pattern of the period. It is divided into rectangular blocks by long streets parallel to the waterfront, and short streets at right angles. The street names are equally standard, including King, Queen, George, Carleton, Montagu and other familiar dignitaries. Church Street and Water Street appear, rather predictably; the only concession to local toponymy is found in St. Mary's Bay Street. Despite this reluctance to depart from tradition, Digby has the distinction of being built out on a peninsula rather than consisting of a rectangle set back from the shore. Being thus surrounded on three sides by water, it has a more individual character than some of the "instant" towns of this period.

During the period beginning in 1783, Morris and his deputies were kept extremely busy planning and laying out settlements all over Nova Scotia. The results of their labours on behalf of the thousands of immigrants who flocked into the province, and of the soldiers whose regiments were disbanded here, are recorded in numerous maps, some other examples of which will be found in later chapters.

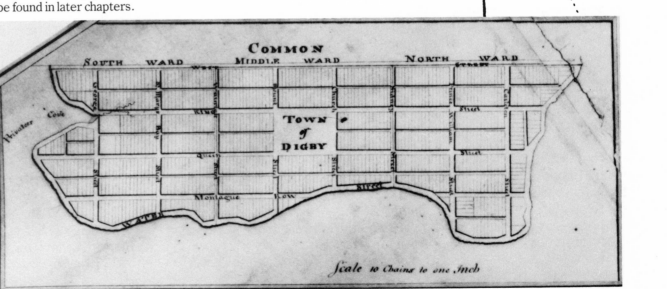

Chapter 3 *Fishing:* The Ports and the Banks

The first regular visitors from Europe to establish a foothold in Nova Scotia were fishermen who came in search of North Atlantic cod. Long before attempts were made at colonization, our harbours and beaches were used as seasonal fishing bases. They also provided shelter and fresh water for fishermen working on the banks further offshore.

Some of the earliest maps of the Atlantic coast of North America reflect the importance of the cod fishery from the sixteenth century onwards. Gastaldi's map of 1556 (Map 1:1, p. 7) shows the fishing banks as a narrow ribbon of sand, extending from Newfoundland to the western end of *"Terra de Nurumbega,"* with a square *"Isola della rena"* (Sable Island) at mid-point. Fish and fishermen are depicted off the shores of eastern Nova Scotia and Cape Breton. Paul Ollivier's North Atlantic chart of 1624, a small area of which is reproduced here (Map 3:1), is more accurate, detailing a chain of banks including the *"grand Banc"* off Newfoundland, the *"Banc d'Accadie,"* and *"B. St. George"* (George's Bank). The Grand Bank was known as the centre of the cod fishery; it lies closest to Europe, and its cold waters teemed with fish. All these banks were to play an important part in the Nova Scotia fishery in years to come.

Fishing was not, however, confined to the offshore banks; cod also abounded on the inshore fishing grounds. Nicolas Denys, in his *Description and Natural History of the Coasts of North America*,[1] identifies and describes three main types of cod fishing: the banks fishery, where vessels normally stayed at sea until they had completed their catch, which was taken back salted but not dried;[2] the seasonal inshore fishery, where temporary base camps were established for salting and drying the catch which was brought ashore daily;[3] and the "sedentary" fishery, based on a community of permanent residents.[4] The seasonal inshore fishery was particularly important in Acadia, where the harbours along the Atlantic coast were temporary summer homes to many Breton, Norman and Basque fishermen before the end of the sixteenth century.

Denys describes in great detail how these fishermen set up camps with processing facilities year after year. Among their requirements were: a sheltered harbour for their vessels, where they could set up *échaffauds* (stages) to clean and salt the catch; space to construct *vigneaux*, or fish flakes, the racks upon which the salted fish was dried; and, preferably, gravel beaches on which to complete the drying process. At the end of the season, all the structures were dismantled, most of the fishing boats hidden away, and the site abandoned until a future season brought back the crews who would set up their camp as before.

When Champlain first arrived in Acadia in 1604, he made individual maps of the first three ports visited by de Monts' expedition—LaHave (Map 2:1, p. 14), Port Rossignol (Liverpool) Map 7:1, p. 96) and Port Mouton (Map 7:2, p. 99). These maps are the earliest detailed representations of what were to become important fishing ports along the South Shore. The plentiful supply of fish at Port Rossignol seems to have impressed Champlain greatly, as the water in his map of the port is full of them. Some of these (perhaps due to the engraver's whim) appear to be dolphins, which seventeenth century Frenchmen classified indiscriminately as fish. The cod, however, is also there, symbolic of the great wealth to be found in these coastal waters. It was at Port Rossignol that, almost 30 years later, Nicolas Denys tried to establish his first "sedentary" fishery.

As we shall see from other maps in this chapter, the harbours of the Eastern Shore were also recognized from an early date as valuable fishing bases. Not far from Canso, which was to become the centre of the Eastern Shore fishery (Map 3:3), the settlers returning from Port Royal in 1607 found a flourishing seasonal fishery in operation. It was described by Marc Lescarbot, a member of the expedition:
Finally, we arrived within four leagues of Canso, at a harbour where a fine old sailor from St. Jean de Luz, named Captain Savalet, was fishing . . . . This worthy man told us that the voyage was his forty-second to these

parts, and one must remember that these Newfoundlanders make but one a year. He was wondrous content with his fishing, and told us that he caught daily a good fifty crowns' worth of cod, and that his voyage was worth to him ten thousand francs. He had sixteen men in his employ, and his vessel was of eighty tons' burden, and able to carry one hundred thousand dry fish.[5]

Port Savalet, marked on maps of New France by Lescarbot and others, is probably the harbour known today as Whitehead.

A sedentary fishery was established in the late 1650s by Nicolas Denys at *Chedabouctou* (Guysborough) (see Map 3:2), and the *Compagnie de la Pesche Sedentaire de l'Acadie* (Company of Acadia) set up one of their bases in the Chedabucto Bay–Canso area in the 1680s. Cape Breton Island also played an important part in the development of the fishery. Nicolas Denys had two bases there, at St. Peter's and St. Ann's Bay, and for much of the first part of the eighteenth century, the French Atlantic coast fishery was centred on Louisbourg (see Map 3:5).

In the meantime, English fishing interests had developed off the Acadian coast, where in the 1680s English boats fished under license from Governor La Vallière, in competition with the Company of Acadia. Some, indeed, fished without licenses, in defiance of the French. With the English right to Nova Scotia officially established from 1713 onwards it became the turn of the French fishermen to be designated "intruders," as in Southack's map of Canso.

Such annotations on maps remind us that international disputes over the right to fish off the coasts of Nova Scotia are nothing new, and that jurisdiction over the resources of the continental shelf has always been hard to establish and enforce. Despite disputed fishing rights, over-fishing and depletion of stocks, and technical advances both in the catching and preserving of fish, the harbours which served the earliest fishermen in this region are, for the most part, still used by their twentieth century counterparts.

Ollivier charts the fishing banks

This portion of Paul Ollivier's 1624 map of the North Atlantic shows much of present-day eastern Canada, from the Ile d'Orléans to Newfoundland and Labrador, and including Nova Scotia. The chart is one of many made during this period to assist mariners crossing the ocean to the New World. The partial compass star visible on the right hand side, and the rhumbs (lines by which sailors could set their course) which crisscross the map, identify even this small section of the chart as an aid to navigation. Although the proportions of the land masses and the shape of the coastline leave something to be desired, it is a remarkably accurate map for this period.

Of particular interest to us is the close attention paid to the banks, or areas of shallow water on the continental shelf, which are shown in some detail. From the early 1500s onward, these banks were visited annually by European fishermen because of the enormous numbers of codfish to be caught there. The Grand Bank (bottom right), where the cold waters of the Labrador current meet the Gulf Stream, has always been the best-known and most productive of the fishing grounds. Ollivier shows also the string of banks lying off the coasts of Acadia and New England. Although some of their names are hard to read, we can pick out *b. St. George* (George's Bank) to the west, and, parallel to the coast of Acadia, we find the *Banc d'Accadie*. Farther east, the word "Sable" is discernable, marking Sable Island Bank.

The banks are indicated by a shaded area surrounded by a dotted line. A similarly defined area along the southern and western coasts of Acadia indicates the shallow water which forms the inshore fishing ground. This, too, was a valuable resource that had been exploited since the latter part of the sixteenth century. A number of ports are indicated along the coast; these were known to fishermen and served as bases for seasonal inshore fishing, before settlement took place.

The detail with which the rest of eastern Canada is represented indicates that Ollivier's map was not intended solely as a guide to the fishing grounds. But the way in which those grounds are depicted makes it clear that European knowledge of them was extensive by the end of the first quarter of the seventeenth century. The importance of the fishing grounds was clearly recognized by the maker of this chart.

Map 3:1 Paul Ollivier. Part of his North Atlantic chart.

The Intendant inspects
Chedabucto Bay

A note on the back of this map tells us that it was sent (to France) by "M. de Meules" in 1686. This note identifies the map as one of a series that recorded the visit of a small party from Québec, led by the Intendant, Jacques Demeulle, on a tour of inspection of Acadia (see also Map 8:1, p. 131). One of the settlements they visited was Chedabouctou (now Guysborough); this map, probably by the King's hydrographer, Franquelin, illustrates the visitors' impressions.

At the time of Demeulle's tour, cod had been fished off the Eastern Shore of Nova Scotia for well over 100 years, and the harbour of Chedabouctou was well-known to seasonal fishermen. Nicolas Denys had established a "sedentary" fishery there in about 1659, and shortly before this map was made the *Compagnie de la Pêche Sédentaire de l'Acadie* (Company of Acadia) had made Chedabouctou the centre of their operations on the Eastern Shore.

The map is oriented with north to the right, so that the fort, established at the head of the harbour, appears at the top. Some of the features observed by Demeulle and his party are marked directly on the map; others are numbered and described by means of a legend.

The *Fort de Chedabouctou*, "2", sometimes known as Fort Saint Louis, stands on a cleared area jutting out into the harbour. The *Bassin de Chedabouctou*, at the mouth of the Guysborough River, is formed by a long beach protecting the anchorage, with a narrow entrance channel. This setting provided shelter for the fishing boats and a harbour for the large vessels that would carry the dried salt cod back to France. The "fort" itself provided a base from which the fishing, salting and drying activities were organized. Larger scale maps of the period show that the building behind the fort was the *saline*, or salt house.

The traffic represented in Chedabucto Bay includes both large commercial sailing vessels and smaller fish-

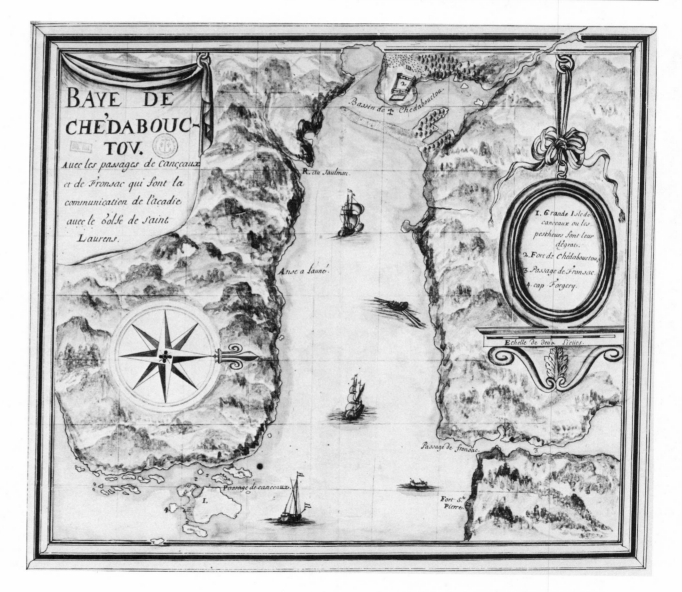

ing boats. Nicolas Denys, in his *Description and Natural History of the Coasts of North America*, describes the daily life of the fishermen, setting out in small *chaloupes* in the morning and returning in the evenings to salt and ready their catch for drying.[6] He also explains that in some instances the fish were found too far along the shore for the fishermen to reach them easily from the base. In order to be able to fish where the cod were most plentiful, they set up *dégrats*, or subsidiary processing stations, which could be moved along the shore as necessary if the fish stocks moved.[7] As we see in this map, the *Grande Isle Canceaux*, "1", (Canso Island) was one of the places where such substations were established. Preliminary processing of the fish there would avoid the long haul back into Chedabucto after each day's fishing.

Canso Island was to remain an important base for both the French and English fishery for many years; this will become clear from later maps. There was a sheltered anchorage between the island and the mainland, shown here by the anchor symbol. On the island itself, there are indications of stages or flakes used for the curing and drying of the fish. The significance of Cape Forgery, "4", is hard to determine except as a landmark and aid to navigation.

Between the islands, a channel named the *Passage de Canceaux* gives protected access from the harbour of Canso to Chedabucto Bay. On the opposite side of the bay, the *Passage de Fronsac* (Strait of Canso) forms the much more significant link, noted in the title, with the St. Lawrence. Canso's strategic position as a port of call, as well as its proximity to the fishing grounds, made it an ideal spot from which to ship fish to Europe, and led to its development as the centre of the east coast fishery in subsequent years.

Two other features on this map have some relevance to the history of fishing in the area. *Fort St. Pierre* (St. Peter's), on the inaccurately defined Cape Breton shore, was the site of another of the many posts Nicolas Denys established for fur trading and fishing in New France.[8] On the south side of Chedabucto Bay, *R[iviere] au Saulmon*, which retains the name Salmon River today, was the source of another valuable fish that would not be commercially exploited for a number of years. Denys describes the river:

Having gone there once to fish, I made a cast of the seine at its entrance, where it took so great a quantity of Salmon that ten men could not haul it to land, and although it was new, had it not broken the Salmon would have carried it off. We had still a boat full of them. The Salmon there are large; the smallest are three feet long. (Denys, *Description*, p. 166)

In the absence of permanent settlers, the salmon were to be left in virtual peace for some time to come. Cod was the important commercial fish: methods had been developed for preserving it, and there was an enormous market for it in western Europe. The exploitation of other species was still in the future.

Map 3:2a   Chedabucto Bay and Canso on a modern map.

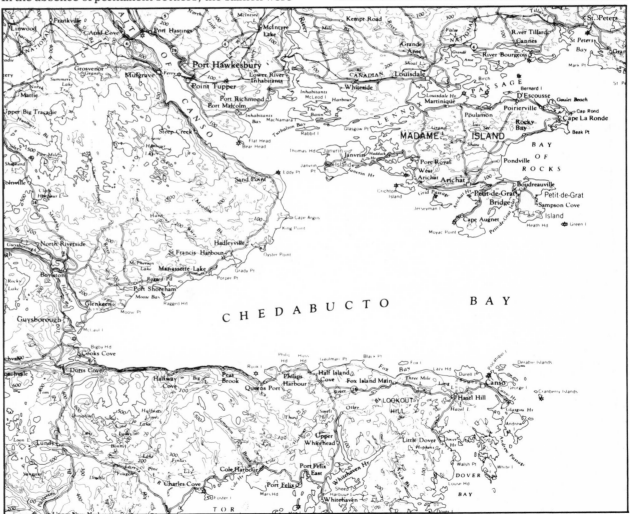

The Disputed fishery at Canso

This map shows in a rough but recognizable fashion the Canso area that appeared as part of the previous map. It records the voyage of HMS *Squirrel*, sent to Canso in 1718 under the command of Captain Thomas Smart to dislodge the French who were still using the area as a fishing base. The cartographer, Southack, was a member of this expedition. He was no stranger to these parts: in 1690, he had led a raid on Fort Saint Louis at Chedabouctou. Although not very accurate in outline, the map offers a degree of credibility with its compass star (with north to the right), its soundings, its bearings for the channel, and circumstantial detail.

From 1713 onwards, Nova Scotia was in English hands, and the New England vessels that had previously fished there under license from the French (or under protest) could now expect to set up uncontested legitimate shore bases. The French, however, were by no means convinced that the Canso Islands were included when the peninsula of Acadia was ceded to the British by the Treaty of Utrecht, and continued to fish in the area.

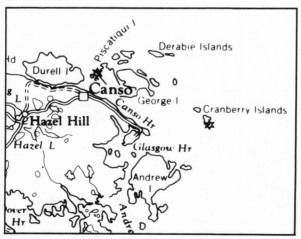

The illustration in the bottom right corner of the map shows fishermen in a small boat, hauling in cod and seining for bait. This scene is typical of the French inshore fishery, which used small boats that returned each evening to the land base, where the catch was processed. The "stages" shown jutting out into the water from the shores of the islands are the *échaffauds* described by Nicolas Denys in the previous century, where the fish were cleaned and salted. Most of them are built near beaches where the fish could be dried. The buildings behind these stages suggest that the temporary camps described by Denys had given way to more permanent structures, even if they were occupied for only part of the year. It is noteworthy that the majority of the stages are marked as belonging to "French Intruders."

Since the English, prior to 1713, lacked shore bases in Acadia, they used larger vessels than the French and fished for long periods without returning to land. The catch was salted on board, and brought back to the home port for drying only when the hold was full. But once Nova Scotia was in British hands, it was possible to establish a shore based fishery, and the small boat depicted with its crew could, in fact, be English. On the bay on the landward side of Canso Island, we find the stage and buildings belonging to "Messrs Hall and Henshaw", who were among the first New Englanders to establish processing facilities on the Canso shore. Earlier in the year of the *Squirrel*'s voyage, Hall and Henshaw had been in Boston complaining that French fishing vessels, under naval escort, had made an expedition "to Cape Cancer and the Islands adjacent. . .and carried off about Twenty Thousand Quintals of Cod Fish."[9]

Despite these problems, Canso was the chief centre for the New England fishery during the early part of the eighteenth century. By 1725, John Henshaw was operating five vessels there.[10] According to Governor Lawrence Armstrong, "the people of New England (as they say) make more fish there than on their own coast."[11] For much of this period, France and England were technically at peace, but mutual harassment limited the development of the Canso fishery. With the renewal of the war in 1740 hostilities escalated, and in

1744 a French raiding force destroyed the entire settlement, taking the inhabitants and fishermen as prisoners to Louisbourg.

It is apparent that, at the time the map was made, Canso was still chiefly a seasonal fishing station. Although each stage has a building behind it, there is no sign of any centrally established community. Hall and Henshaw left 10 men at Canso to "keep possession of their fishery,"[12] but this scarcely constituted a permanent population. Southack shows trees over the whole of the interior of the mainland and most of the islands; no agricultural base existed to support a permanent settlement. The "French House" on the mainland may once have been inhabited year round, but there was no evidence from the map that this was still the case. The island at the entrance to the harbour is marked "Fort," but while forts were undoubtedly constructed, and appear on a 1735 map of the area, they were on what is now known as Grassy Island, and were destroyed in the French raid of 1744. It was not until the 1760s that steps were taken to establish a settlement which would support the fishery on a permanent basis (see Map 2:6, p. 28).

Sailing vessels of different shapes and sizes are shown in the waters around Canso Island. They include a large, three masted vessel in the Road (an area close to the shore where ships could ride at anchor) which may represent HMS *Squirrel*, another ship in the harbour, possibly a merchant vessel loading fish, and a smaller one which appears to be dangerously close to a "Stone Bank." The smaller, single masted boats are presumably fishing vessels; the impression is of a good deal of activity in the area. Indeed, until the *Squirrel* arrived to drive away the French fishermen (and probably shortly after her departure!) Canso was a major fishing centre for *both* nations. The following account, by Captain Ben Young, gives us an idea of this activity. Written in 1720, the year that this map was made, it refers to the voyage of the HMS *Rose* in 1716, an earlier attempt to discourage the French from fishing at Canso.

But what Excells them all is Canso, which is invaluable for its Fishery. Tis here such great quantities of Codd herring and Macrell swarm amongst the Islands that when I was there on his Majesty's ship Rose there was then Ninety six sail of English and 200 French makeing their voyages, the English vessells from 50 to 70 Tonns the French small shallops and when fish is scarce at other places here they are always plenty for on letting the line down they draw up Two and two as fast as they can pull it. . . . When a ship of warr is not there or anything to hinder the French fishing among us that then our fishing vessells cannot take 4 Fish when they will take tenn they fish with fresh and we with Salt Bait we come 180 leagues they but 7; they in small Boats we in Large Sloops. . . . (PAC, NSA, XII, 166–167)[13]

The distances mentioned represent those from Boston and Louisbourg respectively; while not entirely accurate, they give a reasonable basis for comparing the ease of access to the Canso fishing grounds. In fact, the northern (right hand) part of the map shows the "French Shoar" of I. Madam (Isle Madame), capable of providing a refuge if necessary for the French fishermen working at Canso. The note on the map gives "the nearest distance between them" as three and a half leagues.

Although the value of Canso as a fishing station had been known since the late sixteenth century, its isolation and vulnerability to attack were major drawbacks to its commercial development. It was only after the final fall of Louisbourg in 1758 that the threat of a French attack was removed and it then became possible to establish a permanent population in the area. In 1764, a series of maps by Charles Morris announced a new era in the development of Canso and its economy (see Map 2:6, p. 28).

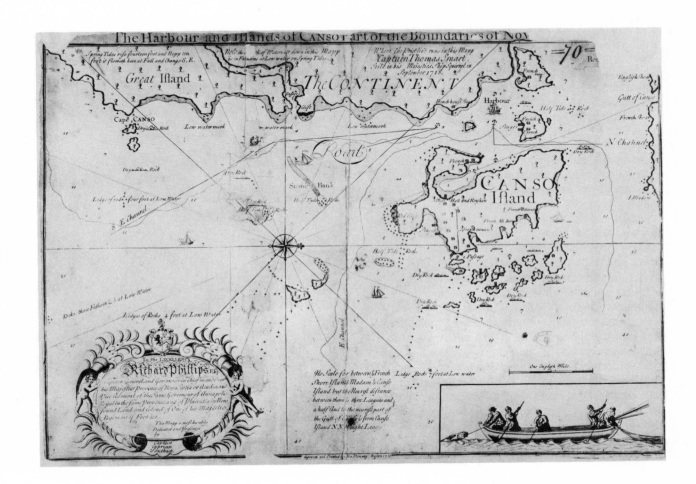

Western Nova Scotia fishing ports

Captain Southack was an enthusiastic, if not always very reliable, mapmaker. His *New England Coasting Pilot* includes maps of the Nova Scotia coast which are even less accurate than his map of Canso. This portion of a large map covers the western half of the province; it includes areas of the coast, such as that around St. Mary's Bay, that Southack seems to have viewed on a very foggy day. His interest, as suggested by the title of his atlas, was primarily coastal navigation; but this map is useful more for its observations about the economic potential of western Nova Scotia and the South Shore than for its guidance to mariners.

Despite his shortcomings as a maker of navigational charts, Southack shows an awareness of the importance to the fishery of the harbours of the southwest coast. The banks that still form the basis of the offshore fishery are identified by name, though not specifically as fishing grounds, while the ports are clearly described in terms of their fishing potential. Every harbour, from Long Island round to LaHave, is annotated with information about navigation, available fish stocks and, in many cases, the suitability of the beaches for making (drying) fish. It is likely that Southack acquired this detailed knowledge of the advantages of particular harbours when, as captain of the *Province Galley*, he was engaged in the protection of the New England fishing fleet in the area.

Great Passage (Grand Passage) or Long Island Harbour is, we are told, navigable for small vessels; it has "great Fishing" and space "to make Fish on." St. Mary's River (Salmon River) is navigable for small vessels and well located: "Cod Fish very plenty two miles of this River," though "very rocky ground" is noted off the coast. Pubenque River, probably Tusket, is navigable and noted for fish, as is Pubencuque (Pubnico) River, while the East and West Passages of Cape Sable Island, despite difficult navigation "but for small

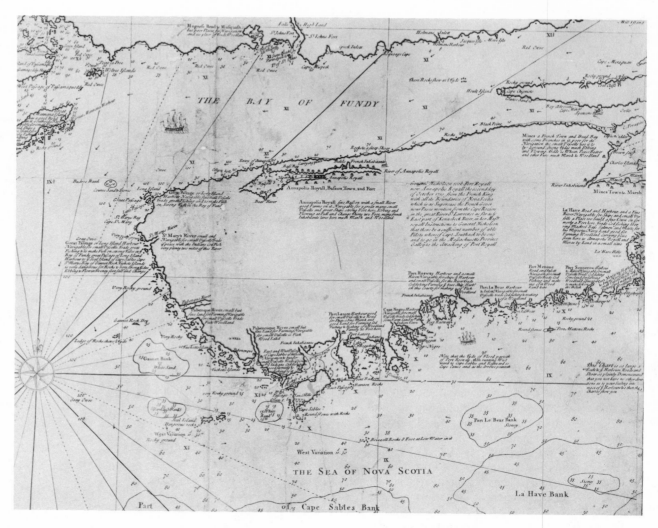

Vessells," provide good fishing, "and the making of it." Port Latore (La Tour) and Cape Negro have similar advantages.

Port Roseway (Shelburne Harbour) earns special praise from the cartographer: the harbour is navigable for ships, and the river for small vessels. The port is "ye best Ship Harbᵣ on this Coast, & for making of Fish." Whether the superlative is intended to include the making of fish is not clear, but Southack certainly

Map 3:4 Captain Cyprian Southack. Western Nova Scotia, Undated. Engraved.

recognized Shelburne's advantage as a deep water harbour. Port La Bear (Port Hebert) Harbour and Inlett and Port Mettone (Mouton) Road and Inlett are navigable for small vessels, and there is cod fishing. This is also true of Port Sennerow (Liverpool), where there is "a fine place to make fish on the beach." Port Matway (Medway) also has small vessels fishing for cod, "and making of it."

Southack reserves his greatest praise for "LaHave Road and Harbour, and a Fine River Navigable for Ships and small Vessells, a Place too bould a fine Town on formerly a Fort here, Trade Cod Fishing, Herring, Mackrel Bass Salmon, and Masts for His Majestys Navy . . . ." Southack also mentions good farming and woodland, as well as inland communications ("Carrying place [i.e. portage route] from here to Annapolis Royal and Mines by land in a small time.") These natural advantages brought prosperity to the LaHave River in the nineteenth century as a fishing and ship building centre, with an agricultural base and excellent transportation links.

The identification of "Indian" and French inhabitants in some of the ports reminds us that it was not until 1713 that the Treaty of Utrecht brought an end to the frequent changes of ownership of peninsular Nova Scotia. Up until the 1750s, the majority of the population still consisted of either Micmacs or Acadians. During the frequent periods of war or unrest between England and France, English vessels had continued to fish in the waters off southwest Nova Scotia, regardless of the political status of the land itself. But they could not count on undisturbed occupancy of the harbours, and therefore developed different fishing techniques from those used by the French. Governor De Menneval wrote from Port Royal in 1688:

They have continued to come to fish here this year, in number, as I am told, over 60 ketches. In truth they do not dry their fish on land at all, and take it back to Eng-land for that when they have enough, so they make several voyages each summer. But they come into the harbours every Saturday on the pretext of getting water and wood, or to shelter from bad weather, and they dress their fish there, which does more harm [to the waters of the harbour] than if they did it at sea or on the grounds; they have had, I am told, a warship on the coast all this summer as an escort. (From PAC, C11D, 2 (1), 187–215)[14] (Translation by the author)

Welcome or not, fishermen from both England and New England were clearly familiar with the ports near their fishing grounds. Once the region was formally in English hands they could use the ports with a little more security, but the presence of the French, and particularly the Micmac inhabitants, did not encourage British fishermen to attempt to set up permanent, but vulnerable, shore bases. It was not until 1761 that Mordow McCleod sought and was granted permission to use a piece of land near the old fort at LaHave as a base for a fishery.

Southack's charting of the Atlantic coast of North America was considered by at least one of his contemporaries as hazardous to navigation.[15] Southack combined apparently careful soundings and some accurate observations with a highly imaginative representation of the actual coastline. But in spite of this rather stylized outline, we are very much aware of the contrast between the Bay of Fundy, whose deep waters and high tides were unsuitable for fishing, and the indented western and southern coasts. The banks and the shallow inshore grounds stand out clearly as the source of the fish that the economy of the ports would be based upon in the years to come. Fishing has continued, from St. Mary's Bay to the LaHave River, up to the present day. With the depletion of the cod stocks and changing technology, the catch has been diversified and freezing has largely replaced drying as a method of preservation. Nevertheless, many of these ports could, until very recently, be distinguished by their "fine place to make fish on the beach."

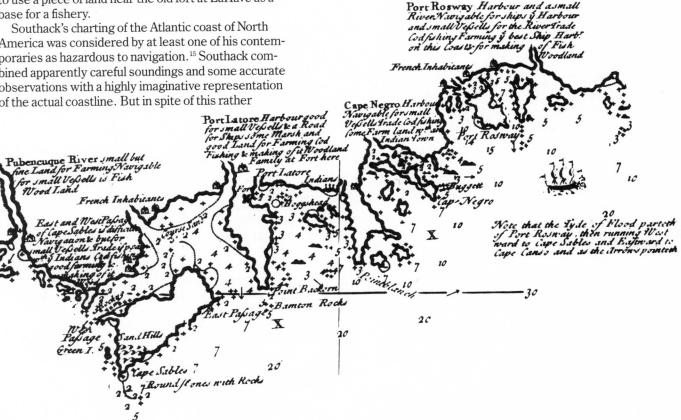

Fishing at Louisbourg

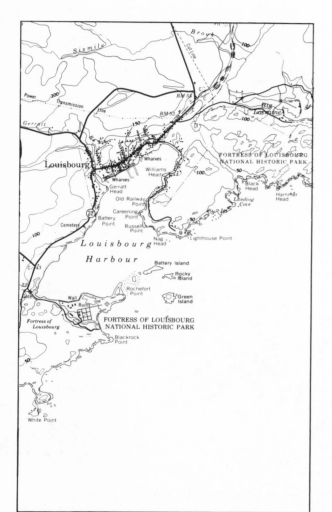

Map 3:5a Louisbourg today.

lthough it is best-known today for its reconstructed fortress, Louisbourg was also a major
fishing port, established by the French after
the Treaty of Utrecht to maintain their access to the
North Atlantic cod fishery.

This vivid drawing, which is not so much a map as a
bird's-eye view of the port, was made at the time when
the major fortifications were being laid out. Most existing maps of Louisbourg are concerned with its
defences, and have clear military and naval significance.
This "View of the Port. . .," while not ignoring the
existing defences and those under construction, is
chiefly notable for its striking details of the fishing
industry as carried on in the early eighteenth century.

Comparison with a modern map will make it clear
that we are looking westward across the harbour from
a point above its entrance. On the peninsula jutting
towards us is the settlement of Louisbourg, consisting
of a few houses clustered around the church, "A". Facing us across the harbour are the old barracks, "B",
and one of the batteries, "E". Other batteries are
established on the tip of the peninsula and on Battery
Island, commanding one side of the harbour entrance,
and also on the northern (right-hand) side of the
entrance. The new barracks, "C", stand just behind
the houses of the settlement, within the planned defensive bastions that are marked out with surveying
poles, "D".

Most of the activity in the harbour, however, is connected not with the construction of the new fortress,
but with the more immediate business of catching and
processing cod. A memoir written at Versailles in 1715
speaks of the urgency of establishing a fishery on Isle
Royale (Cape Breton Island) to replace those lost in
Acadia and Newfoundland by the Treaty of Utrecht.
Louisbourg was recommended as a site for this enterprise, as it had a deep harbour, was sheltered, was

easy to sail in and out of, difficult to blockade from the
sea, and well placed as a port of call for vessels going to
or from the Grand Banks. Above all, "Louisbourg is
situated on a coast most abounding with fish; fishing is
carried on in small boats *[chaloupes]* half a league from
port"[16] (author's translation). Clearly, this advice had
been acted upon by the time the present map was
produced.

The letters "F" to "M" in the key explain how the
fishery was carried on. Comparison with Nicolas Denys'
1672 account of the cod fishery shows that little had
changed, except that the business was now established
around a permanent community, something Denys had
dreamed of, but had never been able to sustain for any
length of time.

The *chafauds*, or stages, "F", that encircle the harbour were the fish processing plants of their day. The
small, single masted *chaloupes* are shown working on
the grounds, "G", and returning to port," "H", where
the catch was cleaned and salted on the covered
stages. When it was ready for drying, it was spread out
on the *vigneaux* (fish flakes), "L", or on *graves*, "I", the
stony beaches which were often used for the second
stage of the drying process. Piles of processed cod,
"M", stacked carefully to protect them from the rain,
await shipment to France, possibly in one of the larger
ships to be seen at anchor in the harbour. These large
vessels also represent the supply ships that the community depended upon for many of its necessities,
including essentials for the garrison and for the
unfinished fortress.

The natural advantages of Louisbourg as a fishing
port outlasted its brief period of glory as the stronghold
of French military power on the Atlantic coast. After
the fall of the fortress, the fishery was taken over by
the English. It continued to form a major part of the
economy of the region, and fishing is carried on in
Louisbourg to this day.

Veüe du Port de Louis-bourg dans L'Isle Royalle

A *L'Eglise au milieu des principales habitations,*
B *Anciens corps de Casernes,*
C *Nouveau corps de Casernes,*
D *Jalons ou doivent être les Fortifications,*
E *Batteries de Canons,*
F *Chafaud pour preparer la Morüe;*

G *Chaloupes sur le fond qui sont la pêche,*
H *Chaloupes qui reviennent de la Pêche,*
I *Grue ou l'on fait Secher la Morüe,*
L *Vigneaux ou l'on fait secher la Morüe,*
M *Piles de Morüe pour les garantir de la playe,*
N *Roche couverte de deux pieds et demy a haute Mer,*

Chapter 4 Farming and Food Production:

The Acadians and their Successors

When European expeditions first travelled to the New World, they brought with them the provisions essential for their return journey across the Atlantic, and for the period they expected to spend exploring, fishing or trading. Their supplies were supplemented on arrival with local fish, game, wild fruit and edible plants. Often, these products were supplied by the natives, for whom fishing, hunting and gathering constituted the normal means of sustaining their semi-nomadic way of life.

Europeans, however, were accustomed to the more orderly agricultural habits of a settled population. It was not long before French fishermen who set up summer bases along the coast of Acadia (see Chapter 3) began to establish gardens to assure themselves of produce for the season. Nicolas Denys tells us that the typical seventeenth century fishing captain "has a garden made on land which provides him with salads, peas [and] beans."[1] The *Rivière des Jardins* (Jordan River) which appears on maps made as early as the sixteenth century may have been a site for such gardens.

Gardens were also established by DeMonts' colonizing expedition of 1604–1607, both at the initial settlement at Sainte Croix and the at the more permanent establishment at Port Royal. Champlain refers to the difficulty of clearing garden sites in a place where "the entire country is covered with very dense forests. . .except a point a league and a half up the river where there are some oaks which are very scattered and a number of wild vines. This could easily be cleared and the place be brought under cultivation. . . ."[2] Champlain's map of Port Royal (Map 7:3, p. 101) shows both his garden, "B", and the area described above,

"H", which was cleared, becoming the first agricultural site in Acadia. Champlain records that in 1606, "the Sieur de Poutrincourt. . . despatched some labourers to cultivate the land at a spot he considered suitable, which is up the river a league and a half from the settlement of Port Royal. . . . There he had wheat, rye, hemp and several other seeds sown to ascertain how they would thrive."[3] Before the expedition left Acadia, it was evident that the experiment had succeeded.

In 1632, Isaac de Razilly established a settlement at LaHave. He brought settlers from France to clear and cultivate the fertile land at Petite Riviere. Before his death in 1636, a crop of wheat had been harvested there.

A great many early maps of Nova Scotia, both French and English, show clearly the "very dense forests" which provided a significant obstacle to agricultural development. The next group of settlers to come to Port Royal, including many of the LaHave pioneers and new immigrants from France, developed alternatives to tree clearing. As we can see from some of the maps in this chapter, these people created the earliest Acadian farmlands by dyking and draining the marshes which lay along the Annapolis River and Basin. The fields produced by this method proved to be exceptionally fertile once the salt had been leached out of the soil, and the dyking system was soon extended to the Minas Basin and Chignecto areas as the population expanded.

Many visitors to Acadia, and even their own administrators, commented on and criticized the Acadians' preference for reclaiming marshland rather than clearing forested uplands. Jean Delabat, a military engineer and cartographer at Port Royal during the last years of the French régime, shared their disapproval, observing that:

The inhabitants, who insist upon cultivating the above-mentioned marshes in preference to the higher lands, because the marshes do not need manuring, build levées and dykes to protect them from the tides; yet the tides do not cease to break through from time to time. If they would use the time they spend in making and repairing their dykes in clearing and improving the high lands, they would receive much greater profits. . . ."
(Description of the River of the Dauphin. . .)[4]

Despite such criticism, the Acadians were probably correct in their choice of soil that they knew to be deep and fertile, as opposed to the sparse soil of the higher land which, even when cleared and manured at considerable cost and labour, would not necessarily be as productive as the marshlands.

The Acadian population carried on mixed farming, primarily to provide for their own communities, but they also supplied food to the French, and later to the English, garrison at Port Royal, as well as to ships from New England. The Acadians also had a hand in the surreptitious provisioning (particularly with cattle) of the French garrison at Louisbourg; their export routes appear on several maps of the mid-eighteenth century (See Map 8:2, p. 134). Halifax, too, was initially dependent on the Acadian farmers for fresh produce.

The 1755 map (Map 4:3) of the Chignecto area marks the limit of Acadian agricultural development at the time of their expulsion. In less than 120 years they had drained, dyked and made productive thousands of acres of land from the Annapolis Basin to the head of the Bay of Fundy. Their principal crop was wheat, but they also grew other grains, peas, cabbages and a variety of vegetables; they also planted orchards.[5] They raised cattle, horses, sheep and pigs, and of course each household had its geese and chickens.[6] In spite of the many accusations of laziness levelled at them, by officials who would have preferred to see them felling trees and cultivating the higher land, the Acadians understood the potential of the marshlands for food production.

It was not until the 1750s that any significant attempt was made to establish an alternative to dykeland farming in Nova Scotia. Then came the settling of the "Foreign Protestants" in Lunenburg, and the allocation of farm lots in the relatively fertile country nearby, as seen in Map 4:4. This area was not far from the spot where farming families were originally settled by Isaac de Razilly at LaHave. In 1753, "Old Labrador's Farm" appears on a map alongside the newly surveyed town of Lunenburg, showing that this piece of land had remained under some kind of cultivation until that date; in 1749, Cornwallis had observed that a few French families were still to be found there.[7]

With the increase of population during the late eighteenth century and thereafter, other agricultural lands were developed with varying degrees of success. Loyalists and other immigrant groups were granted land for farming throughout the province. Farms existed even in such unpromising areas as the Halifax peninsula. On Cape Breton Island, only relatively small pieces of low land were initially found suitable for agriculture and they were usually selected because of their proximity to fishing grounds.[8] The banks of the Mira River, well situated to supply Louisbourg, were among those areas brought into production; Map 5:3, p. 64 shows the *Ferme de l'Hospital*, which was operated for the Fathers of Charity who ran the hospital in Louisbourg.[9] The areas around Nicolas Denys' establishments at St. Peter's and St. Ann's had been cultivated since early days, and Sieur de la Boularderie had a farm at his fishing village at Little Bras d'Or (Map 4:5), but it was left to the Scottish settlers in the nineteenth century to develop the more productive regions of the island.

Over the years, the Annapolis Valley and Minas farms expanded from the dykelands to include higher ground, as the English took over from the French. And with a growing population, agriculture was attempted in new areas of the province. But while a modern map of Nova Scotia still shows a significant proportion of the region covered with "very dense forests," the land drained and cleared by the Acadians and their successors has to a great extent remained in production, and forms a valuable part of the economy of the province.

Acadian farms on Annapolis Basin

This map of the lower Annapolis River includes much of the area depicted by Champlain nearly 120 years before (see Map 7:3, p. 101), from Goat Island to a little way above Annapolis Royal. In the intervening years, this area had been mapped by other French cartographers, including Jean Delabat, whose maps show in great detail what the settlement looked like at the end of the French occupation (see Map 2:3, p. 20). By 1725, the British had been in formal possession of Nova Scotia for 12 years, and had established a garrison at Annapolis Royal (as Port Royal was renamed) to defend the colony. But except for the change of occupancy of the fort and its immediate surroundings, the region remained much as it had been before the British took over.

The "very dense forests" noted by Champlain are still a predominant feature, covering much of the map. Along the river bank, however, we find evidence of considerable change since 1607. In place of deMonts' Habitation, destroyed by Argall's raid in 1613, the "Ruins of the old Scotch fort" that replaced it can be seen. The present fort, shown in more detail in the inset, stands on a point between two rivers, commanding the Basin. Beside the fort, the settlement is shown occupying the peninsula where Champlain's map showed the original area of cultivation (see also Franquelin's map of Port Royal, Map 7:5, p. 107).

On each side of the river, above and below the town, lie the areas described by Champlain on his map as "meadows which are flooded with water at the spring tides." In Map 4:1, these "flooded meadows" have given way to "Plantations along the River," "B". How these plantations were achieved, on marshlands that had not been used for agriculture because of periodic salt water flooding, is also made clear by this map: the lines, "I", along the shore are identified as "Dikes, the Marshes being overflowed at high Tides." A note reminds us that "at Spring Tide it flows upwards of 30 feet."

The lines of the protective dykes can be seen very clearly on this map. The farmhouses stand well back from the river, on rising ground, as a precaution against broken or leaking dykes. Around the farmhouses are the fields of the reclaimed marshlands, which proved to be extremely fertile and productive once rainfall had leached out the salt from the soil. A report written in 1720–21 states:

From Goat Island to five leagues above the ffort, on both sides of the Brittish River are a great many fine farms inhabited by about two hundred familyes. . . . The banks of this river is very pleasant and fruitful and produces wheat, Rye, and other grain, Pulse [legumes], garden roots, herbs and the best cabages of any Place here abounds also cattle and Fowles of all kinds. . . . . (from PAC, NSA, XII, 124–30, 1720–21).[10]

The families who worked these farms were, of course, Acadians, descendants of those who had dyked and drained the land in the seventeenth century. Both French and, later, British officials criticized their lack of ambition: the report quoted above also notes that "their land is not improved as much as might be expected, they living in a manner from hand to mouth, and provided they have a good field of cabbages and bread enough for their families, with what fodder is sufficient for their cattle they seldom look for much further improvement." Just what the Acadian farmers were expected to do with the surplus production which might result from such improvement is not made clear. What is evident is that these "plantations along the river" continued under British rule to produce enough to supply most of the needs of their inhabitants, albeit at a subsistence level.

Comparing this map again with Champlain's, we find that on the river where Poutrincourt's mill once stood there are now three mills (F, G and H): "A Corn Mill to which the Boats come up"—a convenient way of transporting grain from riverside farms; "Ditto and a Saw Mill," where the two sets of machinery were presumably run from the one wheel, and a simple "Saw Mill." The grist mills indicate that grain production had been established by this time.

Other maps make it clear that the farming pattern here extended to the Acadian communities further up the Annapolis River, around the Minas Basin and as far as the Chignecto area. As the descendants of the Port Royal families moved away and formed new settlements, they took with them the skills in dyking and reclaiming marshland that had been developed here, on the banks of the lower Annapolis River. On arrival at a new site, the following technique was used:

The inhabitants make a joint Business of Dyking in several large Tracts, which serve first as common Fields, and being afterwards subdivided into smaller Allotments are capable of the various improvements before-mentioned: Their Dykes are made of large Sodes of Marsh cut up into square Pieces, and raised about five Feet higher than the common Surface, of competent Thickness to withstand the Force of the Tides, and soon grow very firm and durable being overspread with Grass, and have commonly Foot-paths on their Summit, where are both convenient and delightful. . . . (From *The state of trade in the Northern Colonies*, London, 1748, pp. 70–71)[11]

In spite of the disapproval of some French, and many English observers, who felt that the Acadians would have been better employed cutting down trees and clearing forest to create their farms, the labour of building dykes was well repaid by the fertility of the drained soil. The agricultural progress that this map shows was repeated everywhere Acadians settled.

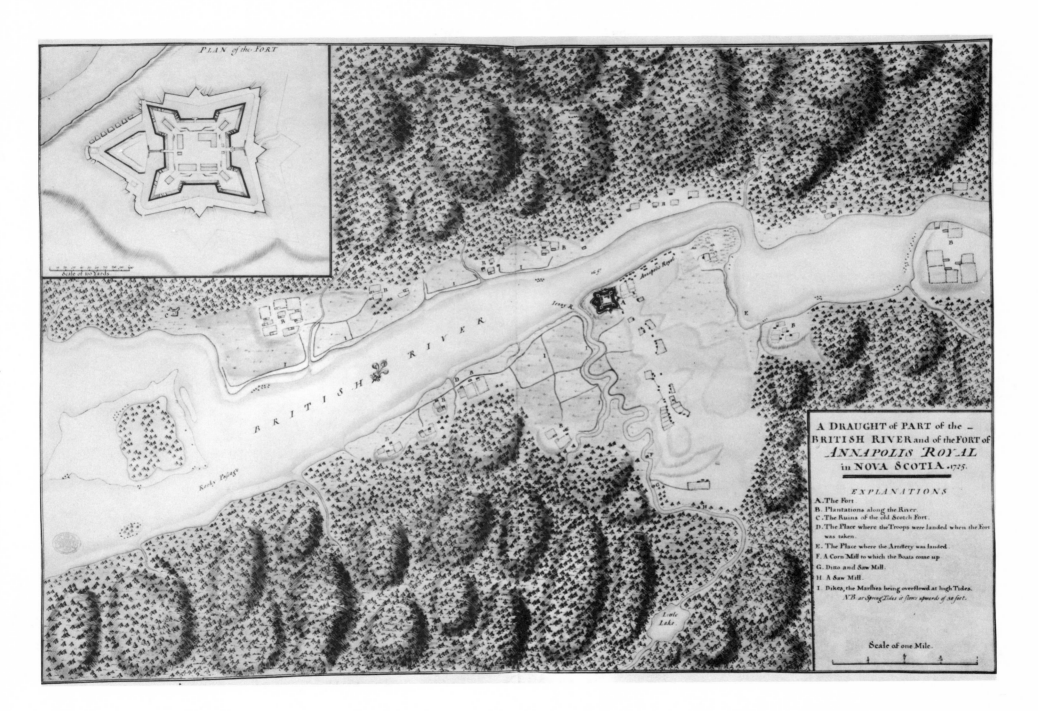

PLAN of the FORT

Scale of 100 Yards

BRITISH RIVER

Rocky Passage

Little Lake

Annapolis Royal

Jenny R.

A DRAUGHT of PART of the
BRITISH RIVER and of the FORT of
ANNAPOLIS ROYAL
in NOVA SCOTIA. 1725.

EXPLANATIONS

A. The Fort
B. Plantations along the River.
C. The Ruins of the old Scotch Fort.
D. The Place where the Troops were landed when the Fort was taken.
E. The Place where the Artillery was landed.
F. A Corn Mill to which the Boats come up.
G. Ditto and Saw Mill.
H. A Saw Mill.
I. Dikes, the Marshes being overflow'd at high Tides.
    N.B. at Spring Tides it flows upwards of 30 feet.

Scale of one Mile.

Annapolis Royal farmlands

The original purpose of this large scale map of Annapolis, which is oriented with south towards the top, appears to have been military and strategic. The notes showing the heights of inland points relative to the fort and the indications of the line of burned houses and felled trees suggest that the author, a military surveyor, was assessing the security of the fort (which is itself shown in some detail) against attack from the land.

At the same time, the map shows clearly the vegetation and relief of the area, the gardens and fields of the settlement itself, and above all the system of dykes which protected the low-lying areas from flooding. This protective system runs from the edge of the ridge of land where Babineau's Field is marked, follows the meanders of Allen's River almost to its confluence with the Annapolis River, and turns to join the fort, which stands on slightly higher land. Beyond the line of houses facing the water, where the level of the land drops again, a short section of dyke runs as far as the wooded rise, and continues again beyond it to enclose more marshland on the eastern side of the town. Some dyking is also shown on the western side of Allen's River, but the system seems to have deteriorated since the making of Map 4:1 in 1725, and the protective line is incomplete.

Notice that the dykes ran straight across the mouths of the numerous small streams that flowed from the peninsula into the rivers on either side. This configuration prevented the salt water from running up the stream beds as the tide rose, and yet there is no indication that the fresh water outlets were obstructed in any way so as to cause flooding behind the dams. Such flooding was prevented by the Acadian device known as the *aboiteau*, which permitted the outflow of fresh water at low tide through an aperture in the dyke. On the outer side of the aperture hung a shutter, hinged at the top; as the tide came in, pressure from the rising

salt water closed the shutter and held it firmly in place, preventing the salt water from entering. When the tide dropped again, pressure from the stream opened the shutter, thus allowing fresh water from behind the *aboiteau* to drain away. By this simple method, the Acadians prevented salt water from overflowing the stream beds at very high tides and damaging their reclaimed fields.

Map 4:2   John Hamilton. "A General Plan of Annapolis Royal. . .," 1753. Manuscript.

The dykes and the *aboiteaux* were the key to the agricultural success of the Acadians, not only in the Annapolis area, but also around the Minas Basin and in the Chignecto area, as Map 4:3 illustrates. As the

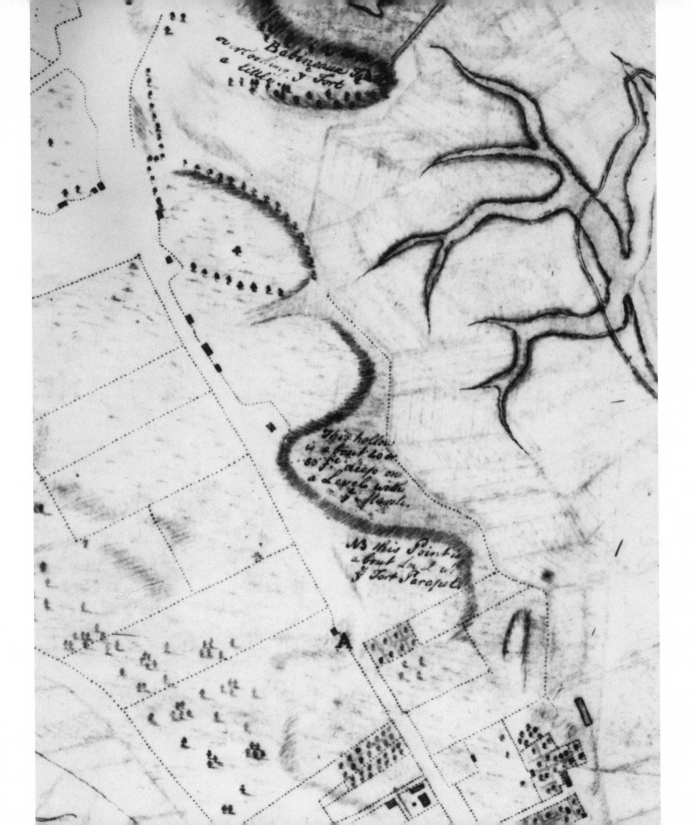

Acadian population increased, from the settling of Port Royal until 1755, it was always low-lying marshlands that Acadians chose for new settlements.

Draining and dyking were skills unknown to British settlers when they took over the Acadian farms. The following request makes it clear how dependent the British were on the help of the Acadians who made their way back to Nova Scotia after the Expulsion.

To His excellency Montagu Wilmot Esquire. March 23d, 1765

The Memorial of the Inhabitants of King's County Humbly sheweth

That the French Accadians who have hitherto been stationed in this Country, have been of great use as Labourers in assisting the carrying on our Business in agriculture and Improvements in General but particularly in the repairing and making dykes a work which they are accustomed to, and experienced in, and we find that without their further assistance many of us cannot continue our

Improvements, nor plough nor sowe our lands, nor finish the Dykeing still required to secure our lands from Salt water, and being convinced from experience that unless those Dyke Lands are inclosed we cannot with certainty raise Bread for our Subsistence.

Your memorialists therefore Humbly pray your Excellency will be pleased to take this matter of so much consequence to us into consideration, to permit the accadians to remain with us the Ensuing Summer . . .which will tend greatly to the encouragement and Success of these Infant settlements. . . .

Signed: 5 names on behalf of inhabitants of Cornwallis, 5 names for Horton, 2 names for Windsor, 1 name for King's County, 4 names for Falmouth Township, 2 names for the township of Newport. (PAC, NSA, LXXVI, 56–57)[12]

Although much of the farming in the Annapolis Valley and Minas Basin areas has now moved to higher ground, dykes still protect many of the low-lying meadows, as they did in the early days of settlement. They are an enduring reminder of the efforts of the Acadians to cope with the phenomenon of the Fundy tides, and to bring large areas of potentially fertile land into production.

Cumberland Basin dykelands

This map shows an area on the Cumberland Basin, on the border between Nova Scotia and New Brunswick, between the present towns of Amherst and Sackville. It was made in or shortly after 1755, when the British forces captured Fort Beauséjour from the French, and renamed it Fort Cumberland. The British stronghold, Fort Lawrence, is located on the map and is also shown in a detailed ground-plan. A view of Fort Cumberland decorates the panel containing "Refferences" to the map. These references and the map itself shows a disparity that can be explained only by inattention on the part of the cartographer. While "A" and "D" correspond to letters on the map, "B" and "C" appear to represent "K" and "L", respectively. The author probably changed his mind about the notation part way through his work, and neglected to adjust the lettering on the map.

Like the two previous maps, this map was clearly made primarily for military purposes. But like them, and many other such maps, its attention to topographical detail makes it a useful record of other features. As well as the forts, settlements are indicated, and drainage and relief are shown. Some of these features are easily recognized on a modern map, although there is a slight difference from standard orientation, with north towards the top left corner.

The forts were built on high land with broad views of the surrounding marshes and rivers; the higher areas on which they were located are visible on a modern map. The rivers are readily identifiable, and the channel between the dotted lines, "A", representing low water mark, remains much as it was in the eighteenth century. A road still leads to the settlement known as Fort Lawrence, from the point, "D", near the mouth of the Missiguash River "where the vessels unload the stores. . . ." Most visible, both to a visitor to the area and to the map reader, are the lines of dykes that still surround the extensive marshlands for which the area is well-known.

The notes to the present map explain that the dykes were established "to prevent the Spring Tides from overflowing the Marshes." (The secondary use of dykes near Fort Lawrence was as a vantage point for Micmac firing on English supply vessels. This use is noted as the reason for the dykes' destruction). The dykes represent the traditional agricultural technique that the Acadians brought to all their settlements around the Bay of Fundy. The dyked area on this map extends from the Tantramar and Aulac Rivers to the LaPlanche, and along both sides of the Hebert River, enclosing the area known as the Elysian Fields, near Minudie.

As in the Annapolis area, the settlements were established on ridges of higher ground. Those shown here include the communities of Westcock, at the mouth of the Tantramar, Beauséjour, scattered round Fort Cumberland, and the remains of the village of Beaubassin, near Fort Lawrence. This last settlement had been burnt by the Micmac, probably on orders from their missionary leader, Abbé LeLoutre. The village was destroyed in 1750 in order to force its Acadian inhabitants to the French side of the Missiguash River, which had become the boundary line between the French and the British.[13]

As the map indicates, the inhabitants of all these settlements had drained and brought into production a considerable area of marshland. The dykes follow the banks of the larger rivers, but cut across the mouths of the smaller streams, indicating the presence of *aboiteaux* to protect the meadows behind the dykes from salt water running up the stream beds. The one major area where reclamation was not completed before the capitulation of Fort Beauséjour and the expulsion of the Acadians from the region, was the Tantramar Marsh, extending between the Tantramar and Aulac Rivers, halfway across the isthmus. This ambitious enterprise had been begun by LeLoutre in 1752; Map 6:4 (p. 81), which was made soon after the construction of the two rival forts, Lawrence and Beauséjour, has written across that area *"aboiteaux projeté."* The escalation of hostilities between the French and the English put an end to what would have been an important extension of the dykelands. As this map shows, dykes had already been constructed along the northern

Map 4:3 Anonymous. Cumberland Basin, with inset "Plan of Fort Lawrence" and "A View of the Fort Cumberland," ca. 1755. Manuscript.

banks of the two rivers, protecting the area of marsh seen in the upper left corner.

Even without the additional resources of the Tantramar Marsh, the inhabitants of the Chignecto area had made great progress since they first came to the region. In the winter of 1685–6, the Intendant, Demeulle, had noted the great potential of the terrain. He wrote that Beaubassin was "remarkable for the number of its meadows, in which more than 100,000 cattle could be pastured."[14] The actual number of cattle noted there by Demeulle at that time was 236.[15] Two years later, Gargas reported that Chignecto was *A place extremely fertile in pasturelands for cattle, but suitable for that only, since grain can scarcely ripen because of the many fogs, which are frequent there. It is only recently that they have cultivated some of the higher ground, and there the grain grows very well.*[16] Gargas listed four horses, two colts, 226 horned cattle, 125 sheep, 40 acres of marshland under cultivation and 16 of upland. Clark estimates that in the years 1748–50, the Chignecto communities owned 7,000 cattle, 8,000 sheep, 4,000 swine, 500 horses and 3,000 acres of dyked land.[17] The raising of livestock had clearly become, as Demeulle and Gargas had predicted, a major part of the economy.

The fact that this valuable farmland straddled the dividing line between the French and the English forts set up in the early 1750s effectively put a stop to any further expansion after that time. Even before their formal expulsion, many of the Acadians had suffered the loss of their homes and property as a result of the fighting. This map represents the limits of their reclamation of the Fundy marshlands, a legacy that has played a notable part in the development of agriculture in Nova Scotia.

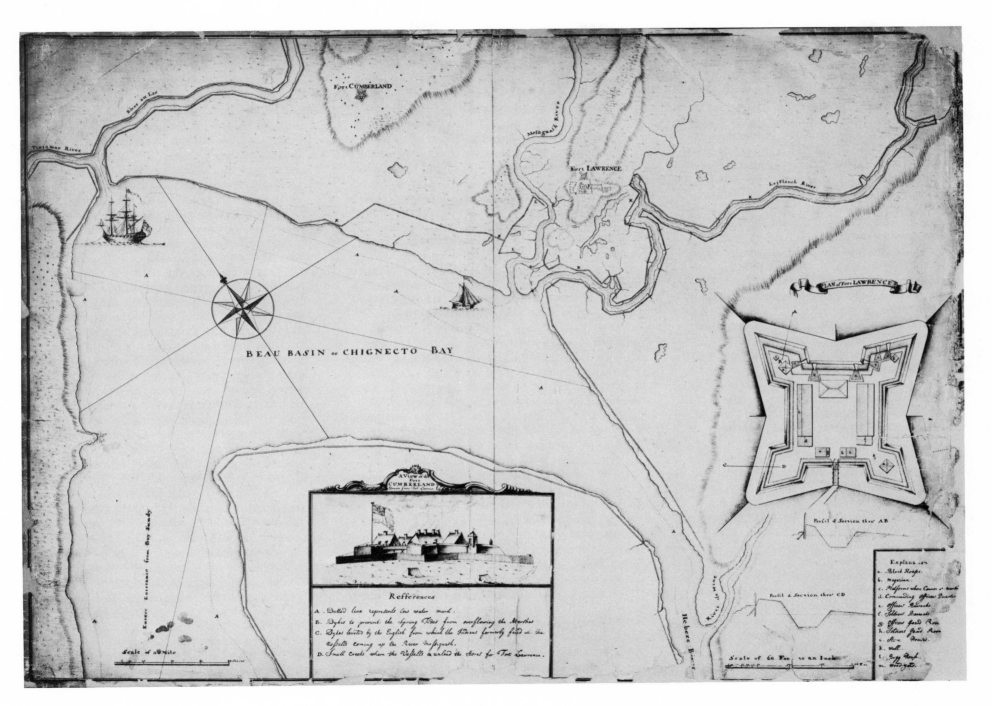

Fort CUMBERLAND

Fort LAWRENCE

Meſaguaſh River

River au Lac

Tintamar River

La Planch River

BEAU BASIN or CHIGNECTO BAY

Entree Entrance from Bay Fundy

Hebere River

River de Mine

PLAN of Fort LAWRENCE

Profil & Section thro' AB

Profil & Section thro' CD

A View of the Fort CUMBERLAND Drawn from Fort Lawrence

Refferences

A. Dotted line repreſents low water mark.

B. Dykes to prevent the ſpring Tides from overflowing the Marſhes

C. Dykes levelled by the Engliſh from which the Indians formerly fired at the Veſſells coming up the River Meſſiguash.

D. Small Creeks where the Veſſells unload the Stores for Fort Lawrence.

Scale of a Mile

Explanation

a. Block Houſe.
b. Magazine.
c. Platform where Canon is mounted
d. Commanding Officers Quarter
e. Officers Barracks
f. Soldiers Barracks
g. Officers Guard Room
h. Soldiers Guard Room
i. Store Houſes
k. Well
l. Cook Houſe
m. Store Houſe

Scale of 60 Feet to an Inch

Lunenburg County farm lots

Taken from a larger map of the County of Lunenburg, this section shows parts of Lunenburg and New Dublin townships. The large map is identified in a note as having accompanied correspondence in 1785 from Governor Parr to Lord Sydney, Secretary of State for the Colonies. It was probably made by Chief Surveyor Charles Morris (II) or one of his deputies. It does not include relief, but shows the coastline, rivers and some lakes in considerable detail. It also identifies the land that had been surveyed there to that time. North lies to the top right corner.

The agricultural potential of the area around Lunenburg and the LaHave River had been recognized for many years. Soon after his arrival at LaHave in 1632, Isaac de Razilly had planted apple trees, established some of the French settlers as farmers at Petite Rivière and pastured cattle behind Oxners Beach, an area then known as *La Vacherie*, which is shown on Bellin's 1744 map of LaHave (Map 2:4, p. 22). In 1721 Governor Philipps described Merligueche (later Lunenburg) as "a harbour only fit for small vessels, but has the best Improvable Land of any other along the coast."[18]

From the initial foundation of the settlement, the inhabitants of Lunenburg were provided with garden lots adjacent to the town site. As soon as they could be surveyed, farm lots of 30 acres each were also allocated. In addition, common land was set aside for grazing livestock. In 1754, a year after the arrival of the settlers, the following enthusiastic report was dispatched by Governor Lawrence:
Everything has gone well at Lunenburg since my last, the Inhabitants are almost incredibly industrious and have already this year planted seven hundred Bushels of Potatoes, they have also sown some Flax seed they brought with them from Germany which comes up very

well and will furnish them with a sufficient quantity of seed that they purpose to make use of as soon as they have properly prepared their land for it. The people have clear'd and cultivated their Town and Garden Lots and have made some progress on their Farm lots to which they seem greatly attach'd they have now in the ground above Two Hundred Bushels of Oats, a great quantity of Turnip seed, and some Barley. They have cut a vast quantity of timber staves and Hoops and built a great number of Boats and Canoes.... (From PAC, NSA, LV, 112–113.)[19]

Although ignoring some of the inevitable problems faced by newcomers to a strange environment, this report gives some idea of the progress being made.

The initial provisions made for settlers appear on this map, as does the record of development of the area over the next 30 years. The garden lots are shown as an irregularly shaped patch east of Lunenburg; Map 7:9, p. 117 shows in more detail how they were laid out. The original farm lots are recognizable by their long, narrow outlines, extending from the Oakland area of Mahone Bay to the east bank of the LaHave River. Larger lots of similar shape, laid out later, are seen in New Dublin township on the west side of the LaHave. Inland from the early farm lots are extensive divisions subsequently surveyed and laid out in 300 acre lots.[20] As the map also shows, there were several commons established by this time, serving different parts of the township. A number of other lots of varying shapes and sizes are identified by the names of their owners. Among these is the huge, 20,000 acre Pernette grant extending from above the falls on the LaHave almost to the river mouth. Some of the lots are associated with saw mills, including Pernette's, Cook's and Mushamuch, whose owner is not named. Others are not identified as to their use, though we know that some shore lots, such as Murdo McCleod's near Fort Point, were used for fisheries.[21]

It seems very likely that a certain amount of farming was carried out on all but the most unpromising of the assigned properties. Land grants of the period normally specified that clearing and other improvements be carried out and that crops be grown. Clearly, the

degree of success that could be expected depended not only on the industry of the settler but also on the type of land received. The hinterland of Lunenburg consists of some areas of fertile drumlin soil, but also of patches of thinner, stony terrain which is considerably less productive.[22] Some of the land granted along the Petite Rivière had been cleared and worked by the farmers established there by de Razilly in the 1630s. On early maps of the area, "Old Labrador's Farm" represented the last traces near Lunenburg of the inhabitants of mixed French and Indian ancestry who had remained there after the rest of the French settlers moved from LaHave to Port Royal. They were reported to have cleared between 300 and 400 acres of land,[23] though only Labrador's farm itself seems to have still been under cultivation in 1753.

Although it is impossible to assess the degree of agricultural development of most of the individual holdings from looking at the map, there are some large lots which are specifically identified as farms. This suggests that their proprietors were engaged in agriculture at more than a mere subsistence level. These farms were owned by some of the leading citizens of Lunenburg, and probably employed a considerable number of people. The most extensive of these is Strasburg's Farm, lying along the east bank of the LaHave from the modern settlement of Dayspring to the site of Bridgewater. Other properties identified as farms include the Moreau family property west of Lunenburg, John Creighton's farm on what is now Heckmans Island and "The Honble Benjamin Greens Farm" between Oakland and Rouses (now Indian) Point.

Common grazing was originally provided on either side of the Lunenburg town site. In "Articles about the Commons, made for the year 1754," quoted in *History of the County of Lunenburg*, it is laid down that:
"The great or horn cattle shall go by turns, one time to the west, the other time to the east side.
"The small cattle shall go from the town pickets to the first garden lots northward of the town, but not higher than the back of the town.
"It is proposed and found very necessary to have forthwith hired a herdsman, one for the horn cattle, and

another for the small cattle, and the inhabitants are to agree with the said herdsmen for the payment, and to bind them to their duty.

"It is proposed about the dogs, that a law shall be made that such as have dogs going over the commons shall keep them in a line, and everybody is to take care that no mischief may happen by the dogs.

"It is proposed that next year some proper expert person be chosen to visit the commons and see what number of cattle they are able to sustain."[24]

Other commons were established with the spread of some of the population from the town itself to the outlying farm lots; Centre Common, South Common and Oakland Common can be seen on this map. After the expulsion of the Acadians in 1755, a considerable quantity of their cattle was brought across from the other side of the province to supplement the existing stock in the Lunenburg area. The practice of establishing common grazing areas does not appear to have extended to the west side of the river when it was settled in the next decade. There, each man seems to have been responsible for providing pasturage for his own animals.

The relatively arbitrary and orderly development of land for agriculture in the Lunenburg area in the mid-eighteenth century makes for a map very different in appearance from those of the Acadian dyke lands. The boundaries of farms were now determined by the surveyor's chain rather than by the natural lie of the land. While the fertile soil that the Acadians had reclaimed and used as farmland was of predictable quality, the rectangular lots laid out around Lunenburg and issued to the settlers, who were then obliged to fell trees and remove rocks to create their fields, were of much more uncertain nature. Despite these problems, much of the land cleared by the Lunenburg settlers was cultivated until fairly recently, and some of it is still farmed today.

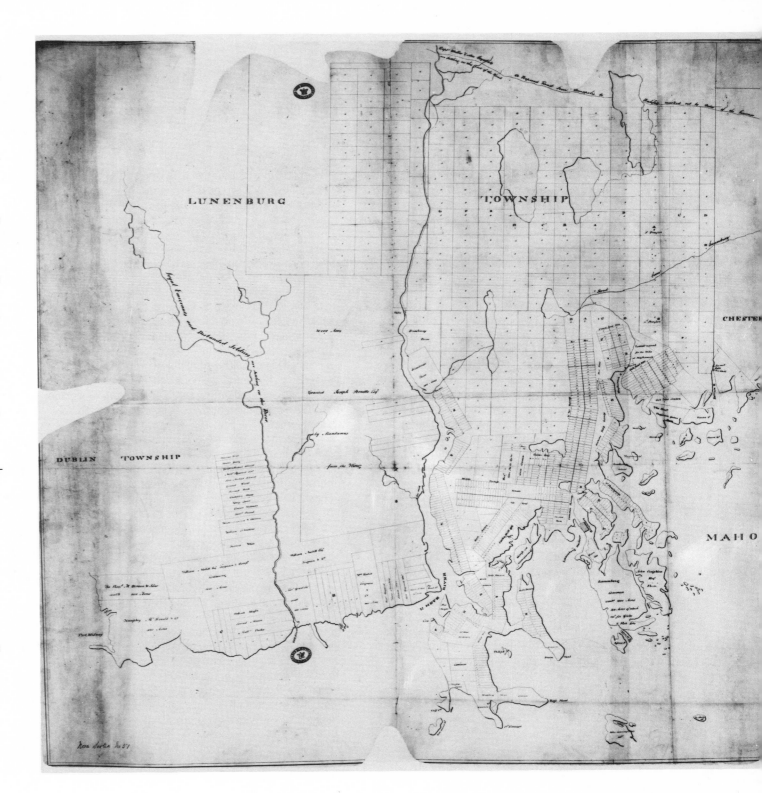

The Boularderie farm
at Little Bras D'or

This 1742 map shows a small French settlement situated at the mouth of the Little Bras D'Or on Cape Breton Island, on the site of the community of Alder Point. Oriented with north toward the right, Boucher's map shows a shoreline that is clearly recognizable on a modern map; it also indicates relief, drainage and, in a general fashion, vegetation. The map also gives an interesting picture of the economy of the small community.

L'Isle Verdronne, now known as Boularderie Island, had been granted by the French crown early in the eighteenth century to Antoine le Poupet de la Boularderie, who took an active part in developing the fishing industry in eastern Cape Breton Island. He built himself a house and cleared land for agriculture here at Little Bras D'Or, where in about 1730 it is recorded that there were 50 workmen employed in cutting wood, building ships and constructing buildings.[25] Thereafter, the population appears to have dwindled, and according to official reports the settlement was in a decline by the time this map was made. Clark concludes that "Boularderie had a good house and the soil was good but he simply was not a farmer and was making a bare living."[26]

Despite this gloomy judgment of Boularderie's efforts, the map shows what appear to be the makings of a reasonably viable community. Unlike some small settlements, this one shows evidence of a mixed economy that included fishing both for food and export, timber cutting for building and coal mining to provide fuel. Gardens and fields provided crops to support the population, and the low-lying areas, particularly those around the ponds close to the shore, probably supplied hay for the livestock. Furs obtained from the Micmac may have supplemented the economy.

The southwest (upper left) part of the map shows the fishing village on the shore of the Little Bras D'Or, with two groups of houses, "N", and the church in between. The majority of the population lived here, or in the other small group of fishermen's houses (also designated "N") on the other shore. Along the water's edge are the stages where the fish were processed (see Chapter 3), and inland are a number of gardens, presumably the responsibility of the fishermen's families. These gardens would have provided vegetables and herbs that probably met most of the needs of the inhabitants.

North of the main settlement the map shows a concession, "D", granted by Boularderie to one *labour-ieur* in 1742. The obliterated word in the legend may have helped to identify this man more precisely; the grant seems to be of significant size, and the gardens already laid out on the edge of the property are fairly extensive. Since the area of woodland, including a pond, was granted during the year this map was made, it is not surprising that there is no evidence of further development.

Still farther north, beyond the two streams that form lagoons behind the beach, is another valley, apparently dry, with a seam of coal, "M", typical of the coastal outcrops found in many parts of the Cape Breton Island coast. This is the same "coal pitt" that can be seen in Maps 5:3, p. 64 and 5:5, p. 68, both made many years later. It is one of a number of small mines developed by the French to supply fuel for their own communities and for the garrison at Louisbourg (See Chapter 5).

Boularderie's personal establishment, "A", was located on the east side of the Little Bras D'Or channel. It consisted of his house and an adjacent group of buildings with gardens, situated fairly close to the shore. From it, a road followed the higher ground around the mouth of a brook, passing another garden and, on the far side of the brook, the cowsheds and stables, "B". The low-lying land around the mouth of the brook appears to consist of marshy meadows that would have provided grazing and hay for the cattle.

Above these meadows lie 34 or 35 *arpents* of cultivated land, divided into several fields, "C", and dominated by a cross. The legend tells us that this land was *en valeur*, that is to say in good order and productive, but unfortunately we are not told what crops were being grown. It seems reasonable to suppose that grain was the most important crop; French settlers in North America continued their European tradition of growing wheat, even given the less than ideal climatic conditions.

The other features of the map which are noted in the legend are the small group of "Indians", "O", (six families in four huts) and the sandbar, "P", across the harbour entrance that restricted access to all but small vessels. The presence of the Micmac suggests that trade for furs was another part of the community's economy. The bar was probably no obstacle to the fishing boats, but would make access difficult for larger trading vessels. It was also a good defence against attack by water, though the distance of the settlement from British bases made this unlikely. The dotted line, indicating shallows where navigation was difficult, explains the location of the fishing stages in places where access was possible.

This map gives an interesting picture of a small, isolated community with a considerable potential for self-sufficiency. At the time it was made, however, self-sufficiency does not seem to have been achieved. Several years later, Boularderie's son apparently made a fresh start with additional farm equipment and labourers brought from France. He claimed to have had some success improving the farm and growing both grain and vegetables, though as Clark points out, some of his statements may have been exaggerated.[27]

The question of why the Boularderie farm was not the success this map might lead us to expect could possibly be answered by a factor that is not represented at all on the map—the inhospitable climate of east-

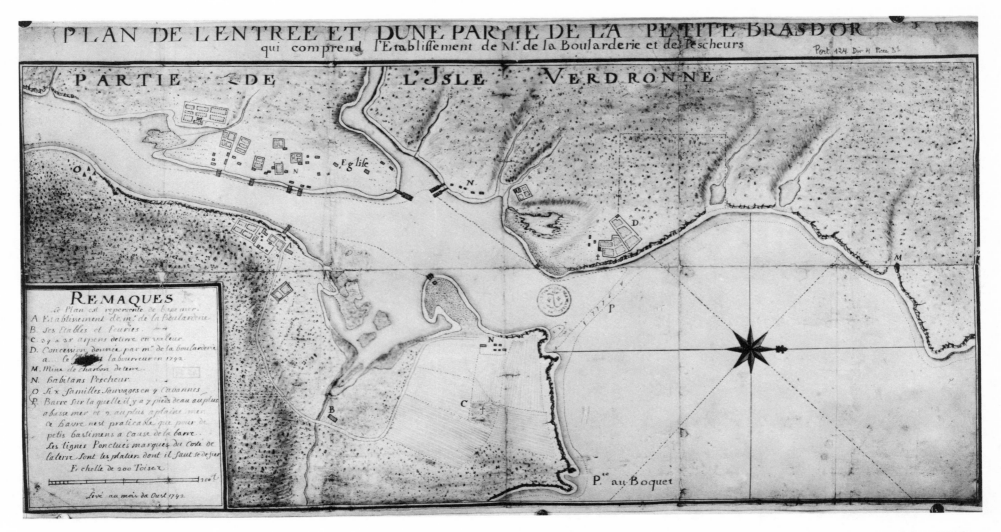

Map 4:5 Boucher. "Plan de l'Entrée et d'une Partie de la Petite Bras d'Or qui comprend l'Etablissement de M. de la Boularderie et des Pescheurs," 1742. Manuscript.

ern Cape Breton Island. Regardless of their skills as farmers, the Boularderies suffered from the disadvantages of a cooler climate and a shorter growing season than most Frenchmen are accustomed to. Although similar in latitude to parts of France, the Atlantic coast of Canada experiences considerably lower temperatures. Furthermore, there is a sufficient difference in climate between Cape Breton Island and the areas of Nova Scotia where the first French attempts at farming were made, that success in one place did not necessarily guarantee success in the other. On Cape Breton Island, French efforts to grow wheat were often unsuccessful, while they were unfamiliar with crops such as oats that are more suitable to the cooler environment.[28] It is no accident that Scottish settlers in the nineteenth century had more farming success, given that the climate of Cape Breton Island closely resembled their own.

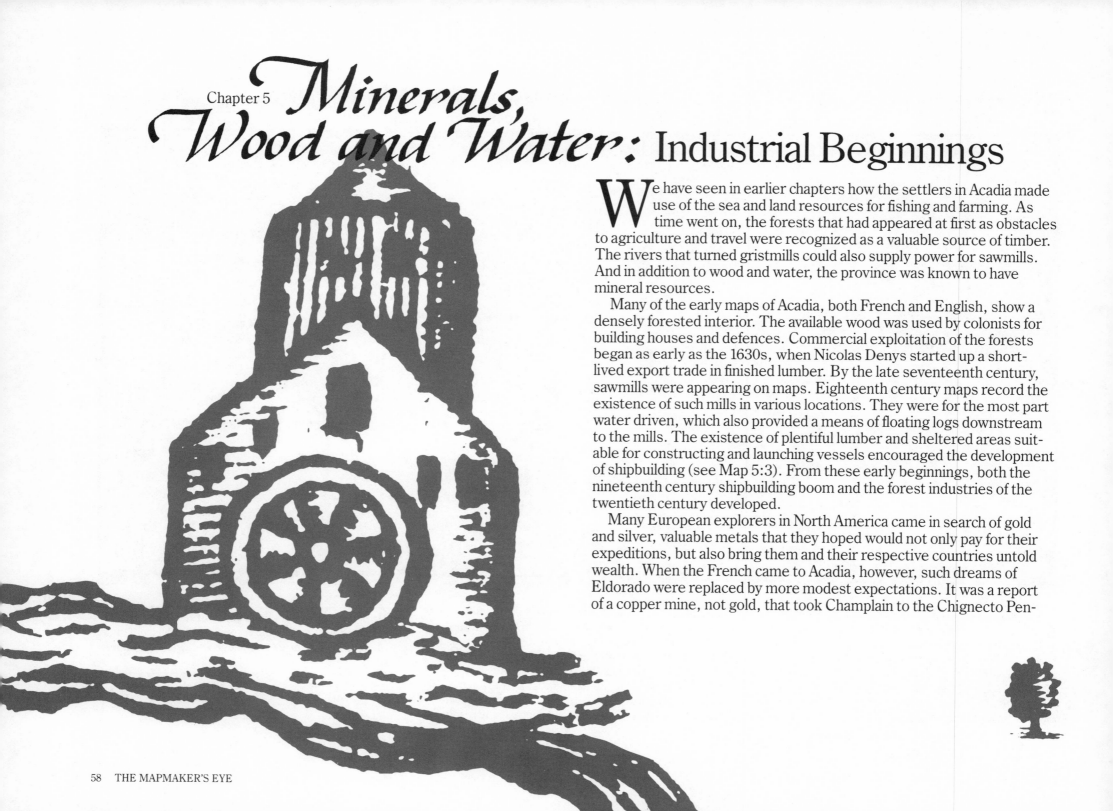

Chapter 5 *Minerals, Wood and Water:* Industrial Beginnings

We have seen in earlier chapters how the settlers in Acadia made use of the sea and land resources for fishing and farming. As time went on, the forests that had appeared at first as obstacles to agriculture and travel were recognized as a valuable source of timber. The rivers that turned gristmills could also supply power for sawmills. And in addition to wood and water, the province was known to have mineral resources.

Many of the early maps of Acadia, both French and English, show a densely forested interior. The available wood was used by colonists for building houses and defences. Commercial exploitation of the forests began as early as the 1630s, when Nicolas Denys started up a short-lived export trade in finished lumber. By the late seventeenth century, sawmills were appearing on maps. Eighteenth century maps record the existence of such mills in various locations. They were for the most part water driven, which also provided a means of floating logs downstream to the mills. The existence of plentiful lumber and sheltered areas suitable for constructing and launching vessels encouraged the development of shipbuilding (see Map 5:3). From these early beginnings, both the nineteenth century shipbuilding boom and the forest industries of the twentieth century developed.

Many European explorers in North America came in search of gold and silver, valuable metals that they hoped would not only pay for their expeditions, but also bring them and their respective countries untold wealth. When the French came to Acadia, however, such dreams of Eldorado were replaced by more modest expectations. It was a report of a copper mine, not gold, that took Champlain to the Chignecto Peninsula (see Map 5:1). Industrial development in Britain in the eighteenth century brought an awareness of the value of an even more mundane mineral, coal. Coal deposits that had been noted in passing by early travellers from France now began to appear on maps of mainland Nova Scotia and Cape Breton Island, as we shall see in this chapter.

The presence of coal was, however, no guarantee of immediate industrial development. Since the 1750s, most of the coal deposits upon which future economic growth would be based were known, and appeared on maps. But mapmakers at the end of the eighteenth century (see Maps 5:5 and 5:6) indicate only sporadic development of mining in the intervening years. This was largely the result of deliberate official policy. The English attitude was clearly spelled out by Lord Halifax and his colleagues:

In regard to the Colliery mentioned in your letter, for working which you have received some proposals. We are of Opinion that it would be contrary to those Rules of Policy, which this Nation has wisely observed in relation to its Colonies, to bring Coals into use in America, as the Use of them would naturally lead them into the Discovery of Manufactures, the raw materials of which we now receive from them, and afterward return in Manufactures. Whitehall, March 6th, 1752. (PAC. NSA. XLVI, 135.)[1]

Although this self-serving attitude delayed the exploitation of the coal-fields for some time, changing colonial policies, the general industrialization of North America and the enormous demand for coal in modern times, particularly during two world wars, ensured that the coal resources shown on maps in this chapter became a major part of the economy of Nova Scotia.

Copper prospecting at
Advocate Harbour

The earliest mapped indication of Nova Scotian mineral wealth is found in this plan made by Samuel de Champlain, probably in 1607, and published as an illustration to his *Voyages*. Oriented with north to the left, it shows the "Port of Mines," the name given by Champlain to what is now Advocate Harbour on the Chignecto Peninsula. As a result of a report that copper could be found there, Champlain visited the area three times, and located some small deposits. Although his finds scarcely merited the name "mines," this name was given to the port, and, later, to the Baie des Mines (Minas Channel and Basin; see Map 5:2). The name was also applied to the settlement on its southern shore which became known, quite unjustifiably, as Les Mines (Minas).

Despite the proliferation of mine-related place names, the size of the copper deposits in the area did

---

Map 5:1a Advocate Bay today.

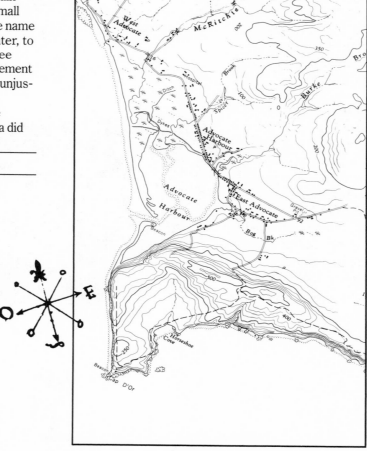

not merit commercial exploitation by either the French or the English. The term "Mine" as used by Champlain referred to the seams of ore, not to any system of recovering the mineral. As he observed: "The truth is that if the sea did not cover these mines twice a day, and if they did not occur in rocks of such hardness, one might expect something therefrom." (*Voyages*, I, p. 375.)

The features shown in the map include the harbour, dry at low tide, where vessels could lie aground, "A". There is a protective sandbar, "C", to one side of the entrance channel, "I", and a pebbly beach, "D", on the other side. The land on either side of the small river, "B", now known as Burke Brook, is shown by stylized trees to be wooded. The equally stylized "range of mountains" known today as Cape d'Or, "M", drops sharply to the water, where the "copper mine", "E", at its foot is noted to be covered twice a day by the sea. This frequent interruption by the tides would make the copper extremely difficult to recover commercially. Another problem which the map demonstrates is that although ships could anchor off the harbour mouth, "G", the extensive sand flats (dotted on the map) that were exposed at low tide along with the copper would have made it impossible to bring the vessels close enough for loading. It is perhaps not surprising that this early indication of mineral wealth in the area did not lead to subsequent development.

Map 5:1 Samuel de Champlain. *Port des mines*. 1613. Engraved.

Les chifres montrent les brasses d'eau.

A Le lieu ou les vaisseaux peuuent eschouer.
B Vne petite riuiere.
C Vne langue de terre qui est de Sable.
D Vne pointe de gros cailloux qui est comme vne moule.
E Le lieu où est la mine de cuiure qui couure de mer deux fois le iour.
F Vne isle qui est derriere le cap des mines.
G La rade ou les vaisseaux posent l'ancre attendant la maree.
I Lachenal.
H L'isle haute qui est a vne lieue & demye du port aux mines.
L Petit Ruisseau.
M Costeau de montaignes le long de la coste du cap aux mines.

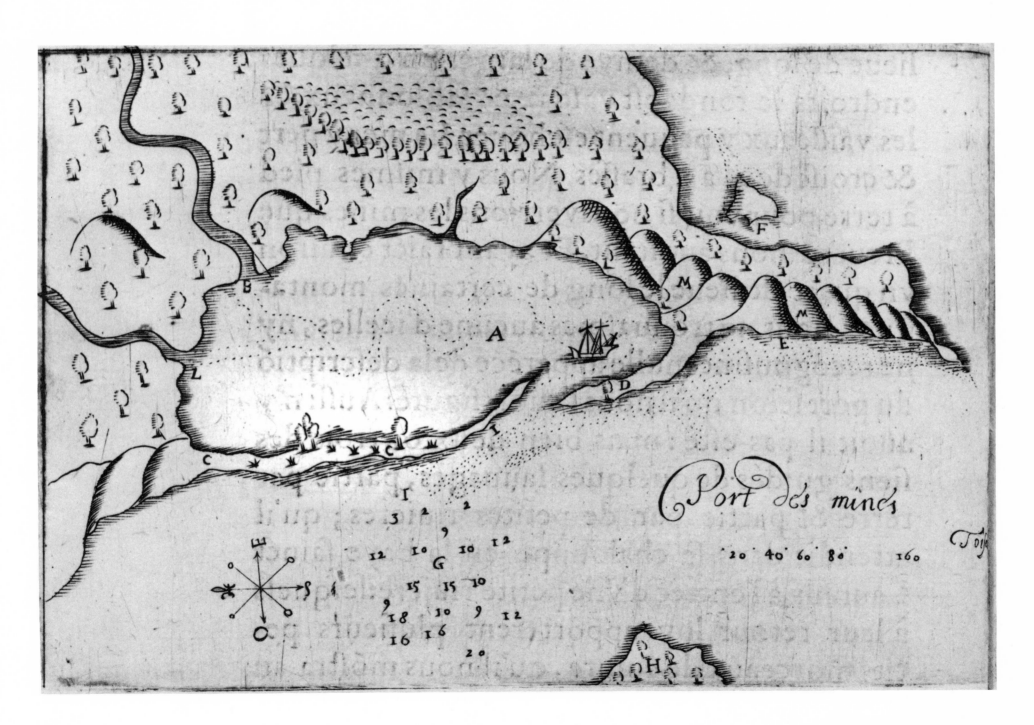

Port des mines

20 40 60 80   160

The Joggins Coalfield

T his map of the Chignecto Peninsula by the deputy surveyors Mitchell and Amhurst includes the area earlier mapped by Champlain (Map 5:1). Shown here as Bladon's Harbour, it lies between Cape Chicanecto "alias Cape Hart," and Cape Dorée, "alias Cape Chandos," now Cape d'Or. No mention is made of the copper deposits but they are commemorated in the name Mines Bason, which had by now become attached to the body of water south of the peninsula (on the upper right side of the map; the

Map 5:2a   The Chignecto Peninsula today.

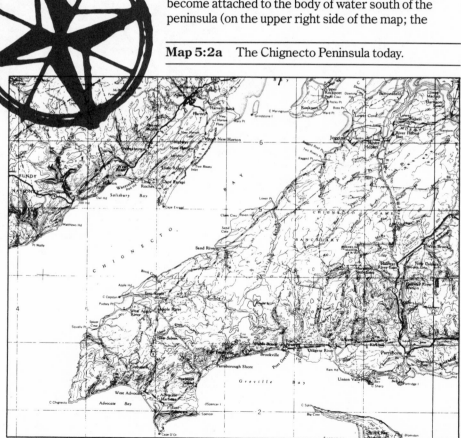

compass rose gives the orientation). The name Cape Dorée suggests the hope that gold, instead of copper, might be found.

On the northern side, the surveyors noted two interesting features. First were the "Coal Clifts," which can be found on a number of other eighteenth century maps, including Southack's coastal survey (see Map 3:4, p. 42). They are marked along a stretch of coast southwest of Grand Nyjagon (Joggins), where coal seams were exposed along the cliff face. Farther east lay Forrest Mine, where coal could be recovered between Joggins and the Carrying Place (River Hebert), the portage route across the peninsula. "Mining" in Nova Scotia at this time consisted of collecting exposed coal from the surface of the ground or the cliff face; the extent of the coalfield back towards Springhill had not been explored. The "coal cliffs" around Coal Mine Point are still visible today.

The location of the coalfield close to a natural overland route did not, as one might expect, lead to its immediate development. The inhabitants of both the Minas Basin area seen on this map and the Chignecto settlement were Acadian farmers who provided neither a potential market nor a likely labour force for the coal mines. Some coal was taken away by ship, but a report of 1720–21 suggests that this was not a very satisfactory exercise:

Within seven leagues of Cape Chignecto which with Cape Doré divides the Bay of Fundy into two branches there are very good coal mines, and easily come at but want of shelter makes it dangerous. For the vessells which come to receive it, they being forced to anchor in the open bay. (From PAC, NSA, XII, 137–3)[2]

The development of this resource would have to await a considerable increase in the colony's population, as well as encouragement from the authorities in London, who, as we have seen, were not at all anxious to permit any activity which might lead to the industrialization of the colonies.

Map 5:2   George Mitchell and Edward Amhurst. "A Map of a Peninsula Situate in ye Bay of Fundy. . .," (1735). Manuscript.

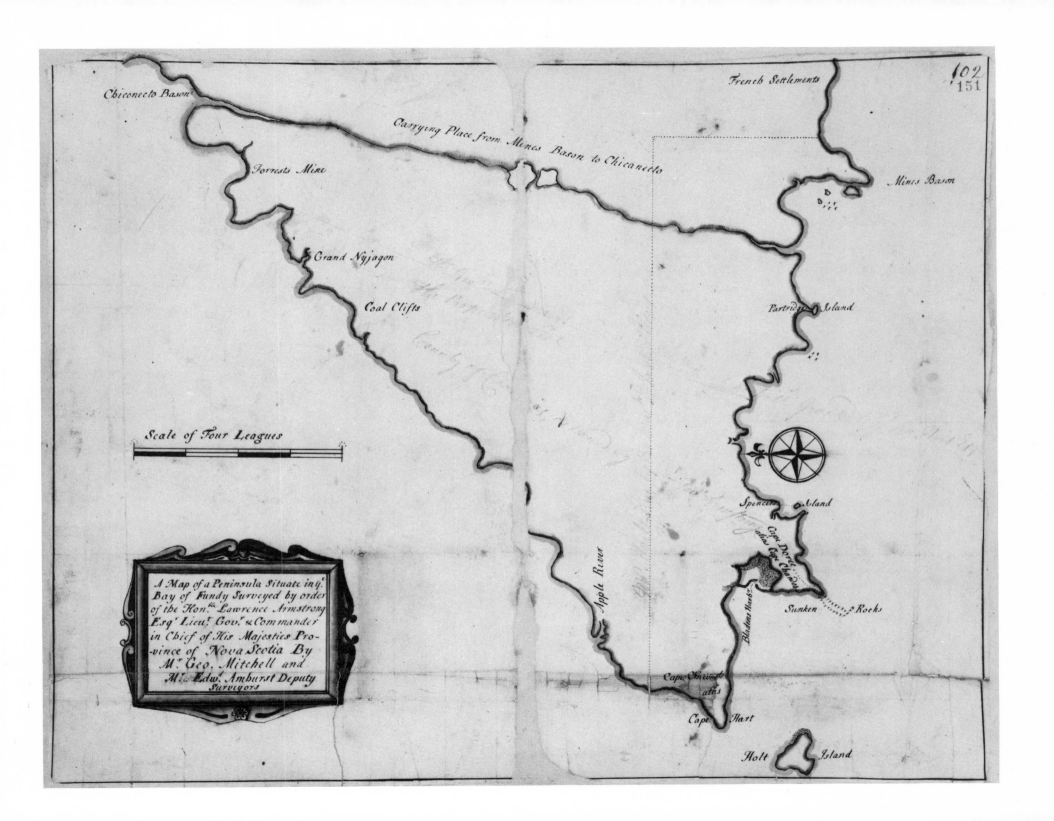

Chiconecto Bason

French Settlements

Carrying Place from Mines Bason to Chicanecto

Forrests Mine

Mines Bason

Grand Nyjagon

Coal Clifts

Partridge Island

Scale of Four Leagues

Spencer Island

Cape Dorie alias Cape Chariot

Apple River

Bladens Harbr

Sunken Rocks

A Map of a Peninsula Situate in ÿ
Bay of Fundy Surveyed by order
of the Honble Lawrence Armstrong
Esqr Lieut Govr & Commander
in Chief of His Majesties Pro-
vince of Nova Scotia By
Mr Geo. Mitchell and
Mr Edw. Amhurst Deputy
Survÿors

Cape Chenieto
alias

Cape Hart

Holt Island

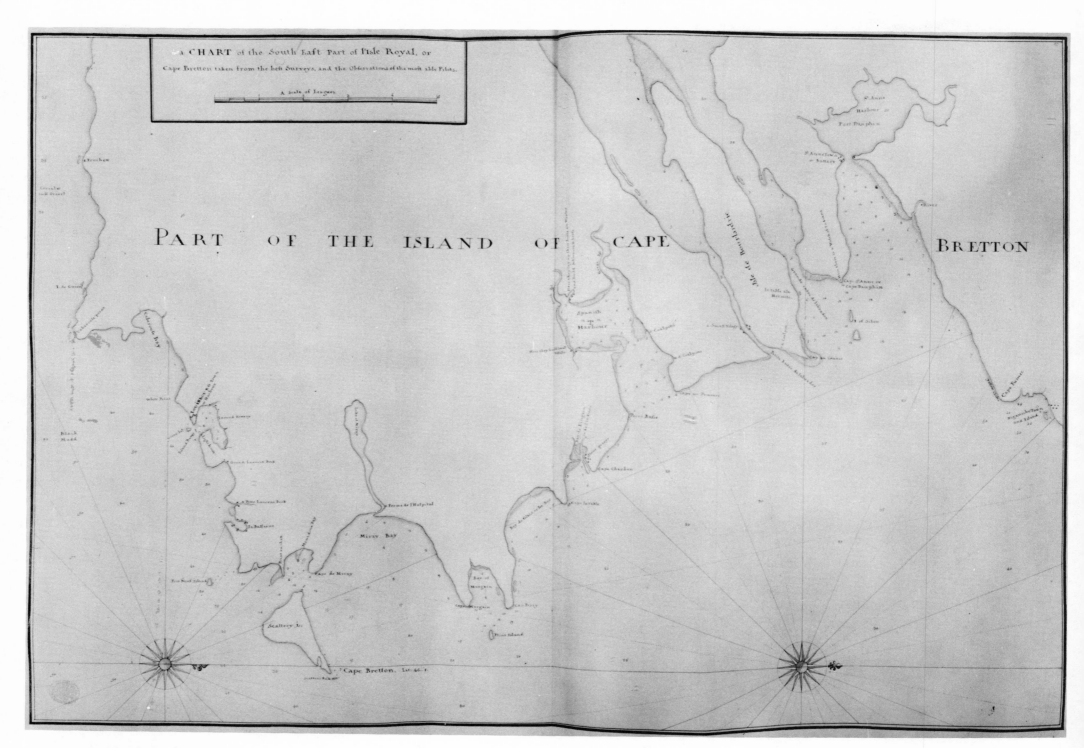

Cape Breton's
industrial origins

This map, probably made in the 1750s, provides an interesting early glimpse of what was to become the chief industrial area of Cape Breton Island. It is not dated, but represents the French development of the area before the final fall of Louisbourg in 1758. It is an English map, based, according to the title, on most reputable sources, and probably compiled in the office of the chief surveyor of Nova Scotia, Charles Morris. It is oriented with north towards the right, and gives a recognizable if rough representation of the coast from Fourchu to Niganiche (Ingonish).

The settlements south of Mira Bay were, then as now, fishing communities. Even Louisbourg, the capital of the colony, with its fortifications, battery and lighthouse, all visible on the map, remained primarily a fishing town (see Map 3:5, p. 45). Indeed, fish was by far the most valuable commodity exported from Cape Breton Island during the period of French occupation.

Between Mira Bay and Lingain (Lingan), the only settlement marked is the hospital farm near the mouth of the Mira. However, records show that there was a scattered population elsewhere along the shore, mostly engaged in fishing. But from Lingan northward, and particularly around Spanish Harbour (now Sydney Harbour) in the centre of the map, there is evidence of considerable activity.

At the time this map was made, much of the coal in the area was exposed and easily accessible without extensive digging of shafts. Cape Charbon, now North Head, near Lingan on Bay de l'Indiene (Indian Bay) took its name from these clearly visible coal deposits. Similar outcroppings of coal occurred elsewhere along

Map 5:3 Anonymous. "A Chart of the South East Part of l'Isle Royal, or Cape Bretton taken from the best Surveys, and the Observations of the most able Pilots." Undated. Manuscript.

the coast. Along the more sheltered shore of Spanish Harbour, it was found close enough to the water for loading onto ships.

The existence of coal in this region had been known to Europeans for some time, and small amounts had been shipped to various destinations in Europe and North America. It was close enough to Louisbourg to supply the garrison there, and might have been shipped on a regular basis to France by the supply ships that frequently visited the port. The failure of the French to develop this resource seems to have been based, at least in part, on a fear that the coal might ignite in transit.[3]

As we see from this map, there were three "coal pitts" in operation at this time. They were all close to the shore, where it would be possible to bring ships in for loading; this was the only practical means of transporting such a bulky commodity even the short distance to Louisbourg. Two of these mines appear on the northern shore of Spanish Harbour, at approximately the sites of North Sydney and Sydney Mines, while the third can be seen near the mouth of the Little Bras d'Or, identified as Petite Entre de Labrador.

Nicolas Denys had noted the availability of coal all along the coast here and had attempted, without much success, to exploit it; he had specifically remarked on the "hill of very good coal four leagues farther within the river"[4] (Sydney Harbour), as well as at the inlet of Little Bras d'Or. Allowing for a somewhat exaggerated estimate of the distance of the coal from the mouth of Spanish Harbour (Sydney Harbour), it appears that by the mid-eighteenth century both these sites were being worked.

At Lingan, although there is no evidence of actual mining of coal at this date, there were "stone quarys." This is one of the areas on Cape Breton Island where limestone is available; local stone had been used in the construction of the fortress town of Louisbourg.

At the head of Spanish Harbour, two separate shipbuilding sites are identified. The first, sheltered behind the Southeast Bar which is clearly drawn but not named, is labelled "Here they build small Vessells." Across the South River, on Barachois Creek, (also unnamed) we read that "Here they lay up thier boats in Winter and build Schooners & boats." The first record

of boat building in this area was of a 15–ton sloop built in 1750.[5] Our map shows a continuation and expansion of this activity.

The existence of boatbuilding facilities presupposes a supply of cut lumber. This particular map does not show the forest that is the natural vegetation of much of the region, and which is evident in Map 5:4. Maps 5:5 and 5:6 indicate the existence of a sawmill in the North Sydney area later in the century; it may already have been in existence by the 1750s, or there may have been others on the very streams where the boat yards stood.

An inhabitant of Spanish Harbour in the 1750s would no doubt be startled at the degree of industrialization of the area by the twentieth century. The harbour itself was soon to replace Louisbourg as the commercial and administrative centre of Cape Breton Island. With its natural resources, the area needed only a period of peace and some encouragement from the English authorities for industries to develop. Later maps in this chapter will show some of the subsequent steps towards this development.

Coal on the
Cape Breton coast

This section of map extends from Cape Dyson, called "by the French Cap la Table" (Table Head, north of Glace Bay) to part of Gage (Mira) Bay. Enough of the place names have survived, in either their English or alternative French forms, for them to be easily located on a modern map. North is at the top, and the large scale allows for a considerable amount of detail to be shown. The map resulted from a survey of Cape Breton Island conducted by Captain Samuel Holland between 1765 and 1767.

At this time, the forest extended almost to the shore, and was broken only by a few streams and ponds. A number of small inland lakes that are visible on a modern map are not included here; the surveyors had presumably not traced the streams very far back. Closer to the shore, Dyson Pond (now Big Glace Bay Lake) is shown, as is Hussey Lake, which no longer exists; it was apparently formed by a sandbar, since washed away, across the present False Bay. The silting and sandbars in Granby (Morien) Bay are still evident, while a small pond and a stream running southward from Manning Cove (Schooner Pond Cove) seem to indicate a change in the drainage pattern between 1767 and today.

The most notable feature of the coastline was clearly the frequent occurrence of "coals." Coal had been known to exist in this area for as long as it had been known in the Spanish Harbour area. These exposed deposits were the surface indications of the deeper seams that were to shape the development of mining in the future. At this time, however, coal was simply shovelled from shallow pits or hacked from the cliff-face.

The annotations "coals" or "coal vien" (vein) occur at intervals along the entire coastal area represented in this map. But only on the coast of Granby (Morien) Bay do we find evidence of active mining. Near Herbert Point, the site of Port Morien, appears the note "Coal mines workt at present for the King" and, on the shore, there is a "Coal Wharf." This coal deposit had supplied fuel for the garrison at Louisbourg from the 1720s. The site is still visible in Port Morien, known as the Old French Mine.

Dyson Bay later reverted to a form of its original French name, and is now known as Glace Bay. The coals observed along the shore there became the basis of the major mining industry for which the town became known. Another mining town, Donkin, was established at the site a little further east where coal was also observed. Mining continued for some time in the Morien area. As the demand for industrial coal increased, the easily worked exposed seams were exhausted, and the deep undersea mines of modern times took the place of surface pits.

Map 5:4   John G. Goldfrap. Part of "A plan of the sea coast from Gage Point to Cumberland Cape. . .with the coal mines in that extent. . .," [1767]. Manuscript.

Near the western edge of the map two areas are marked respectively "Ruins of Fort William at the Burned Coal Mines," and "Burning Coals." Open coal seams in this area were frequently ignited, either accidentally or on purpose. As a result of such a fire, Fort William, a British fort, had burned down in 1752.[6] Its location is marked on this map, close to the coal seams concerned. The coal deposits here, and the gases associated with them, have always been particularly inflammable. From the early French incidents of coal burning in transit to the disastrous colliery fires of more recent times, fire has posed a continual threat to the development of the industry.

This map, showing one of the major mining regions of Nova Scotia, gives an idea of how impressive the visible coal deposits must have been to the English newcomers to Cape Breton. It is interesting that the map also shows the result of one of the phenomena that has made the commercial exploitation of this resource so dangerous.

An account of mining on Cape Breton Island written by Governor Franklin in 1766 reminds us that fire was not the only hazard encountered while exploiting the coal seams. Probably referring to the Morien mines "workt at present for the King," he wrote:

That there is a wharf convenient for the loading the coals close to the Mines; that the Mine at present is in good order; well propped, and the vein appears to be good and large; I am told that the vein is about 12' thick and half a mile wide; that about twenty men may be employed daily; vessels from Eighty to one hundred tons burthen may take in their loading from the wharfe between the 1st of June and the 15th of October with Safety when the wharfe must be taken down and rebuilt in the spring, the Bay being so open, and the Draughts of Ice so violent as to carry it away in the winter season. (PAC, NSA, LXXVIII, 112–113)[7]

Despite the problems presented by fire and ice, this period saw the official recognition of the potential of the Cape Breton Island coal deposits.

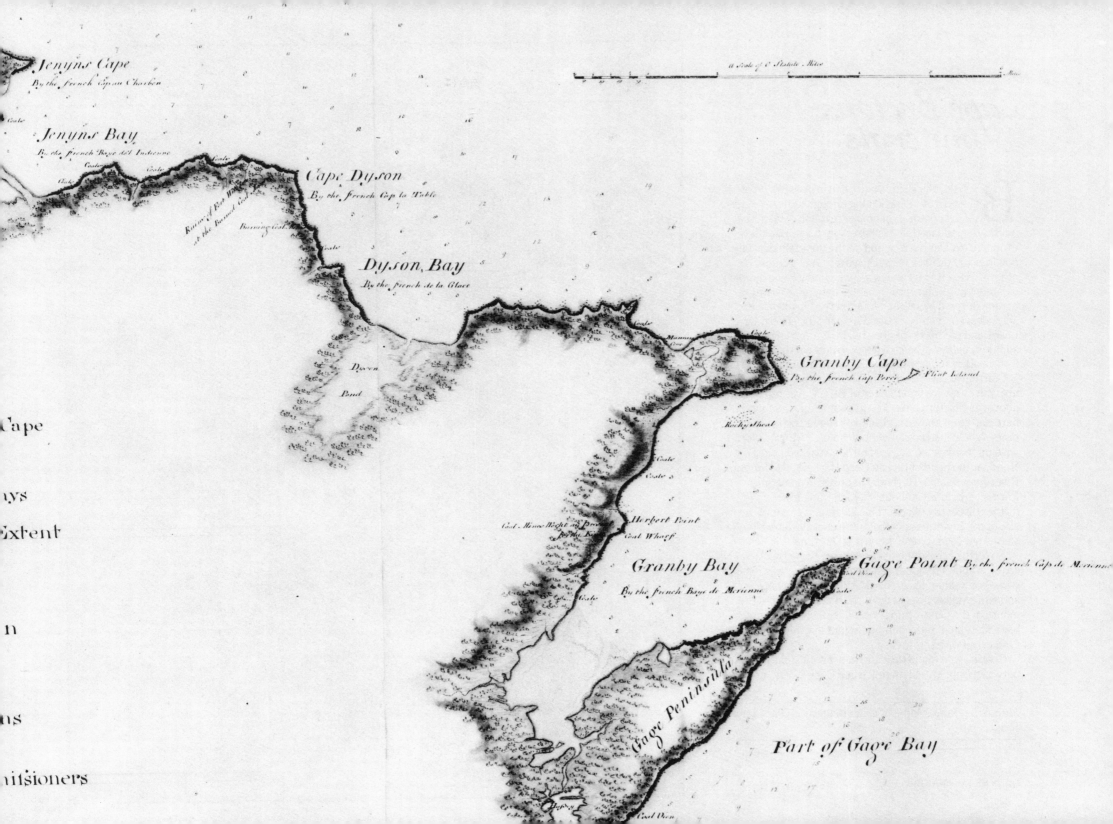

Jenyns Cape
By the French *Cap au Charbon*

Jenyns Bay
By the French *Baye de l'Indienne*

Coale

Coale   Coale   Coale

Ruins of East Works
at the Burnt Coal

Burning Coal Mine

Cape Dyson
By the french *Cap la Table*

Dyson Bay
By the french *de la Glace*

Coale

Coale

Manning Cove   Coale

Granby Cape
By the french *Cap Percé*   Flint Island

Dyson

Pond

Cape

Rocky Shoal

ays

Coale

Coale

xtent

Coal Mines Right at Present
for the King

Herbert Point

Coal Wharf

n

Granby Bay
By the french *Baye de Marianne*

Gage Point By the french *Cap de Marianne*

Coale

Coale

ns

sioners

Gage Peninsula

Part of Gage Bay

A Scale of 6 Statute Miles

Cape Breton's minerals

By 1794, the British had been in possession of Cape Breton Island long enough to have examined its natural resources in detail. The notes on this map tell us that it is based on the work of Governor J.F.W. DesBarres, and on the mineralogical discoveries of "the late Dep[y]. Surveyor Gen[l]. Nugent & others." Des Barres' maps are well known as examples of late eighteenth century cartography, and the information derived by James Miller has produced a remarkably accurate picture of the coastline, the Bras d'Or Lakes and the major rivers of Cape Breton Island. In addition, many of the coal deposits known today, as well as other mineral discoveries, are recorded.

Starting at the Gut (Strait) of Canso, near the present causeway, we find Plaster of Paris Cove, otherwise known as Plaster Cove. The gypsum deposits found here had been known and used by the French at the time of the construction of Louisbourg.[8] Moving clockwise up the west coast, we find coal marked near Port Hood, at the head of Just au Corp Harbour. At Hunting River (now Mabou Harbour) deposits of "coloured Earths" are noted and, just beyond Cape Mabou, a further discovery of coal. This location is close to the site of the Inverness coalfield; the coal at Mabou itself seems not to have been known at this time.

No further coal deposits are shown along the west coast. But on the upper reaches of the Margarie (Margaree) or Salmon River, black and yellow ore appear, and more yellow ore occurs a short distance from the mouth of the Cheticamp River. These ores have not been identified, but a number of metallic minerals are associated with this area.

Coal is again found near the mouth of a small river between Cape (St.) Lawrence and Cape North, and

---

Map 5:5   James Miller. "Cape Breton," 1794. Manuscript.

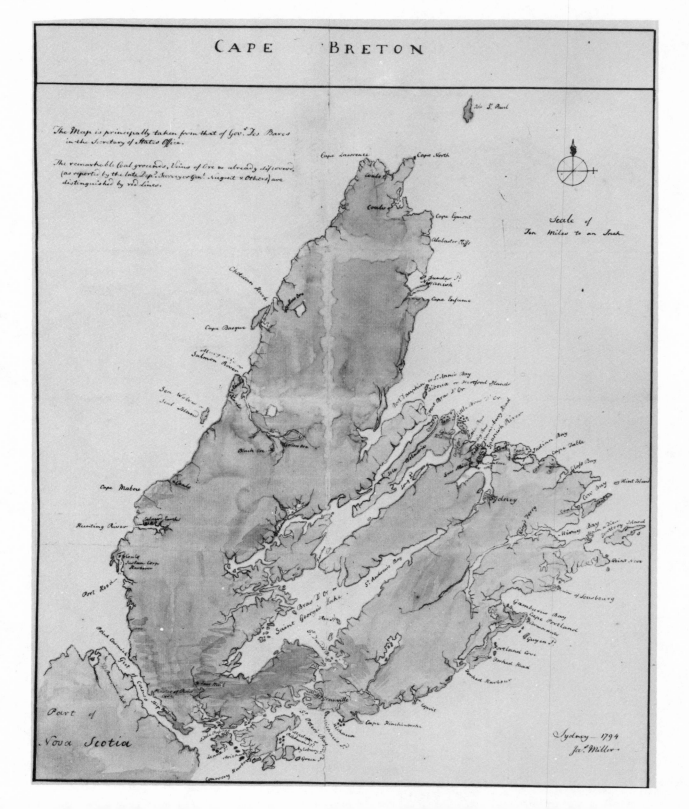

between Cape North and Cape Egmont, though the amounts available did not lead to commercial exploitation. Further south, however, the coal deposits seen in earlier maps are very much in evidence. They are located along the shore of Isle Boladrie (Boularderie Island) from Great Bras d'Or to Little Bras d'Or. A note inland from them mentions coals at the nine foot stratum; it is not clear whether this refers to the shore deposits or to different seams. Further deposits are shown between Little Bras d'Or and Spanish River (Sydney Harbour), with a note about coal at the six foot stratum. On the northern shore of the harbour itself, the word "coalery" (colliery) denotes the continued working of the "coal pitts" of Map 5:3.

There is evidence of other resource development on the northwest side of Sydney Harbour, where a sawmill is shown on a stream running into the harbour at what is now North Sydney. This mill, the colliery and the boat yards seen in Map 5:3 mark the beginnings of the industrial development of the Sydney area. Ship building continued under British rule; in more modern times, the ready supply of coal and the location of Sydney Harbour within easy shipping distance of the Newfoundland iron ore deposits encouraged iron and steel manufacturing.

Further to the east, the frequent annotation "coal" defines the rest of the mining region. Coal is shown all along the coast in places familiar in the history of mining in Cape Breton Island—Victoria, New Waterford, Lingan, Dominion and Glace Bay. There is an unexpected gap on the northern side of Cow (Morien) Bay, where Map 5:4 showed a coal mine and wharf. It is probable that in compiling this map, James Miller accidently copied the word "coal" onto the south rather than the north side of the bay.

Miray Bay marks the limit of the Sydney coalfield. The small populations both at Main à Dieu and the ruins of Louisbourg were chiefly engaged in fishing,

and their way of life was to develop differently from that of their neighbours on the coalfield. The population of the Sydney area would grow considerably during the next 150 years, as it took on the characteristics of a busy industrialized region.

The only other indication of industrial activity found on this map is on the southwest corner of the island. There, some way inland, on an unnamed stream that is actually the River Inhabitants, we find an isolated sawmill. It is known that the Acadians who settled in this region earlier in the century did some lumbering,[9] this mill seems to represent a continuation of the activity by their descendants or successors.

Clearly, the protectionist policies of the British authorities that prevented coal from being used to develop local manufacturing caused considerable delay in the commercial growth of the coalfields of Cape Breton Island. Nevertheless, this map shows an awareness of the resources on which industrial development would eventually be based.

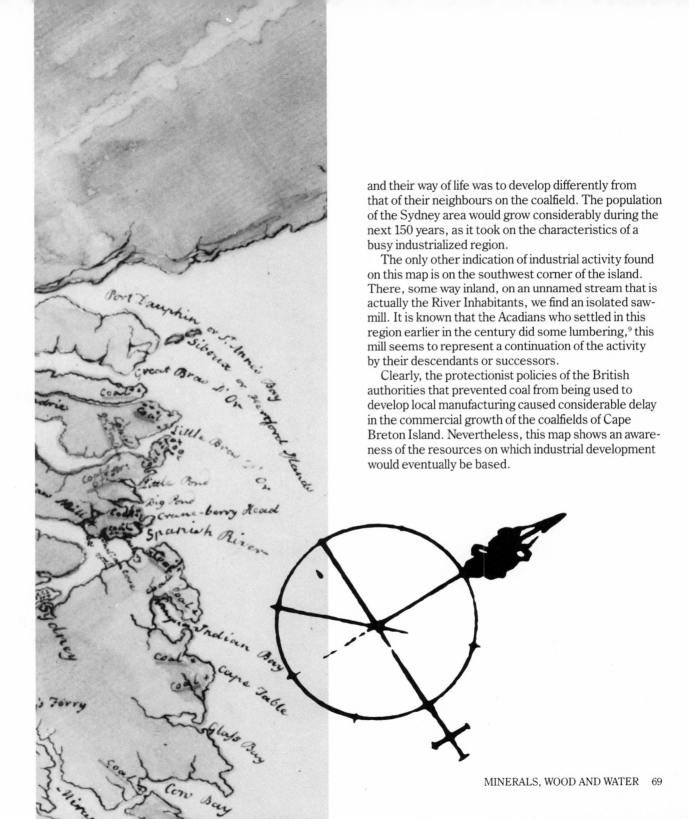

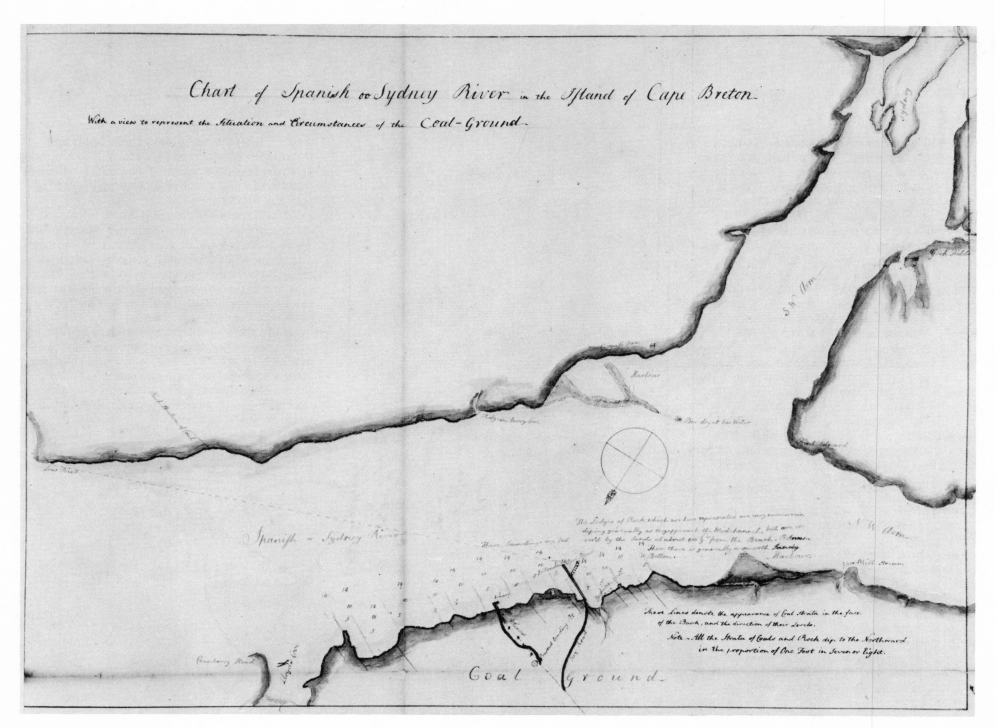

Chart of Spanish or Sydney River in the Island of Cape Breton.

With a view to represent the Situation and Circumstances of the Coal-Ground

Spanish or Sydney River

Coal Ground

Mining develops at Sydney

This large scale map of Sydney area was made in the same year as Map 5:5. Oriented with north towards the bottom left-hand corner, it shows in some detail the "Coal-Ground" of the North Sydney–Sydney Mines area, as well as the harbour itself.

The most interesting features of the map illustrate the mining activity. As we saw in earlier maps, coal had been located and mined in this spot for many years. By this time, a number of coal seams had been identified, of which only one was actually being worked. Along this seam, in the present North Sydney area, several pits are shown. Four of them apparently represent exhausted workings, or at least pits where access to the coal was becoming difficult or unsafe. A note on the map observes that "the Strata of Coals and Rock dip to the Northward in the proportion of One Foot in Seven or Eight." Apparently, when the coal seam ran too deep, and the shaft become too dangerous, digging was abandoned and another pit, slightly inland, was opened up further along the seam. When this map was made, the "Present trading Pit" was some way from the shore, linked by a road to the wharf where the coal was loaded onto ships.

The map indicates plans for further development of the area. A new pier and "Intended Pier Head" are shown, roughly in the middle of the North Sydney group of coal seams, linked by the "Key Road" to a point inland from the pit being worked. They were obviously designed to serve subsequent workings, along both the original seams and those yet to be developed. The pier lies parallel to the "ledges of rock" indi-

cated off the shore, and was evidently built on one such ledge. The deeper water between the ledges and the smooth, sandy bottom described would make it possible for vessels to moor safely alongside the pier. The new pier and pier head represented an advance over the simple wharf that had served the coal mine until then. The ice problems described in connection with Goldfrap's map (5:4) were less acute within the harbour than on the more exposed shores of Morien Bay. The construction undertaken at this period marked the beginning of the development of more permanent installations to serve a growing industry and Sydney Harbour formed the natural centre.

Farther along the shore, near Lloyd's Cove, more coal seams are shown. This is the site of the present Sydney Mines, shown in map 5:3 as "coal pits," where a mine was located in 1788 (Map 7:13, p. 127). No commercial activity is indicated there at the time of this map, but it was to become an important part of the development of the region.

Because of the open nature of Spanish or Sydney River, as Sydney Harbour was called, two other "harbours" are shown on the map, where vessels could escape from storms, wind and ice. One was on the North West Arm, probably at the site of the present Yacht Club, while the other, on the South West (now South) Arm, was the sheltered anchorage behind the Southeast Bar, which is unnamed on this map.

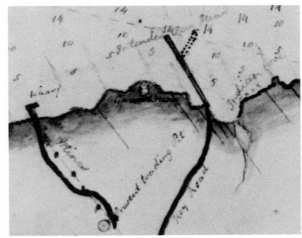

Map 5:6 Anonymous. "Chart of Spanish or Sydney River in the Island of Cape Breton With a view to represent the Situation and Circumstances of the Coal-Ground," 1794. Manuscript.

The mouth of Saw Mill Stream can be seen inland from the harbour on the North West Arm. The mill here, apparently the one shown on the previous map, was well situated to supply lumber for both the coal mines and other construction.

Across the harbour from the Coal Ground, there is still no sign of any commercial activity. Toward the harbour mouth, however, a "Rich Stratum of Coal" is identified. It is in this area that the future Victoria Mines were to be developed. Otherwise, there is little evidence of the development that the east side of the harbour would eventually see. Pidgeonberry Cove and Cornish Town may have been havens for small fishing boats at this time, but industry was confined to the mining area.

The map shows how Sydney, at the head of the South Arm, enjoyed a protected position which led to its selection as the site of the main settlement and garrison town of the region. Though not yet industrialized, it served as the administrative centre of Cape Breton Island (See Map 7:13, p. 127). As time went on, its key location at the heart of the mining region led to its development as a distribution and marketing centre, as well as the major port for the region. North Sydney, for its part, became not only a mining town but also an important link in the transportation system as the terminal of the ferry service to Newfoundland.

Map 5:6 is valuable for its record of the early development of mining, and its indication of the methods employed in that development. It also shows the potential for industrial growth in the region, with its ample coal resources, the suggestion of the availability of lumber, and harbour facilities that were already being developed. All these features formed the foundation for the establishment of the industrial region of Cape Breton Island as we know it.

Chapter 6 *Forts and Harbours:*
Military and Naval Strength

O ne of the first concerns of newcomers to any unknown territory has always been security against the possible hostile acts of the existing inhabitants who might justifiably resent their intrusion. Some form of physical barrier was also desirable against the wild animals which might threaten an isolated group of adventurers. Moreover, in an age when territorial rights in North America were disputed among Europe's colonizing nations, it was necessary to defend against attack both by official expeditions from other countries and by independent marauders, on whose illegal activities their governments might turn a blind eye. Finally, disputes between rival companies of the same nationality over trade and territory concessions gave rise from time to time to bitter fighting between fellow countrymen, who thought nothing of raiding each other's posts. Fortifications were, therefore, an essential part of the early settlement of Nova Scotia.

The earliest example of a fortified settlement on the Acadian mainland was the Habitation of Port Royal, which Champlain's map (7:3, p. 101) shows as a group of buildings within a palisade. His detailed drawing of the "abitasion" shows more clearly the lookout post and gun platform, designed to detect and repel unwelcome visitors. Small forts, many of which have since vanished, were subsequently built by other colonists. The foundation of Charles de LaTour's Fort St. Louis near Port LaTour can still be seen, but Fort Sainte Marie-de-Grâce, built at LaHave by Isaac de Razilly, has been lost to erosion. Its site, however, is clearly established by a number of maps made by both French and English cartographers during the seventeenth and eighteenth centuries. Maps also show the location of the Scottish Fort Charles, built in 1629 by Sir William Alexander's settlers near the site of the Habitation (Map 4:1, p. 49); the forts set up by Nicolas Denys and his successors to protect fishing stations at Canso, St. Peter's and St. Ann's; the English fort established at Grand Pré in the 1650s to subjugate the Acadians, and others of which little or nothing remains.

As well as providing a valuable historical record of long-vanished forts, maps also tell us something of the development of existing ones. We see how the original French and Scottish forts at Port Royal were replaced by a series of structures on the site of the present Fort Anne, as each country's forces in turn occupied and fortified the area. The early defences of Halifax are shown, and their development can be traced, on maps of the mid-to-late eighteenth century. The numerous maps sent back to France with reports during the fortification of Louisbourg gave a sufficiently clear picture of the operation that the modern reconstruction of the fortress could be based on them.

While some maps represent the forts that were actually constructed, others record proposals by optimistic planners that were rejected or modified, usually on financial grounds. These include an ambitious plan by an anonymous French official in the early eighteenth century for the refortification of LaHave on a much larger scale; Pasquine's and Saccardy's schemes for rebuilding and enlarging the fort at Port Royal; proposals for a fort at St. Ann's, abandoned in favour of Louisbourg; and John Brewse's grand scale plan for the fortification of Halifax, with encircling walls and bastions.

Many of the maps in this book were made by members of either the British or the French military. Some show not only ground plans, but also sections through the defensive works of the forts they depict; they are clearly the work of competent engineers. Others give strategic details of campaigns, such as the landing places and positions taken up by troops attacking a fort. These glimpses of military history, and of battles lost and won, give the maps a particular interest.

Not all confrontations between rival claimants to the new territories took place on land. Good harbours were essential not only for the fishing fleets and the ships providing communication and supply routes among the settlements, but also for the fighting ships that protected them. Sites such as Port Royal, Halifax and Louisbourg served as both military and naval bases, and were selected as much for their harbour facilities as for their other strategic advantages. Not only were troops transported by sea — the only means of communication in much of the region — but the ships also took an active part in the fighting, attacking enemy vessels and blockading enemy strongholds. The ships that appear in a number of the maps in this book are not merely decorative, but represent a very valuable part of the defensive capability of the colonists.

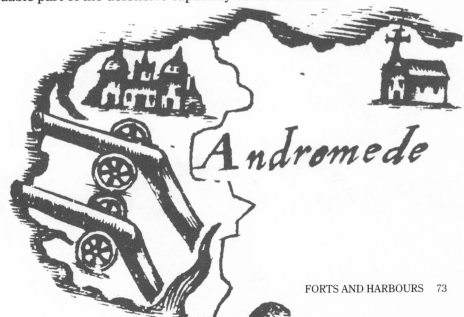

New fort plans for Port Royal

Maps 6:1 and 6:2 Pasquine. "P[l]an pour la reparation du fort du Port Royal en l'acadie," 1688. Manuscript. Vincent de Saccardy. "Port Royal d'Acadie," 1690. Manuscript.

The history of the fortification of the present site of Annapolis Royal goes back to the relocation of the chief settlement of Acadia by Charles de Menou d'Aulnay between 1636 and 1640. D'Aulnay's fort, constructed on a site commanding the river mouth, was subjected to attacks by Charles de LaTour in 1640 and 1642, and was taken by the British in 1654. In 1670, Port Royal was occupied by French forces in accordance with the Treaty of Breda, but sixteen years later, when Intendent Demeulle came to Port Royal, the fort was still in ruins (Map 7:5, p. 107).

In 1688, an engineer named Pasquine was sent out from France to examine the defences of the Acadian colony, and on his return drew up this plan (Map 6:1) for repairing the fort. A light dotted line indicates the remains of the original structure, which shows a seaward bastion undermined by erosion. The heavy line shows the proposed reconstruction, and the incomplete key describes its details.

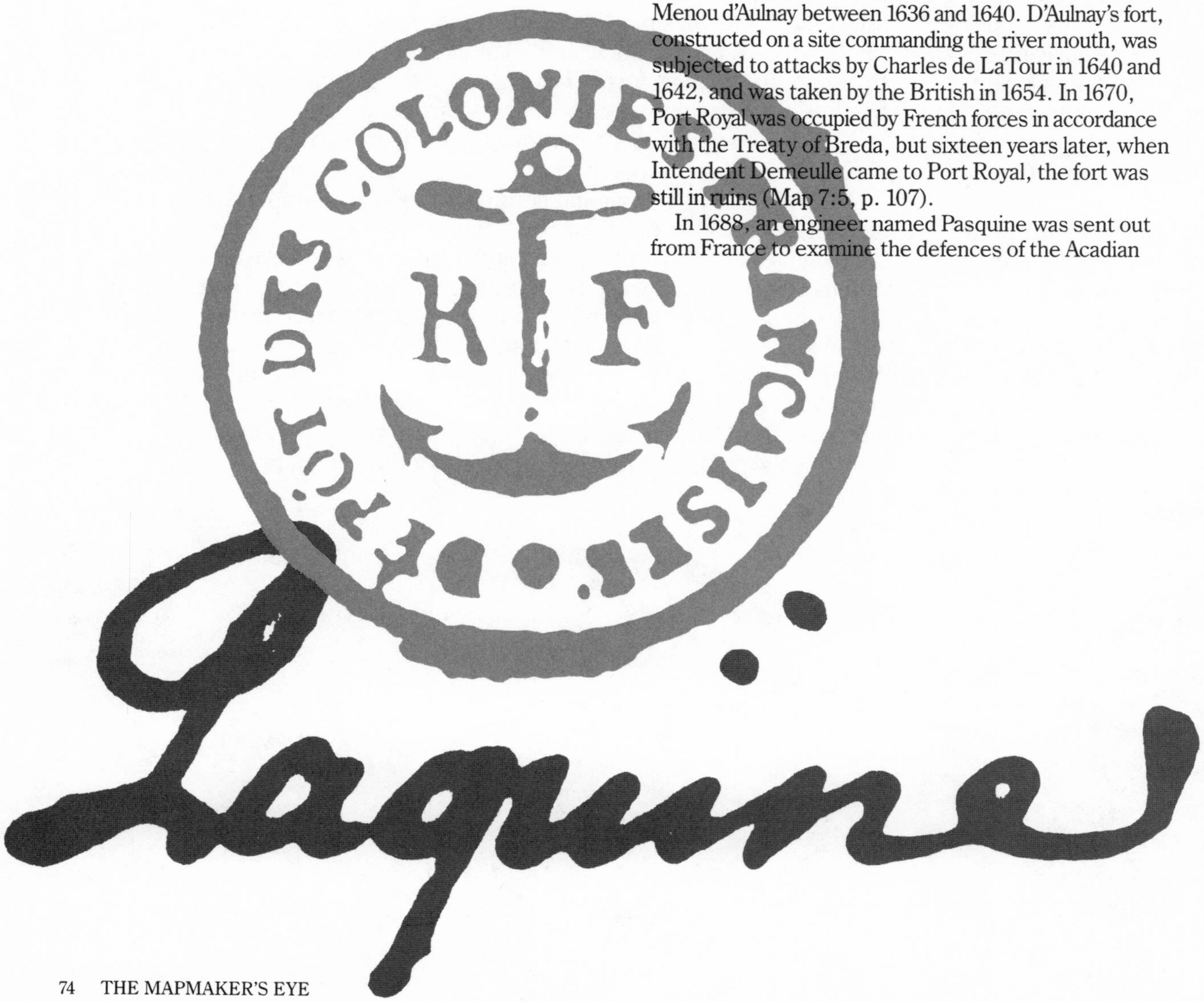

No attempt was to be made to rebuild the lost bastion. Instead, a series of posts, "G", were to be driven into the seaward slope to protect it from further erosion, and the outer wall would form a simple right angle, "H", at that corner. The bastion would be replaced by a curved gun platform or cavalier, "E", with a parapet, "F", behind the seaward angle. A ramp, "D", was to give the soldiers access to the rampart or parapet, while a second ramp, "C", was to allow cannon to be taken up to the platform, "if it is constructed." A barrack building, "B", was proposed for the inland corner of the fort. The barracks and the gun platform were tentative proposals. Clearly, Pasquine's instructions were to recommend as cheap a job as possible. The mill, "A", which had appeared in Franquelin's map two years previously, was apparently still standing and seems to have been included on this map simply as a means of locating the proposals for the fort.

The other key letters on the map presumably refer to a covering document identifying the remaining features. The line "O"–"N" represents the location of the cross section, while the other letters refer to the outer defensive walls and bastions. The plan as a whole is a very modest project for reconstructing the small fort much as it had been, apart from the modifications at the erosion site. As such, it gives us an idea of the extent of D'Aulnay's fort and pinpoints its location, as well as outlining Pasquine's proposals for a new structure.

The plans drawn up by Vincent de Saccardy in 1690, following his visit to Port Royal the preceding year, were much more ambitious (Map 6:2). Saccardy had noted the unprotected state of most of the buildings in

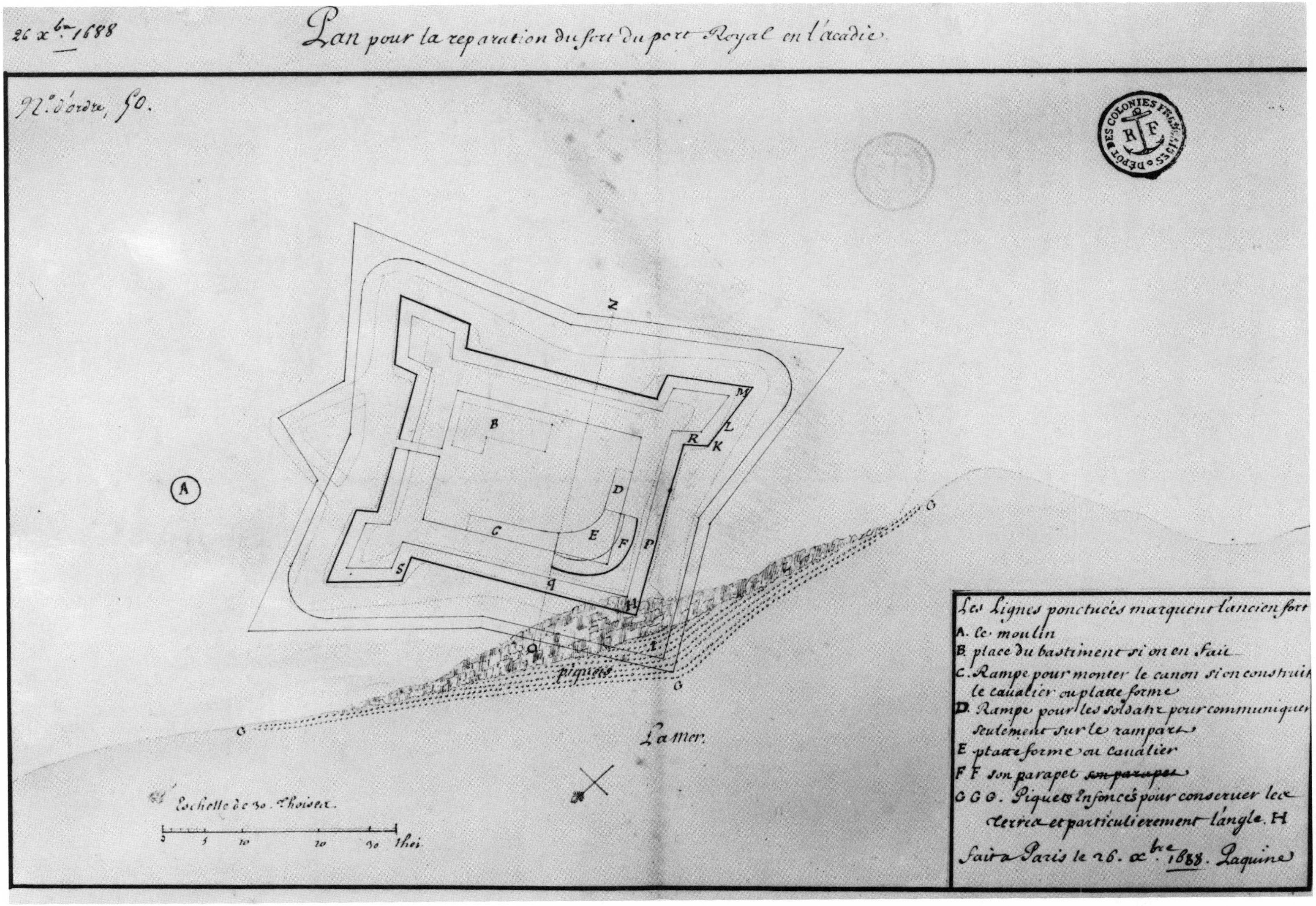

26 xᵇʳᵉ 1688

Plan pour la reparation du fort du port Royal en l'acadie.

Nᵒ d'ordre, 90.

N

M

B

L

R K

A

D

C

E F P

S

q

H

O

piquets

O

La Mer.

Eschelle de 30. Thoises.

5   5   10   20   30 thoi.

Les Lignes ponctuées marquent l'ancien fort
A. le moulin
B. place du bastiment si on en fait
C. Rampe pour monter le canon si on construit
le caualier ou platte forme
D. Rampe pour les soldatz pour communiquer
seulement sur le rampart
E ptatte forme ou caualier
F F son parapet ~~son parapet~~
G G G. Piquets Enfoncés pour conseruer lee
terrée et particulierement l'angle. H

fait a Paris le 26. xᵇʳᵉ 1688. Laquine

the settlement, and proposed replacing the old, ruined fort, "A", with a much larger structure, "B", that would include dwellings and essential services within the walls. He was very critical of the existing state of both the defensive and civilian buildings:

I inspected the old fort, which was not even large enough to be a simple Acadian dwelling. It was more than a quarter undermined by the sea and was crumbling everywhere.

The governor's house and church are in bad condition outside, which made me resolve to make a fort which should enclose these places, for it would cost more to tear them down and rebuild them than it would to add a fort. (La Rochelle, 12 Jan. 1690)[2]

In spite of Saccardy's suggestions of economy, the changes that he proposed and set in motion were both extensive and expensive. The new fort would cover a much greater area than the existing defences, which would disappear under one corner of the new structure. It would be roughly trapezoid in shape, with a bastion at each corner. Once again, there would be a modification of the shape of the bastion at the erosion site, to keep the defensive wall well back from the edge of the water. A large detached bastion and other works would face the existing town site, "C". A few buildings are shown within the walls. The other letters describe the surrounding terrain: "D" represents the land behind the fort "of the same height until out of range of the cannon", "E" is the uncultivated marshland, and "F" a natural division between the two areas. "G" represents the area exposed at low tide, "H" the sea (i.e. the river mouth) and "I" the *Riviere des Moulins* (Allain's River).

Saccardy demolished the remains of the old fort and began to lay the foundations of his new project, without authorization, before returning to France. Predictably, his scheme was rejected as being too costly. By the time Saccardy returned to Port Royal in June 1690, the

unprotected settlement had already fallen to a British expedition led by Sir William Phips.

This disastrous period in the history of Acadia reflects the unwillingness of the French government to spend any money on the protection of its colony. Maps 6:1 and 6:2 propose two different solutions to the problem of defending French interests in Acadia, but both were doomed to remain buried in the files of the bureaucracy until it was too late. It was not until 1702, after Acadia had once again been restored to France by treaty, that a third engineer, Jean Delabat, was sent out to build a new fort to protect Port Royal.

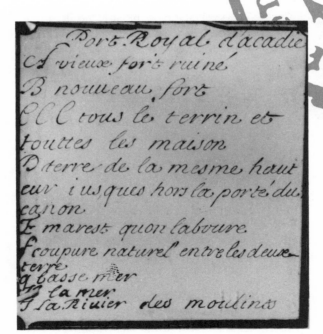

Port Royal falls to the British

In this map, oriented with north to the left, we have a first hand impression of Annapolis Royal, formerly Port Royal, as it appeared to the British forces when they captured it in 1710. We also see something of the surrounding countryside: the cultivated farmlands with their dwellings on either side of the Annapolis River below the fort, and the areas of marshland and forest. The fort itself had, eventually, been reconstructed by the French in the early 1700s and had repelled a number of British attacks in the years before its final surrender. It is shown here in some detail.

The key to the map not only tells us more about the features depicted, but also describes something of the campaign by which the fort was finally captured. The attacking force, under Colonel Nicholson, came by sea and entered the mouth of the River Dauphin (Annapolis) by the channel to the north of Goat Island (1) at the bottom of the map. The rocky passage on the other side of the island, as shown on the map, was unsuitable for large vessels. As they approached Port Royal, the British passed "A Small Settlement" (2) consisting of houses, fields and "Large morasses which by draining & damming out the heigh tyds made a great part arable" (3). These were among the first marshlands to be reclaimed for agriculture by the Acadians (see Chapter 4). Beyond these farmlands are the areas on both sides of the river "Where our whole body of men landed" (4). Though still separated from the fort by the Annapolis River and by "la Petiete Rivier" (Allain's River) the figure "5" shows an attack route that had been used before by British forces: "A large marsh and a small river which is foardable at Allen's mill."

The fort itself (6), which can be seen also in Jean Delabat's maps of Port Royal (Map 2:3, p. 20), shows the reconstruction that was eventually undertaken, under Delabat's supervision, in 1703. Less extensive than Saccardy's project, it nevertheless incorporated some of his proposals, and was a definite improvement over Pasquine's modest plan. It was a star shaped structure, with four main corner bastions and a detached fifth bastion looking downriver. It stood far enough back from the shore to be proof against any foreseeable erosion.

The fort is described in more detail in the "Explanation of the Figure." The four conventional bastions consisted of the "Bastion du Roy in it a large Store house for provision & a Small Cavalier" (7); "Bastion Dauphin in it a bake house a smiths forge & a Small Cavalier" (8); "Bastion De Bourgogne in it a Magazin of powder & over that a Magazin for Small arms" (9); and "Bastion De Berry in it a Magazin of powder" (10). The cavaliers, or gun platforms, served to cover the landward approaches to the fort, while the detached bastion (15), was equipped with "a Battery of twelve Guns to defend the River Dauphin."

Within the fort, as Saccardy had proposed, were some of the more important buildings. They included not only "A large house for lodging part of ye garryson over ye dry Store" (11), as one might expect in the interior of a fort, but also "The Governours House" (12), "The Lieut Governours House" (13) and "The Chapel" (14).

Outside the fort and unprotected were "The Severall Houses & Inclosures of the Inhabitants" (16) that made up the settlement of Port Royal. There is also a symbol in the form of a cross which appears to correspond with the cross that is marked between the parish church and the centre of the community in Franquelin's map of 1686 (Map 7:5, p. 107). Sir William Phips claimed to have cut down the cross in his raid of 1690,[3] but no doubt the pious Acadians were quick to restore it. The church itself had been replaced by the chapel inside the fort. The windmill that appears on Franquelin's and Pasquine's maps had also vanished, its site apparently incorporated into the extensive outer works of the fort. Delabat's maps indicate that a high proportion of the houses in the settlement had been burnt by the English during their attacks on Port Royal. As a result of several years of intermittent warfare, the settlement that Colonel Nicholson occupied was much diminished and most of its former inhabitants had moved to outlying settlements.

The remaining notes in the "explanation" refer again to the campaign by which Port Royal was taken. The place "where we landed our Cannon & ammonition" (17) lay on the bend of the river above Hoggs Island (18), which was in fact not a true island, but a piece of higher land rising above the surrounding river and marshes. This spot, on the outer edge of a meander of the river, would have deep enough water close to the shore to allow the vessels carrying arms and equipment to unload. The besieging forces established themselves at "The Incampment of the Severall Regiments" (19) in a line behind the fort, isolating its defenders

from their Acadian neighbours further up the river. As the title tells us, the fort "Surrendered to Her majesties armes under the Command of the Honourable Collonel Francis Nicholson after Eight dayes Siege in October 1710."

The British occupation of Port Royal gave them effective control over the Acadian population of the surrounding area. The Treaty of Utrecht in 1713 confirmed their possession of Nova Scotia, and the fort became a British stronghold, renamed Fort Anne. As we see in Map 4:1, p. 49, made in 1725, it remained for some years much as it had been at the time of its capture. During the second quarter of the eighteenth century, however, it was expanded by the addition of two more detached bastions, on the northeast and southeast sides, and by an enlarged battery on the seaward side. These improvements can be seen in the 1753 "General Plan of Annapolis Royal" (Map 4:2, p. 50). By that time, of course, Halifax had been established as the centre of both civilian administration and military activity. But throughout the first half of the eighteenth century, Annapolis Royal remained "the principall place of strenght in Nova Scotia."

Map 6:3 Anonymous. "Plan of Annapolis Royall Ffort the principall place of Strenght (sic) in Nova Scotia in America. . .," 1710. Manuscript.

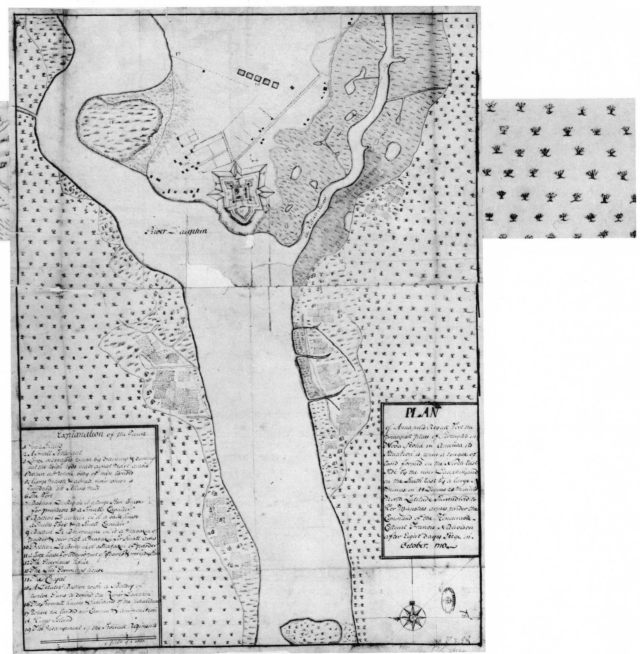

The rival Chignecto forts

Although this map bears no date, it was evidently made in the early 1750s, after the construction of the three forts, and before the capitulation of the French forces in 1755. It sets the scene for the final mainland confrontation in the long struggle between France and England for the control of Acadia and its inhabitants.

The Beaubassin (Cumberland Basin) area had become a major Acadian settlement consisting of a number of villages scattered around the basin; a small group of Acadians also lived at Baie Verte, on the other side of the isthmus. The population consisted of families, originally from Port Royal, who had developed new farmlands here in the 1670s and 1680s. For much of the early part of the eighteenth century they lived fairly comfortably under British rule, having taken a modified oath of allegiance that did not require them to bear arms against the French or their Micmac allies.

The Chignecto area formed a natural link, and the Missaguash River a natural boundary, between British Nova Scotia and what is now New Brunswick, which in the early 1750s was still claimed, and largely controlled, by the French. The officially neutral Acadians found themselves caught in this strategic zone where, whatever their sympathies, their lives were bound to be disrupted. In 1750, many of those living south of the dividing line (on the British side) were persuaded or coerced by the French to abandon their homes and farms and move to the French side of the river. The burning of the village of Beaubassin, on the orders of the French missionary Abbé LeLoutre, forced its remaining inhabitants to take permanent refuge in French controlled territory.

This map shows the consolidation of military forces on both sides of the boundary that occurred in the early 1750s. In 1750 the English established *Fort Laurent* (Fort Lawrence) on the site of the abandoned village of Beaubassin in response to the growing threat of a French attack on the peninsula of Nova Scotia, and ultimately on Halifax, its new capital. This move was immediately matched by the French, who began the construction of *Fort de Beauséjour* in 1751. The two forts stood a short distance apart, on adjacent ridges above the marshlands.

The building of Fort Beauséjour proceeded so slowly that in 1754 it was reported still to be unready to withstand an attack.[4] One of the reasons for the delay in completion can be seen on this map. Abbé LeLoutre did not confine his activities to the cure of souls. As well as taking an active political role in the struggle for the loyalty of the Acadians, he had organized the drainage of new marshlands for the expansion of the community (see Chapter 4). LeLoutre diverted some of the manpower which might have been employed in the construction of the fort to the building of a new dyke[5] and the *"aboiteaux projeté"* which is marked here between the *R. du Lac* (Aulac River) and *Rre de Tita-mare* (Tantramar River).

Ready or not, by the time this map was made *Fort de Beauséjour* faced *Fort Laurent* across the *R. de Mesa-gouche* (Missaguash River), "which separates the ground occupied by the English from that of the French." The French, moreover, had established another fort on the opposite site of the isthmus, near the village of Baie Verte. *Fort de Gaspareaux*, established in 1751, was connected to Fort Beauséjour by an overland route, which superseded the original portage trail seen in earlier maps. This route to the Gulf of St. Lawrence formed a valuable link between the Beaubassin communities and France, *Isle Royale* (Cape Breton), *Isle St.-Jean* (Prince Edward Island) and Québec. Supplies could be brought in by sea through the Gulf, instead of passing through the Bay of Fundy, where they were likely to be intercepted by English vessels from Annapolis Royal or New England. In spite of this potential life line, Fort Beauséjour was still dangerously isolated both from France and from Québec and the French colonies in the region.

Map 4:3, p. 53, illustrates the disadvantages of the locations of both forts. The British ship anchored at the mouth of the Tantramar River demonstrates how easily Fort Beauséjour could be blockaded and supplies prevented from reaching it from the Bay of Fundy. On the other hand, the French, or their native allies, had found a means of interfering with ships supplying Fort Lawrence. The vessel at the mouth of the Missaguash River is clearly heading for the "small creeks" where they would "unload the Stores." But ships using this route were vulnerable to French attack from the vantage points provided by the "Dykes leveled by the English from which the Indians formerly fired on the Vessels coming up the River Messiguash." Although beyond the range of Beauséjour's cannon, supply ships had to endure sniper fire from behind the dykes, whose strategic value had not been lost on the French.

Map 4:3 also shows both a ground plan and section of Fort Lawrence, as well as a "View of the Fort Cumberland," as Beauséjour was renamed after its capture by the English. Using Fort Lawrence as a base, and with the assistance of 2,000 volunteers from Massachusetts, the British forces attacked their French counterparts in June 1755. Greatly outnumbered, and unable to summon assistance in time, both Beauséjour and Gaspereaux capitulated after only two weeks of fighting. Beauséjour, now Fort Cumberland, was enlarged and strengthened and became the principal British fort in the area. Shown in the "View" with the British ensign flying, it was to remain an active military base in time of war until after the War of 1812.

These two maps give us some idea of the strategic positions of the forts. Although Fort Lawrence and Fort Beauséjour were different in design, their sites were in many respects similar. The British, in fact, clearly preferred the location of Fort Beauséjour, with its commanding view out toward the Bay of Fundy. Controlling Fort Beauséjour enabled the British to keep a tight rein on the surrounding Acadian population as the time of the expulsion drew near. It also helped the British deal with the continuing resistance of groups of French, Acadians and Micmacs up until the end of the Seven Years' War in 1763. These forts appear on a number of maps, French and English, made both before and after the last major battle for Acadia.

Map 6:4 Anonymous. "Carte Particuliere de l'Ishme de l'Acadie ou sont situés les Forts de Beauseiour, Gaspareaux et Fort Laurent Anglois," undated. Manuscript.

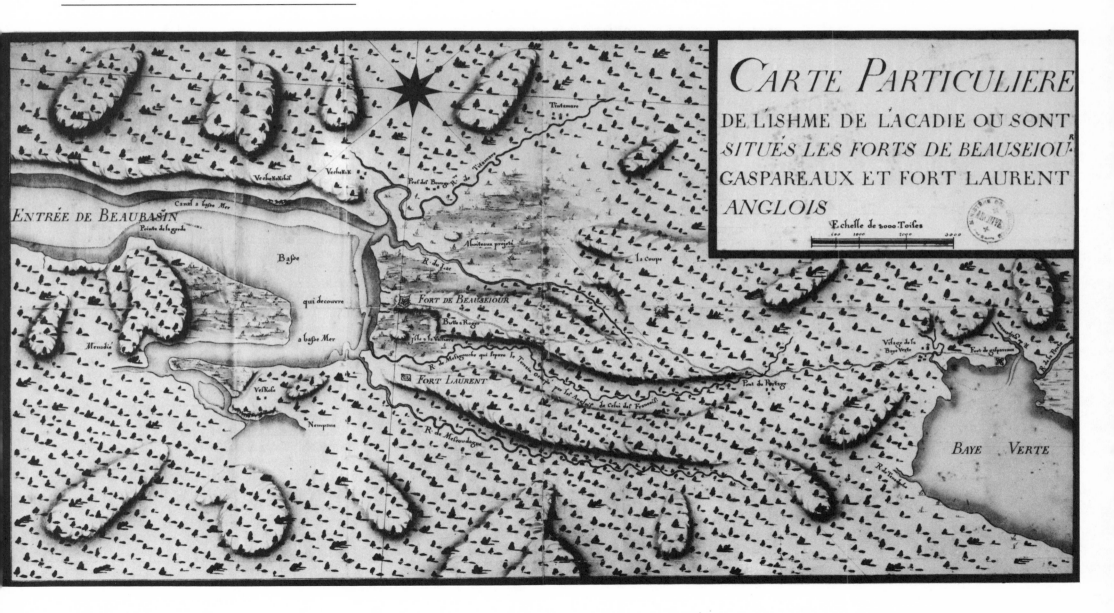

CARTE PARTICULIERE
DE L'ISHME DE L'ACADIE OU SONT
SITUÉS LES FORTS DE BEAUSEIOUR
GASPAREAUX ET FORT LAURENT
ANGLOIS

Echelle de 2000 Toises

ENTRÉE DE BEAUBASIN

Canal à basse Mer

Pointe de la garde

Basse

qui decouvre

à basse Mer

Menadic

Veskose

Nempasie

R. de Mescoudagne

FORT LAURENT

R. de Messgouche qui separe le Terrein Occupé par les Anglois de celui des François

FORT DE BEAUSEIOUR

Butte à Roger

Isle à la Valliere

R. du Lac

Aboiteaux projeté

Pres des Bourgs

R. de Titamare

Titamare

la Coupe

Village de la Baye Verte

Fort de gasparreau

Pont du Portage

BAYE VERTE

R. de Tentoube

The defences of Halifax

T his plan of Halifax, with proposals for fortifying it, was made in the summer of 1749, at about the same time as Moses Harris' maps (see Map 7:7, p. 113). Both authors show the small town that was laid out immediately upon the arrival of Cornwallis and his settlers, with the proposed sites of the principal buildings. Harris' map (inset Map 2:5, p. 26), illustrates the town's initial defences, consisting of a palisade and a series of five small forts. These structures were, in fact, far from complete when Harris' maps were first published: by October 1749 only two forts had been finished, and a temporary barricade had been thrown up in place of the planned palisades. It was not until the following year that the palisades were completed, and the remaining forts built.[6]

Those temporary defences were designed by the author of this map, John Brewse, Cornwallis' chief engineer. They served their purpose in deterring native attacks, but represented only a primitive form of the defensive system which Brewse had in mind. His more elaborate project is shown in this map, which

Map 6:5 Jn°. Brewse. "Project for Fortifying the Town of Halifax in Nova Scotia," 1749. Manuscript.

bears a note stating that it was sent to London "with Col. Cornwallis's Letter dated y^e. 17th Octob^r. 1749." (According to Cornwallis' letters of July 24 and August 20, 1749, it was in fact sent in August, having been omitted from the July letter.[7]) Although never completed in detail, Brewse's proposals formed the basis for some of the subsequent defences of Halifax.

Like many plans of Halifax, this map is oriented with north towards the right. It shows only the town site and a very small portion of the adjacent shoreline, as well as George's Island.

Brewse's proposal involved strengthening the initial defences by replacing the palisades with earthworks and a ditch, as in the "Section Thro a.b," and constructing bastions instead of the five stockaded forts. An additional bastion and battery, "G", of ten 24–pounders were to be built on the shore to the south of the town, and a demibastion to the north. In addition, three smaller batteries, "F", of four 4–pounders each were to be constructed along the waterfront. To strengthen the landward defences, three redans were proposed facing to the northwest, the presumed direction from which a land attack might be expected.

As well as providing for defences surrounding the town itself, Brewse recognized the strategic position of George's Island, "K", in intercepting attackers approaching by sea. He proposed the construction of a rectangular fort, and two batteries, "L" and "M", of sixteen 24–pounders and six 18–pounders respectively.

Although the landward defences of Halifax were not completed according to Brewse's plans, some of his other projects were developed in general accordance with his proposals. Between 1750 and 1755, considerable work was done on the installation of batteries on George's Island. In 1755, on Brewse's advice, Lawrence had three batteries constructed along the waterfront, including many more guns than had originally been proposed.[8] These batteries remained in place for a number of years, and can be seen in later maps in this chapter.

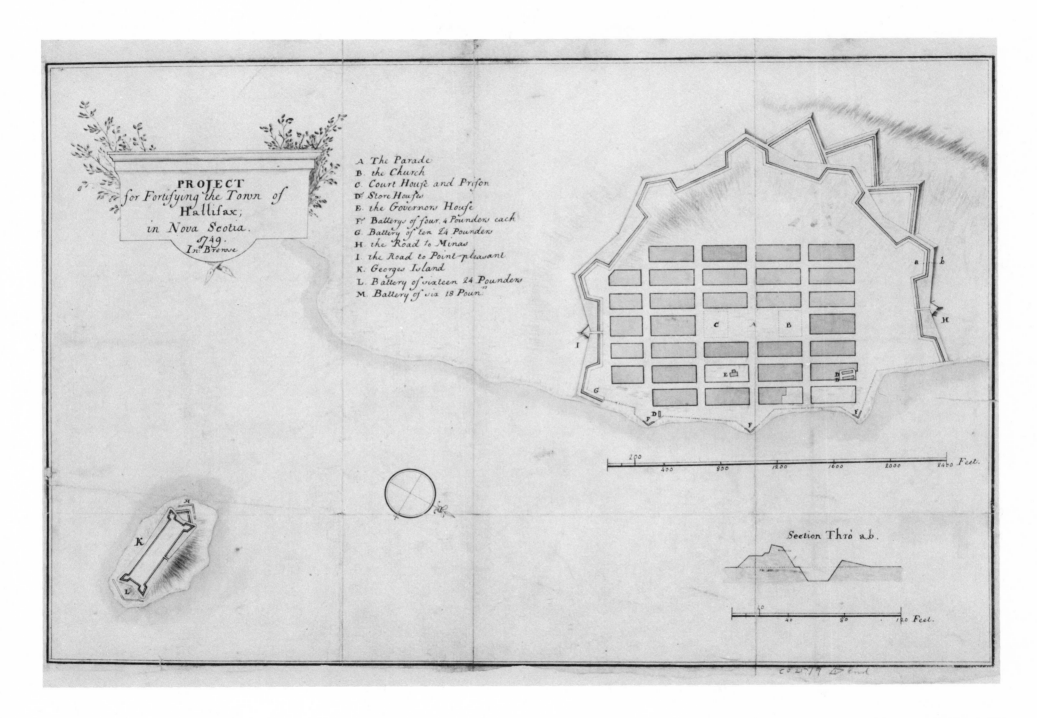

PROJECT
for Fortifying the Town of
Hallifax;
in Nova Scotia.
1749.
In. Brewse

A The Parade
B the Church
C Court House and Prison
D Store Houses
E the Governors House
F Batterys of four, 4 Pounders each
G Battery of ten 24 Pounders
H the Road to Minas
I the Road to Point-pleasant
K Georges Island
L Battery of sixteen 24 Pounders
M Battery of six 18 Poun.

Section Thro a.b.

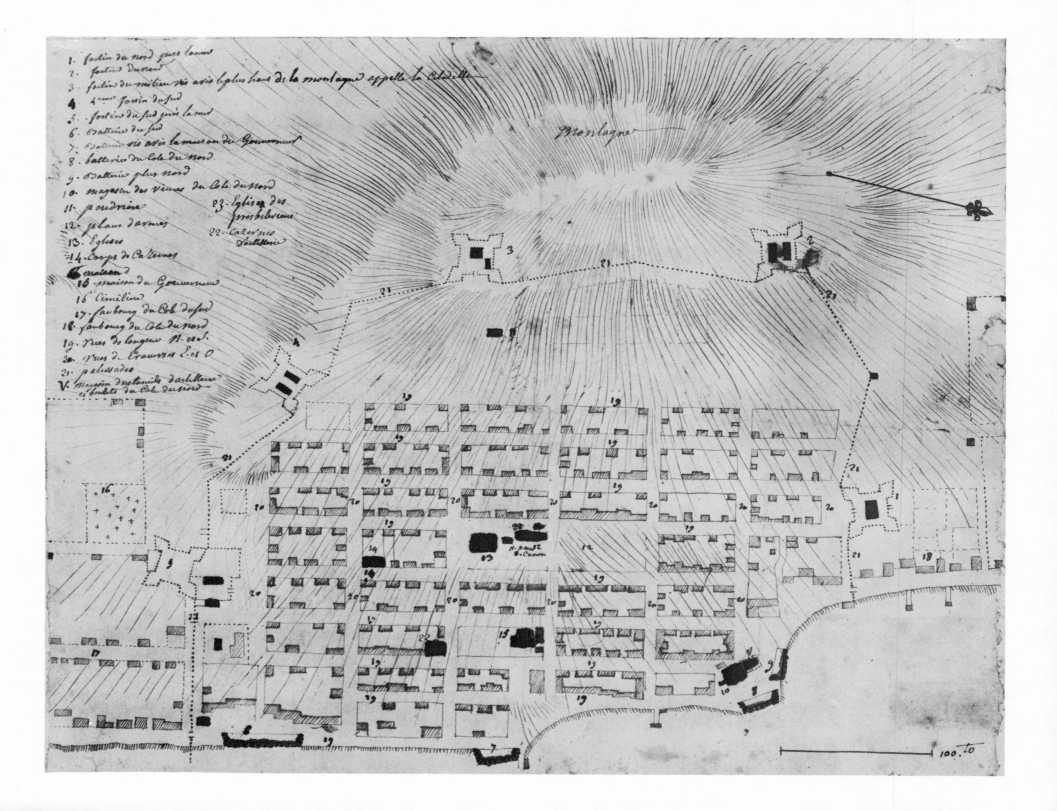

A spy reports on Halifax

This map was made in 1755 when Vaudreuil was a prisoner in Halifax. It was described by Admiral Boscawen in November of that year as "A Plan of Halifax with a scheme of attacking it from Canady. Taken out of a Wash Ball that was in a French Officer's Chest, going to Louisbourg."[9] A wash ball was a cake of soap, and its owner was clearly a spy. The cloak and dagger circumstances of the map's origin were part of the final stages of the long dispute between the French and the English over possession of Nova Scotia. Although war was not formally declared until the following year, tensions rose in 1755 with the capture of Fort Beauséjour and the expulsion of the Acadians. Despite these setbacks, the French had not given up hope of capturing Halifax, with help from their

stronghold in Louisbourg, and this map seems to represent a part of the intelligence gathered for this purpose.

Although some of the information found on the map could have been derived from published maps such as those put out by Thomas Jefferys (see Map 2:5, p. 26), other details were undoubtedly gathered on the spot. The map identifies not only the forts (1–5) shown on earlier maps, but also the newly established shore batteries (6–9) and the Artillery Barracks (22) with their field pieces on the Grand Parade (12).[10] A second barracks (14) is shown in the block south of the Parade, a powder magazine (11) on the slope below the Citadel (3) and two storehouses (10 and "V"), one for provisions and one for munitions, near the waterfront at the north of the town.

The Church (13) is, of course, St. Paul's, correctly located at the south end of the Parade instead of the north end as it appeared on earlier plans. The Governor's House (15), the "Presbyterian Church" (marked 22 but keyed 23, located southeast of the Grand Parade),[11] the cemetery (16) and the houses of the north (18) and south (17) suburbs are all depicted with

some care. The streets parallel and at right angles to the waterfront are, for some unknown reason, labelled 19 and 20 respectively. The entire map, down to the variety of shapes of the buildings (whose accuracy we now have no means of determining), appears to have been drawn up with the meticulous attention to detail necessary to serve as a guide to an invading force.

The landward defences as shown here represent the original palisade and forts, begun in 1749 and completed the following year. They had not been replaced by John Brewse's more elaborate plan. The forts are shown in some detail, with their corner bastions and barrack houses inside, except for the "south fort near the sea" (5) where the buildings are shown standing separately within the palisade. The waterfront batteries originally planned by Brewse were installed, according to a slightly different design but under his supervision, in 1755. The accuracy of their representation in this map is confirmed by British maps of the same date. The map as a whole provides an interesting picture of the fortifications of Halifax from the point of view of a potential invader.

Map 6:6 Unsigned; attributed to François-Pierre de Rigaud de Vaudreuil. A Plan of Halifax. . . , 1755. Manuscript.

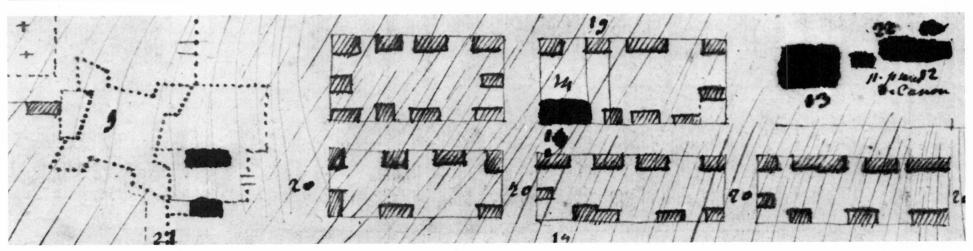

Naval yard and its defences

This map is part of a survey of Halifax and the surrounding area carried out by Captain Charles Blaskowitz and drawn up by Henry Castleman. It includes additions to the defences, seen in the previous map, that were built because of the threat of renewed hostilities at the time of the American Revolution. The complete survey extended from Purcell's Cove to just north of the Narrows, and includes the Northwest Arm, part of McNab's Island, and the Dartmouth shore. It shows relief, drainage, settlement patterns, farms, fisheries, and even some out of town taverns.[12] It also depicts the fortifications of the area in some detail. Although much of the map is self-explanatory, a number of items are identified by a table of references not included in this extract, but which will be quoted when necessary.

The waterfront of the town itself was bristling with wharves in 1784, much as it had been 10 years before (see Map 2:7, p. 31). But the batteries that had formed a major part of the town's defences at the time of DesBarres' survey were no longer operational. Among the wharves, the letters "c", "d" and "e" represent, respectively, "The Remains of the South Battery, the land of which is granted away"; "The Remains of the Middle Battery, in the Rear of which was a large Square reserved for Public Uses; the part of which stained yellow has been lately given up by the Town, and is now inclosed for Government Uses"; and "The Remains of the Lower Battery, in the Rear of this, are the Ordnance Storehouses, the inclosing of which was lately objected to by the Magistrates of the Town." These batteries had been made redundant by the establishment of a more extensive series of defences closer to the harbour mouth. The use of the land behind them then became a subject of the inevitable debate between different levels of government. The Ordnance Yard behind the Lower (North) Battery had been badly overcrowded since 1755, when two build-

ings were shown there (see Map 6:6). By 1766 it was distinctly congested,[13] and the opportunity to expand was clearly welcome.[14]

"McLean's, or the Principal Battery" is listed as "b" in the references. It occupied the site of what DesBarres identified as the South Battery, also known as the Barbette Battery,[15] which together with the guns of George's Island defended the western channel of the harbour.[16] Farther along the shore, a series, "a", of "Batteries and Intrenchments thrown up at different times for the Defence of the Harbour" extended along to Point Pleasant; two more batteries faced onto the Northwest Arm.[17]

The Naval Yard was located to the north of the town. Although doubts had been expressed from time to time about the yard being too far from the main defences of the settlement,[18] construction had continued, and in about 1755 extra defences were built to protect it. These, keyed "f" and "h" respectively, consisted of "Fort Coote, being a Blockhouse with an Intrenchment thrown up round it," on the shore to the north of the Yard and three "detached bastions thrown up for the Defence of the Naval Yard," as landward defences.[19] The notes state that only the remains of these survived in 1784.

The other defences on the Peninsula consisted of three significant forts visible on the map. Fort Massey

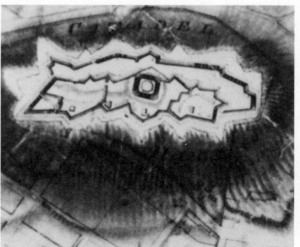

Map 6:7 Charles Blaskowitz/Henry Castleman. Section of "A Plan of the Peninsula upon which The Town of Halifax is situated, shewing The Harbour, the Naval-Yard, and the several Works constructed for their Defence," 1784. Manuscript.

was established between 1776 and 1778 to the south of the town, overlooking Freshwater Brook, whose hollow might provide shelter for attacking troops. Fort Needham, at the northwest corner of the map, was built in 1778 to defend the Naval Yard and the northern approaches to the town.[20] The third and most extensive fort was the Citadel.

The original "Citadel" had been one of five small forts, connected with a palisade, that formed the original defences of Halifax. It was rebuilt in 1761, and consisted of "a system of much elongated, irregular, polygonal fieldworks of earth and sod."[21] In about 1776, the fortifications were further developed and become "a maze-like system of rambling polygonal earthworks"[22] whose irregular outline is clearly seen on this map. The central wooden blockhouse, visible here, was used as a keep and barracks.

Although the Citadel was by far the largest of the structures defending Halifax, it was not necessarily the primary deterrent to potential invaders. The formidable defences of George's Island, consisting of two levels of earthworks, stand out clearly on this map. The chief responsibility of the island's guns was to defend the eastern channel and the outer harbour; some of them reinforced the Principal Battery on the Halifax side. The Eastern Battery can be seen at the bottom of the map, on the Dartmouth Shore. One of the earliest defensive works to be established on the harbour, it completed the firepower of George's Island in defending the eastern channel.[23]

The defences shown on this map were the last to be built for some time. A period of peace discouraged further development, and it was not until the final years of the century that improvements were initiated by Prince Edward (later Duke of Kent), Commander in Chief at Halifax from 1793–1800, which changed the face of Halifax once again.[24]

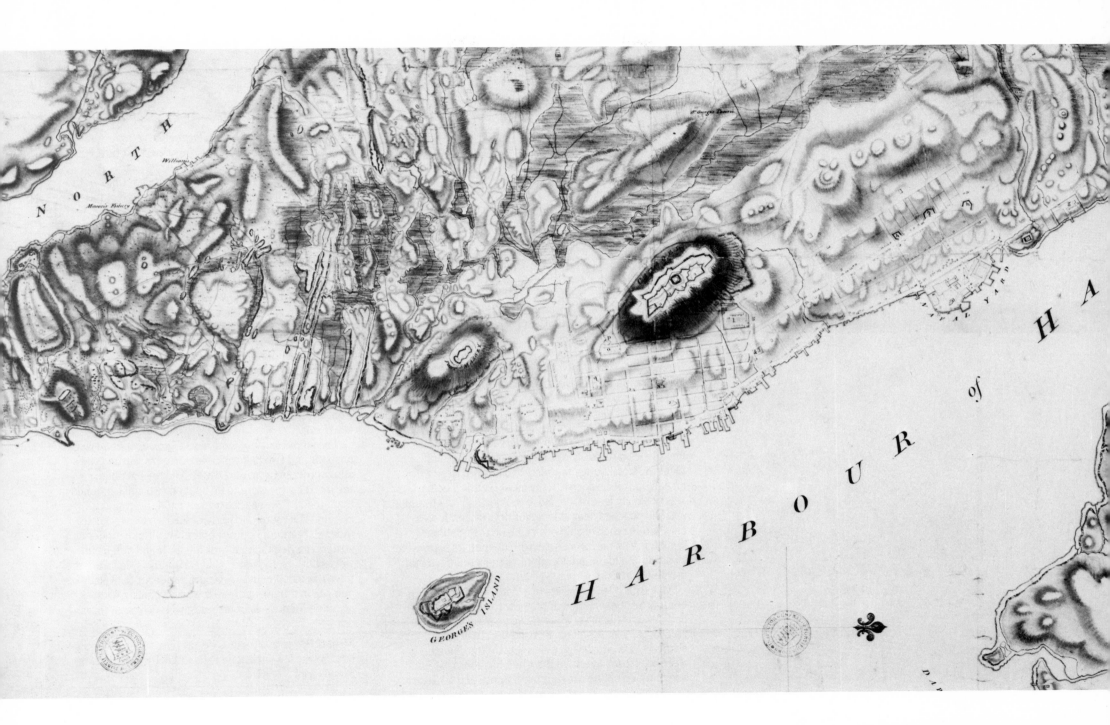

NORTH

Williams

Morris's Redoubt

St George's Tavern

GEORGE'S ISLAND

HARBOUR of HA

Construction begins at Louisbourg

Map 6:8 illustrates the plans put forward in about 1720 by the French engineer, Jean-François de Verville, for the development of the town and fortifications of Louisbourg. Verville came to Louisbourg in 1716, and in the following year undertook the planning that would establish the settlement as the chief stronghold of Cape Breton. In 1719 Louisbourg was formally named the capital of the colony, and serious work on its fortifications began.[25] A comparison of this map with Verrier's map of 1745 (Map 6:9) shows that the construction that was carried out essentially followed Verville's plans.

The Fortress of Louisbourg was built as a result of the provisions of the Treaty of Utrecht which, in 1713, awarded mainland Nova Scotia and the Newfoundland fishing base of Placentia to the British and left the French with *Ile St Jean* (Prince Edward Island) and Cape Breton Island. Deprived of their administrative and military base at Port Royal, and the fishing stations at Canso and Placentia, the French decided to replace them with a base on *Ile Royale* (Cape Breton Island) that would serve both their military and commercial needs.[26] Strategically placed between France and Québec, Louisbourg was also well located to serve as an entrepôt for trade with the West Indies. The harbour was normally free of ice, close to good fishing grounds, and had beaches near at hand for drying fish. It was also within reach of ships working on the offshore banks. It was therefore selected, despite its somewhat swampy and fogbound location, as the site for a major fortified settlement.

Map 3:5 (p. 45) consists of a "view" of Louisbourg before the construction of the new town and its fortifications. For the first two or three years after Verville's arrival, the fishing village remained virtually unchanged. The surveying poles seen in the distance were only forerunners of the great bastions that we see outlined on the present map. Some of the batteries of guns included in the view were, like so many features of optimistic colonial reports, proposed but never installed.

As the title of Map 6:8 suggests, it describes both existing and planned features, though some of the planned elements were not completed exactly as shown. Although not identified as such here, the dark shaded structures, by convention, are those already existing or completed. The plan as a whole gives a clear idea of Verville's proposals for the defence of Louisbourg from both land and sea.

The Grand, or Royal Battery, directly opposite the harbour entrance on the north shore, was one of Verville's earliest constructions. The other was the important Island Battery that defended the harbour mouth itself. As the map shows, between them they covered the approaches and much of the interior of the harbour. Later maps show that the battery on the tip of the peninsula was not actually developed, while the waterfront defences were constructed in a somewhat modified form.

The landward defences were to consist of two large bastions and two half bastions, linked by curtain walls and protected by an outer wall. The full bastions, as the map shows, were to be built on two small mounds that stood between the town site and the country behind. The more northerly of the two was by far the more elaborate, and was apparently already under construction when the map was made. It had defensive works both on the outer side and on the side facing the town, so that it could serve as a citadel or final place of defence in the event of the town itself falling to an attacker. Visitors to Louisbourg will recognize this as

Map 6:8 Jean-François de Verville. "Plan de Louisbourg Avec les Ouvrages Faits et les Projets," 1720. Manuscript.

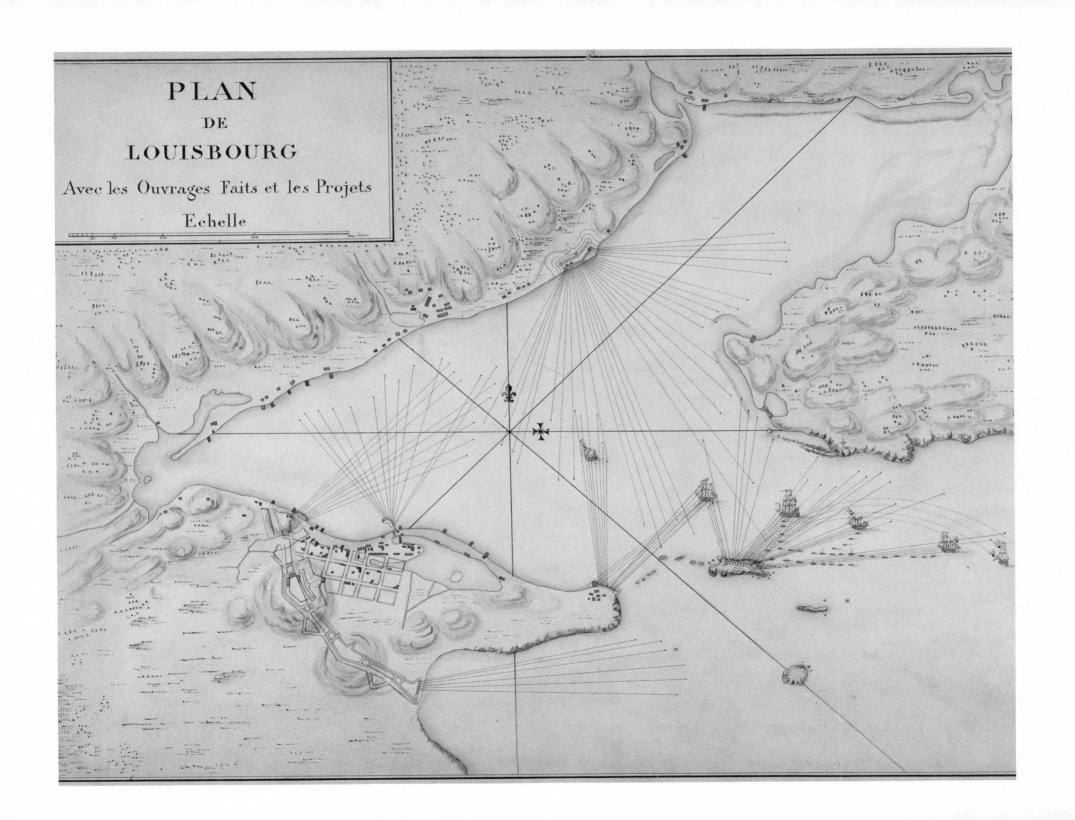

PLAN
DE
LOUISBOURG
Avec les Ouvrages Faits et les Projets
Echelle

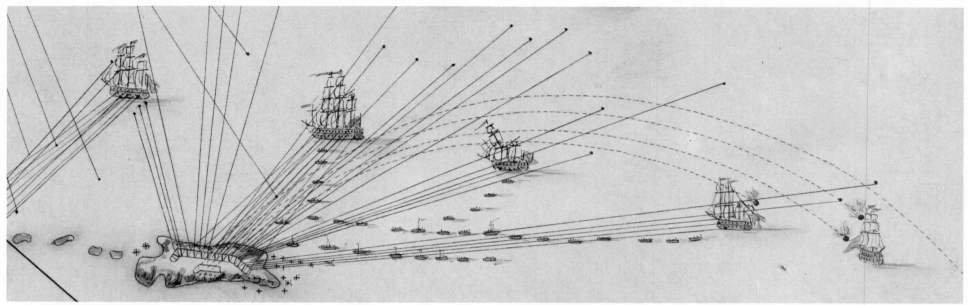

the now reconstructed King's Bastion, which incorporates the main barracks and the Governor's lodging,
Château St. Louis. The two half bastions were to
defend the main entrance to the town (the Dauphin
Bastion and Gate, visible today) and the otherwise
undefended seaward side of the town.

The buildings of the town consisted, in part, of the
houses of the original settlement, which were built in a
rough arc facing the shore. Together with the other
buildings around the harbour and the fish stages along
the shore, they represented the community as it was
in the days when fishing was its only economic base.
The rectangular blocks so typical of eighteenth century
town planning in North America were laid out as shown
on the map, and apparently some of the new buildings
had already been completed. Nevertheless, the map

clearly shows Louisbourg in a transitional stage between the former fishing village of Havre à l'Anglois
and the important fortress that was eventually to stand
on the site.

A final interesting feature of the map is the illustration of an enemy attack on the harbour, and the damage
inflicted on the invading force by the projected batteries. Approaching ships had no choice but to sail
through the channel to the north of Battery Island; the
map shows the rocks blocking the eastern approach. A
landing force of small boats appears to be making its
way to the island beneath the cannon fire; apparently it
was feared that the guns there might be attacked in
this way, though the boats appear extremely vulnerable. During the siege of 1745 the British did, indeed,
make an unsuccessful attempt to land troops on the

island in this way, under cover of darkness, but from
the opposite direction.[27]

The construction of a major fortification such as this
was obviously a long-term project, even without un-
foreseen delays. In fact, the work was slowed down for
a number of reasons. The inhospitable climate of the
area was a contributing factor: there were serious
construction problems as a result of the alternate freezing and thawing of mortar and masonry. In addition,
conflicting instructions were issued from time to time
by the French authorities, who were predictably
unhappy at the enormous cost of the project. Ineffi-
ciency, corruption and discord among the local administrators did nothing to improve matters, and it was not
until 1738 that the fortifications as outlined on this map
were virtually complete.

Fortress Louisbourg

É tienne Verrier was appointed chief engineer at Louisbourg, working under Verville, in 1724.[28] Between that time and the fall of the fortress in 1745, he was responsible for a number of plans illustrating the progress of construction, along with additions to the defences originally outlined by Verville. This plan shows the full extent of the fortification of the town, together with some of the principal buildings. It is oriented with north to the bottom, in contrast to the previous map. It includes, in a cartouche, a similarly oriented map of the entire harbour and adjacent coast. It is signed "Verrier fils," indicating that some of the engineer's work was at this time delegated to his son.

The plan shows that there had been very little modification of Verville's designs during the lengthy period of construction. The massive ramparts that formed the landward defences consisted of an inner and an outer wall with four bastions, much as they had appeared on the earlier map. The waterfront had been built up with a sea wall, and furnished with defences on each side. These works had been finished, or were near to completion, by 1738.[29] Beginning in 1739, walls and bastions were added on the eastern side of the town, along the shore and cutting across the peninsula to the harbour, so that the town was completely encircled.

Notes on the map and a key within the title cartouche provide details of the features shown, allowing us to reconstruct something of the appearance of the fortress. A visitor entering the town from the land would pass through the *Porte Dauphine* (Dauphin Gate, "A") between the Dauphin Bastion and the *Éperon* (spur) whose guns guarded the waterfront. The bastion, which guarded the entrance to the town, contained a guardhouse, "M", and its own powder magazine, "L". Not far from the gate stood the block, "H", which consisted of store houses for provisions, the bakery, the armoury and the artillery storage shed; in one corner was "the lodging of the chief engineer," "G". The next

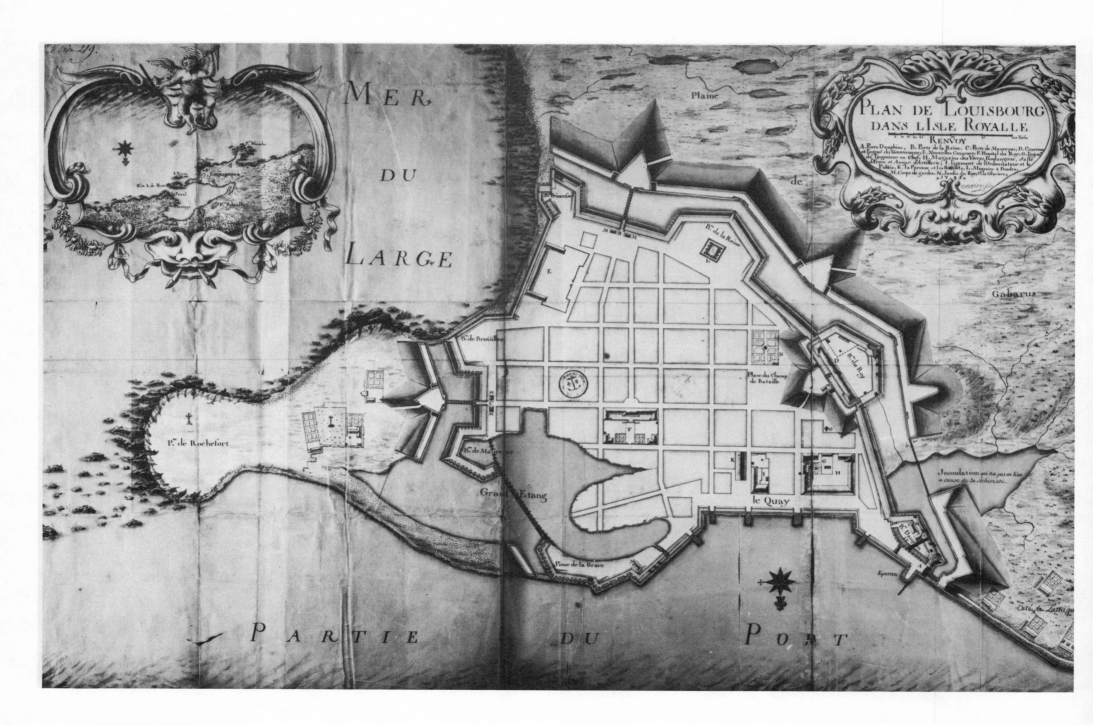

block included the house of the *Ordonnateur* (controller of finances) and the courthouse, "I". Across the street lay the parish church and the quarters of the Recollets, "K", who served it. Farther to the east was the hospital, "F", which with its garden and anciliary buildings occupied an entire block.

Dominating the town, the *Bastion du Roy* (King's Bastion) was the most impressive of all the defensive works. Together with the barracks and Governor's lodging, "D", it formed what was known as the Citadel. As the map shows, it was protected on the town side as well as the outer side, enabling the occupants to repel any attackers who had penetrated the encircling defences. Walls and a moat stood between the town and the citadel. In front of the drawbridge that formed the single entrance to the Citadel, the walled parade square with its guardhouse, "M", was built up in such a way as to expose attackers to fire from within. Although work had begun on this major part of the fortifications as early as 1720, it was not completed until after 1733.

Below the citadel was a public square, the *Place du Champ de Bataille*, and the King's Garden, "N"; to the northwest of this open space was the ice house, "O".

Southeast along the curtain wall lay the *Bastion de la Reine* (Queen's Bastion), another impressive structure which contained the main powder magazine, "L". The bastion itself seems to have been constructed in a simpler fashion than originally called for by Verville. Between the Queen's and the Princess Bastion was a second gate, the Queen's Gate, "B", with its guardhouses, "M", on each side. This gate provided access to the outer fortifications. The Princess Bastion commanded both land and sea approaches to the fortress. The completion of the Queen's and Princess Bastions represented the fulfilment of Verville's original project for the fortification of the town itself.

The eastern walls, with the Brouillan and Maurepas Bastions, formed the second stage of the defensive plans. A third gate, the *Porte de Maurepas*, "C", stood between the two bastions. It gave access to the outer

On a representé en noir les Ouvrages qui ont été faits a cette place pendanque les Anglois en ont fait le Siege dans la presente année 1745.

Quatre Embrazes qui ont été ouvertes dans le parapet de la face du Bastion du Roy pour battre la batterie des ennemis marquée B, a la Carte.

Le flan du même Bastion a été retably plusieurs fois, mais a la fin ruiné par la Batterie ennemie C, a la Carte. On avoit établi sur ce flanc un mortier qui bombardoit les batteries de l'attaque.

Six Embrazes qui ont été ouvertes au parapet de la face du Bastion Dauphin et au Redant, pour battre les batteries des ennemis marquées C, D, a la Carte. On avoit établi sur cette face un gros mortier et deux petits pour bombarder les dites batteries.

On avoit masqué avec de la pierre de taille la Porte Dauphine, démoli le pont, et rempli les corps de gardes a coté de cette porte, pour retarder la breche, laquelle a la fin a été très considerable par le feu des batteries ennemies marquées D, E, a la Carte.

On a retabli plus.rs fois les parapets de l'Eperon, mais la batterie marquée E, a la Carte, les avoient entierement ruinés, ainsi que la batterie Dauphine dont il ne restoit que trois embrazures vers le fer a cheval.

On avoit pratiqué dans le Bastion Dauphin un retranchement en terre et pareillement un autre dans la fausse Braye pour deffendre la breche en cas d'assaut.

Les flancs du Quay ont été retably plusieurs fois, mais a la fin ruinés par la Batterie ennemie marquée E, a la Carte.

Trois embrazures qu'on avoit ouvertes dans le parapet d'une des faces du Quay qui battoient la Batterie ennemie E, marquée a la Carte, et on avoit établi deux mortiers a la piece de la grave qui bombardoient la dite batterie, et celle de la batterie Royale.

defences commanding the tip of the peninsula. A new barracks, "E", is shown behind the eastern wall, and guardhouses, "M", beside the gate. The new defences made use of the *Grand Étang*, the pond, lying behind the beach, that effectively hindered access to the town. In this map, the ditch between the inner and outer walls on the eastern side is shown as full of water from the pond. A British map[30] made after the capture of the town suggests that the necessary deepening of the ditch to receive this water had not, in fact, been carried out. A bridge across the pond connected the Maurepas Bastion with the *Piece de la Grave* (beach artillery), completing the landward encirclement of the town. A line of closely planted stakes on the bridge appears to have protected those using it against enemy fire.

The inset map gives a general view of the entire area. The Royal Battery and the Island Battery are much as they appear on the previous map. A lighthouse (*Le Fanal*) was begun in 1731 to ensure the safety of naval, commercial and fishing vessels entering the port. A careening place for repairing ships was set up on the eastern side of the harbour entrance in 1740.

The existence of a number of maps of Louisbourg made possible the accurate reconstruction of part of the Fortress that was begun by the federal government in the 1960s. Positive identification of its buildings supplemented the work of the archaeologists who investigated the actual site. For the amateur historian as well as professional researchers, these maps provide a detailed text of the planning and construction of the major French fortress in North America.

Chapter 7 *Habitation and Settlement:* Community Growth

The first settlements to appear on European maps of North America were, of course, those of the native inhabitants. Although their semi-nomadic way of life did not give rise to towns and villages like those the explorers were familiar with, early mapmakers attempted to illustrate their presence as best they could. Gastaldi's 1556 map of the Atlantic coast (Map 1:1, p. 7) depicts the natives inhabiting crude shelters; unfortunately, the outline of the map is too inexact to give us any clear idea of their location, if, indeed, the cartographer was aware of it. But Champlain's maps of individual harbours, made during the early 1660s, show very precisely some of the traditional native camping grounds along the South Shore of Nova Scotia. His maps of LaHave (Map 2:1, p. 14) and Port Rossignol (Map 7:1) clearly locate and illustrate native camps and dwellings. A number of mid-eighteenth century maps, such as Map 8:2 (p. 134) also show the location of native settlements and missions.

The earliest known European settlement in Nova Scotia was also recorded by Champlain, whose early maps provide an interesting record of the settlement process. His map of Port Royal (Map 7:3) shows in considerable detail the area surrounding the Habitation set up in 1605 by the Sieur de Monts on the northern shore of the Annapolis Basin. In the late 1630s, the transfer of the population of LaHave to the site of the present town of Annapolis Royal resulted in the creation of a second Port Royal settlement, which was mapped in extraordinary detail by a series of cartographers. A 1686 map by Franquelin (Map 7:5) shows the community as it appeared to the visiting intendant Jacques Demeulle and his party. In the early 1700s, the French engineer Jean Delabat made several maps, (including Map 2:3, p. 20), showing houses, gardens and farms, as well as the fort, with the names of the inhabitants and details of the damage done during the English raids. Subsequently, English mapmakers gave their own versions of the condition of the settlement (Maps 4:1, p. 49, 4:2, p. 50, 6:3, p. 79), which, until the founding of Halifax, served as the administrative centre under both French and English rule. Meanwhile, Acadian settlements had spread up the annapolis River and on to the Minas Basin, Cobequid and Chignecto areas. Maps such as Morris' 1748 survey (Map 7:6) show the location of these communities.

The year 1749 saw the beginning of a new series of maps showing the establishment of Halifax on the hitherto undeveloped Chebucto Bay. A planned town from the start, the layout of its central area is recognizable from the earliest maps, which show both the street-plan, much as it remains today, and the original fortifications (Map 7:7). The rapid expansion into the north and south suburbs is reflected in subsequent maps, such as DesBarres' 1777 Map 2:7, p. 31.

The growth of the population of Nova Scotia in the second half of the eighteenth century resulted in the foundation of new settlements to house different waves of immigrants. The newly-appointed Surveyor

General, Charles Morris, and his deputies and successors conducted systematic surveys of potential sites, and produced a spate of plans for proposed settlements. Among the earliest areas surveyed were the South Shore, from Port Medway to Halifax, and the Lawrencetown area seen in Map 7:10. A number of plans of Lunenburg, such as Map 7:9, appeared beginning in 1753 when it was selected as a home for the Foreign Protestants. The arrival later in the eighteenth century of further immigrant groups such as the early Scottish settlers, the Loyalists and the members of regiments disbanded after the American Revolution, is reflected in numerous surveys of the township sites where land was granted to these newcomers. (See Maps 2:8, p. 32, 7:11, 7:12). Some of these maps also record the location of other groups such as Blacks and returned Acadians who now form part of Nova Scotia's population.

Maps and surveys of the island of Cape Breton, like those of the mainland, also illustrate the changing settlement patterns. English and French maps record both the isolated fishing stations set up by Nicolas Denys in the seventeenth century (Map 3:3, p. 41), and the later foundation of the fortress of Louisbourg (Map 6:8, p. 89). With the selection of Sydney as the capital of the separate province of Cape Breton, under Governor DesBarres, maps of the late eighteenth century (such as Map 7:13) show the location and layout of this new settlement.

The maps reproduced in this chapter represent only a selection from the many that illustrate stages of growth in the population of Nova Scotia, and the settlements established to accommodate that population. Whether the growth was by normal demographic expansion, or by immigration, it has been consistently reflected in maps. Almost every community in the province can find some information about its origins in cartographic form. Most of these early maps include features still recognizable today, and maps made at intervals over the years provide interesting links between past and present.

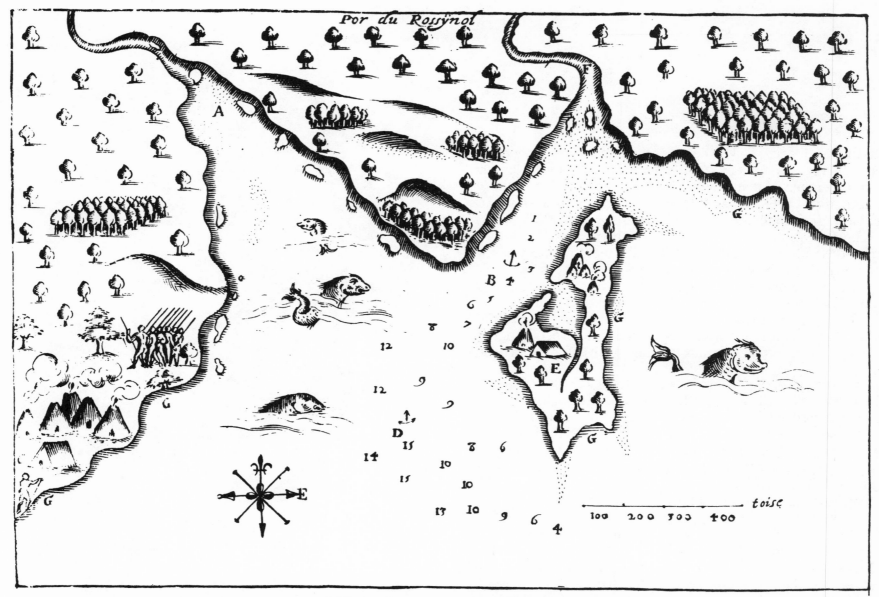

Por du Rossÿnol

Les chifres montrent les brasses d'eau.

A Riuiere qui va 25. lieuës dans les terres.
B Le lieu où ancrent les vaisseaux.
C Place à la grande terre où les sauuages font leur logement.
D la rade où les vaisseaux mouillent l'ancre en attendant la marée.
E L'endroit où les sauuages cabannent dans l'isle.
F A chenal qui asseche de basse mer.
G La coste de la grande terre.
Ce qui est piquoté demontre les basses.

Micmac at Port Rossignol

The earliest maps made by Champlain after deMonts' expedition arrived in Acadia record the new arrivals' impression of native settlements. This map of Port Rossignol (Liverpool), like that of LaHave (Map 2:1, p. 14), shows the location of the settlements and the structures of which they consisted. These are the familiar circular wigwams and rectangular cabins, represented here more realistically than the European-style cottages of the LaHave map. The group to the west of the map, at "C", is described by Champlain as "the mainland site where the Indians make their dwellings," while the wigwams and hut at "E" represent "the place where they camp on [Coffin] island." The native population was semi-nomadic, spending the winters hunting in the forest while summers were spent on the coast at traditional camping grounds. The island site surrounding a sandy bay would be a good source of the shellfish that formed an important part of the Micmac diet.

These sites were clearly occupied when Champlain and his companions arrived in May 1604. Smoke is rising from within several of the wigwams, while near the mainland site some of the inhabitants are shown, armed with poles or spears. Whether these weapons were for hunting or for defence, if necessary, against the new arrivals is not at all clear.

Other features of the map include the river, "A", "which goes 25 leagues inland." This is of course the Mersey River, one of the traditional native routes from the Annapolis Basin *via* Lakes Kejimkujik and Rossignol to the South Shore (see Map 8:1, p. 131). Like the Indian campgrounds shown on the LaHave map, the settlements here mark the end of the canoe and portage trail across the peninsula.

Other features of the map record the visit of the French expedition. Soundings, the anchorage point, "B", and the roadstead, "D", where the ships waited for the tide, mark their route. Champlain's investigations allowed him to determine the coastline, "G", a channel, "F", which was dry at low tide (near Beach Meadows) and the location of rocks and sandflats. The proximity of good fishing, which was to encourage Nicolas Denys to establish his first sedentary fishery here in the 1630s,[1] is suggested by the fish shown in the water. W.F. Ganong describes the codfish in the map as "representative of the well-known abundance of that fish in this place"[2] while dismissing the dolphins as an engraver's decoration. They may, however, be that artist's impression of the common harbour porpoises that Champlain perhaps observed and drew in his original map.

Port Rossignol was so named by the French because of the presence not of nightingales, but of a certain Captain Rossignol whom they found illegally trading in furs with the natives whose presence is recorded here.[3] The subsequent growth of a fishery in the area is not surprising in light of Champlain's map, and the forests that he represented symbolically support the pulp and paper industry which is the chief economic base of the modern community. But at the time when the map was made, the native inhabitants occupied their traditional camping ground undisturbed, and settlement by Europeans was still some way off in the future.

Map 7:1 Samuel de Champlain. *Por du Rossÿnol*, 1613. Engraved.

Map 7:1a Liverpool and Port Mouton today.

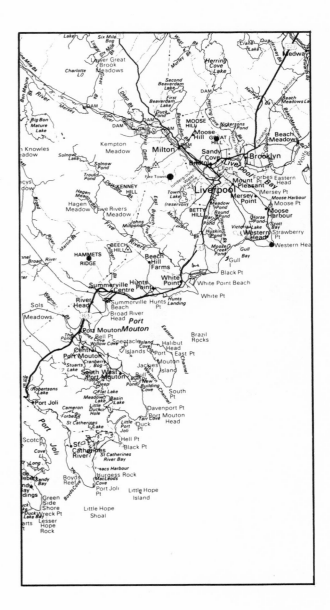

French at Port Mouton

Port Mouton was the third harbour visited by deMonts' expedition and recorded by Champlain in 1604. His map of the area, oriented with north to the right, represents the first harbour where the travellers established a shore base after reaching North America. Their huts lie between the point, "B", identified as the place where they established their dwellings, and the small pond, "C". The shelters are, naturally enough, European in style, with walls and pitched roofs.

The reason for the choice of this site is clear. As well as the hills and forests familiar from Champlain's other maps, there is an area described at "L" on the legend as being of "brush and very small heather" *(bruyères)*. The letter is omitted from the map, but the location is indicated by the small tufts of vegetation that contrast with the trees found elsewhere. This area, lying between the larger "pond," "F", (now Stewarts Lake) and the point, stands out equally against the surrounding forests on modern maps. It was in this relatively open country that the expedition constructed temporary quarters.

The advantages of this site went beyond that of not having to clear away trees in order to establish a camp. Champlain noted in his account of Port Mouton: "Here are great numbers of hares, and plenty of waterfowl in consequence of the ponds there."[4] After the long voyage, the availability of fresh food must have been particularly welcome. Examples of the local wildlife appear on the map, and consist of one rabbit or hare, or possibly two—the second animal is too compact to be identifiable, but Ganong considers it to be a second hare—and some kind of antlered animal which may be a moose.[5] There are also some waterfowl swimming on the large pond. Some years later, Marc Lescarbot was to describe the same visit and note that "near the said Port Mouton is a place so full of rabbits that they ate hardly anything else,"[6] but when he himself passed through, he noted that "we had no time to hunt the rabbits, which are found in great numbers not far from the said harbour."[7]

Also identified on the map are the places, "A", where the ships moored; within the harbour, opposite the campsite, and to the lee of a wooded island, "D", at the entrance to the port. A river, "E", with fairly low water (Broad River) and a fairly large stream, "G", coming from the pond are recognizable on a modern map, as are the little islands, "H", in the harbour. The seacoast, "M", extends from White Point almost to Port Joli.

The group of human figures on the map suggests the presence of a native band in the area, but there is no indication of the location of their encampment. No doubt they, too, were aware of the abundance of game for the hunting.

Port Mouton served only as a temporary stopping place for the French expedition. From there they continued around the coast to establish their permanent quarters first at Sainte Croix and eventually, and more satisfactorily, at Port Royal. When Marc Lescarbot visited Port Mouton on his way to Port Royal in 1606, he found the buildings still standing.[8] This map is an interesting record of the first foothold established by the French in what was to be their colony of Acadia.

Map 7:2 Samuel de Champlain. *port au mouton*, 1613. Engraved.

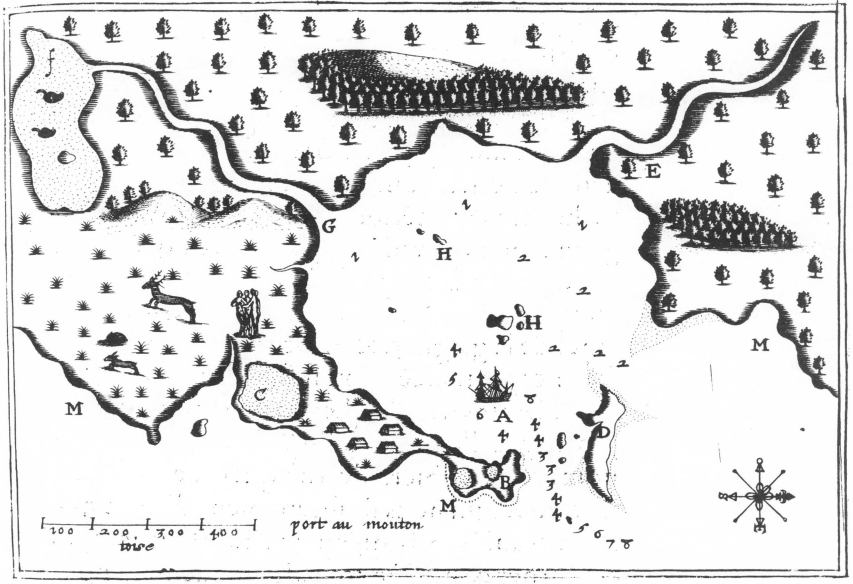

Les chifres montrent les brasses d'eau.

A Les lieux où posent les vaisseaux.

B Le lieu où nous fismes nos logemens.

C Vn estang.

D Vne isle à l'entree du port couuerte de bois.

E Vne riuiere qui est assez basse d'eau.

F Vn estang.

G Ruisseau assez grand, qui vient de l'estang f.

H 6. Petites isles qui sont dãs le port.

L Cãpagne où il n'y a que des taillis & bruyeres fort petites.

M La coste du costé de la mer.

DeMonts' settlement at Port Royal

This map of the Annapolis Basin and river is one of the most detailed and interesting of the series that Champlain made to illustrate his *Voyages*, published in 1613. It shows clearly the site on the north shore of the Annapolis Basin where the members of the expedition, led by Pierre du Gua, Sieur de Monts and including Champlain, established a settlement. This *habitation*, "A", now reconstructed, represented the first formal French presence in Nova Scotia; it was the official base for French trade and exploration from 1605 until the expedition was recalled in 1607. The map also gives a great deal of information about the natural features of the surrounding area, and of the modifications made to it by settlers.

As in Champlain's other large scale maps, the forest that covered most of the country is shown here by symbolic trees, scattered singly and in clumps over most of the land area. Relief is indicated by round topped hills; the escarpment of the North Mountain is singled out for particular notice as the *costes de montaignes*, "O". Along both sides of the river are meadows, "L", which are described as being flooded by the spring tide, and along the shore we find mud flats, "F", which are dry at low tide. These features are all clearly visible on modern topographical maps, although some of the areas once subject to flooding are no longer marshy, having later been dyked and drained for agricultural use by Acadian settlers.

Many early maps exaggerate the size of rivers and streams, and this map is no exception. As well as the Annapolis River itself, which Champlain calls *Riviere de l'Equille* (the name has survived in the town of Lequille, outside Annapolis) he names the *Riviere du moulin*, or Mill river, now Allain's River, and the *Riviere sainct Antoine*, now Bear River. The *Ruisseau de la Roche* (Deep Brook), indicated by "q" on the map, and "Q" in the legend, and "another stream," "R", are only two of many otherwise unidentified streams running

into the basin from the south. Of those entering from the north, only the *Ruisseau de la trutiere*, "X", just to the west of the Habitation, is named. By contrast to the well watered shores of the Annapolis Basin, the coast of the Bay of Fundy, described by Champlain as *La coste de la mer du port Royal*, "N", is unbroken, except for the *entrée du port Royal*, "E", now known as Digby Gut. At the head of the *Riviere du moulin*, at the eastern edge of the map, the letter "T" indicates a "little lake," most of which appears to be off the map, that seems to have no counterpart in a modern map; the lakes from which Allain's River flows are considerably further upstream.

Two islands are identified in Champlain's map: Goat Island, "D", is described simply as "the island at the entrance to the Riviere de l'Equille," while Bear Island, "P", is referred to as an "island near the St. Antoine River."

Despite some inaccuracies and exaggerations, the natural features that led the colonists to choose the site for their settlement are clearly visible. The harbour provided by the Annapolis Basin was invaluable for a community that depended almost entirely on

Map 7:3   Samuel de Champlain. *Port Royal*, 1613. Engraved.

water transport for food supplies and reinforcements. The channel indicated by the soundings on the map allowed access to the settlement, while the narrowing of the passage at Goat Island would bring potential intruders within range of its defences. The North Mountain protected the harbour and sheltered the habitation from the north wind. Streams close to the settlement ensured a fresh water supply, the meadows nearby could be made into gardens, and the land between the two rivers provided arable soil, close at hand, where wheat could be grown. The hunting and fishing offered by the forests, rivers and the basin itself, provided further sources of food. Champlain states simply that "Having searched well in all directions, we found no place more suitable than a somewhat elevated spot, about which are some marshes and good springs."[9]

Map 7:3a   The Annapolis Basin today.

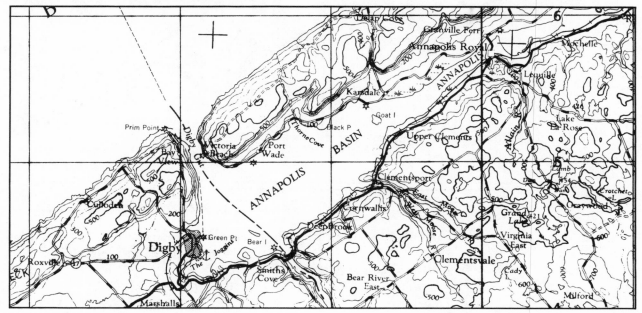

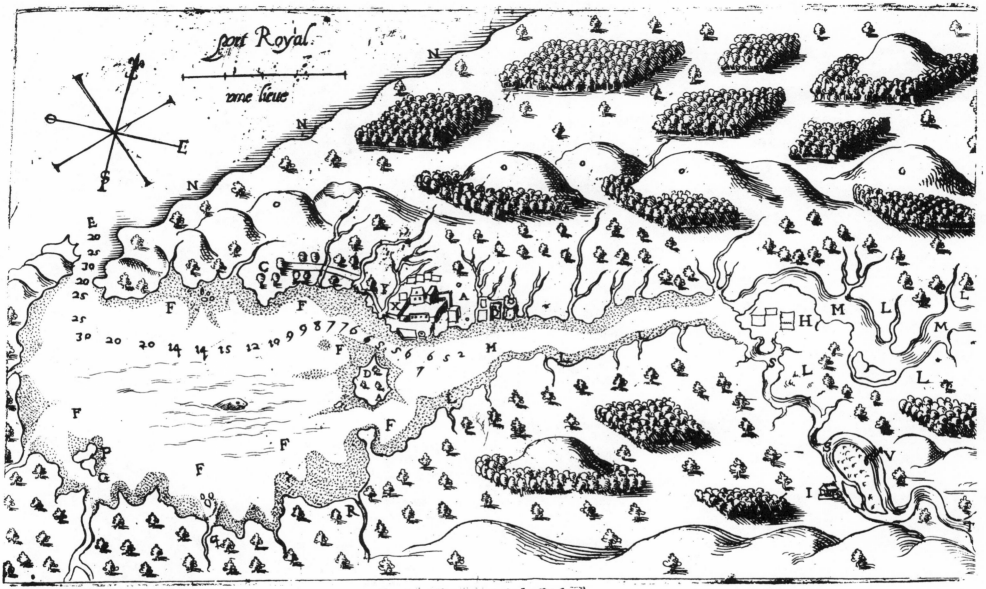

Les chifres monstrent les brasses d'eau.

A Le lieu de l'habitation.
B Iardin du sieur de Champlain.
C Allée au trauers les bois que fit faire le sieur de Poitrin court.
D Isle a l'entrée de la riuiere de l'Equille.
E entrée du port Royal.
F Basses qui assechét de basse mer

G Riuiere sainct Antoine.
H Lieu du labourage où on seme le blé.
I Moulin que fit faire le sieur de Poitrincourt.
L Prairies qui sont innôdées des eaux aux grandes marées.
M Riuiere de l'Equille.

N La coste de la mer du port Royal.
O Costes de montaignes.
P Isle proche de la riuiere sainct Antoine.
Q Ruisseau de la Roche
R Autre Ruisseau.

S Riuiere du moulin.
T Petit lac
V Le lieu où les sauuages peschent le harang en la saison,
X Ruisseau de la trutiere.
Y Allée que fit faire le sieur de Champlain.

Having selected the site, the French then proceeded to do what they could to make it habitable. The results of their efforts are shown on this map, where the Habitation itself is represented roughly as a group of buildings and a palisade. A larger scale drawing of the buildings appears elsewhere in Champlain's *Voyages*;[10] that version was the basis for the modern reconstruction. The present map, however, speaks more eloquently of the isolation of this little community in a strange and potentially hostile land, and of the endeavours of its members to achieve security and a measure of self-sufficiency.

The palisade around the buildings was a precaution to discourage intrusions by the local natives who, in fact, turned out to be generally friendly. Nevertheless, there was always the possibility of attack, not so much from neighbouring bands as from visitors from farther afield, including rival European colonists.

To the east of the Habitation, by the water, we find "B", the "garden of the Sieur de Champlain." Champlain himself writes that this was only one of a number of gardens made by the colonists during the first year at the settlement.[11] The others are not identified; the series of squares to the north and west of the Habitation may represent gardens constructed by Marc Lescarbot.[12] Champlain describes how he created his garden:

I also, in order not to remain idle, made one which I surrounded with ditches full of water wherein I placed some very fine trout; and through it flowed three brooks of very clear running water from which the greater part of our settlement was supplied. I constructed in it near the seashore a little sluiceway, to draw off the water whenever I desired. This spot was completely surrounded by meadows, and there I arranged a summer house with fine trees, in order that I might enjoy the fresh air. I constructed there likewise a small reservoir to hold saltwater fish, which we took out as we required them. (Voyages, v.I, pp. 371–372)

This early description of ditching and draining the marshy land along the shore in order to grow crops sets the scene for the future agricultural activities of the Acadians. The stocking of fish ponds to ensure a constant supply of fresh fish was a common European practice. Champlain's account shows how European techniques were transplanted to the New World.

The cultivated land, "H", between the two rivers represents the first steps towards agricultural self-sufficiency, without which no colony could survive. Although Champlain uses the words *"lieu de labourage"* it is not certain whether ploughs were used in Acadia before the end of the seventeenth century.[13] The term could simply mean "tillage" by more primitive tools such as spades and hoes. But the statement that wheat was sown there indicates the desire to grow a staple crop, and the establishment of the water mill, "I", by Jean de Poutrincourt[14] in 1606–1607 shows that wheat was being grown on a large enough scale to warrant such construction. The fields appear to be located on the slightly higher land away from the river banks, where the soil could be worked without fear of flooding, and where houses were later built.

To the west of the Habitation, lying parallel to the shore, is a walk, "Y", which Champlain had made. It is described by him as leading to the Troutery brook;[15] it appears likely, therefore, that the "X" identifying this brook has been misplaced by the engraver.[16] The path was later continued by Jean de Poutrincourt; his extension, "C", is described as a "walk through the woods," and was apparently constructed for exercise and recreation.

Unlike some of Champlain's maps, this one gives no indication of any native settlement in the area depicted. Their presence in the vicinity is attested to by the location, "V", of the place "where the Indians fish for herring in season." Written accounts, by Champlain and others, make it clear that native tribes frequented the area and often visited the Habitation.

The reference to their presence reminds us that the fur trade with the natives was the economic base of most settlements in New France during the seventeenth century. With this potential source of revenue, and with the natural advantages indicated on the map, it seems very possible that the settlement, despite its isolation and distance from France, could have flourished. The premature withdrawal of support from the French authorities cut short what appears to have been a viable attempt to establish a self-sufficient community on the shores of the Annapolis Basin. Later maps illustrate the outcome of subsequent attempts to colonize the area.

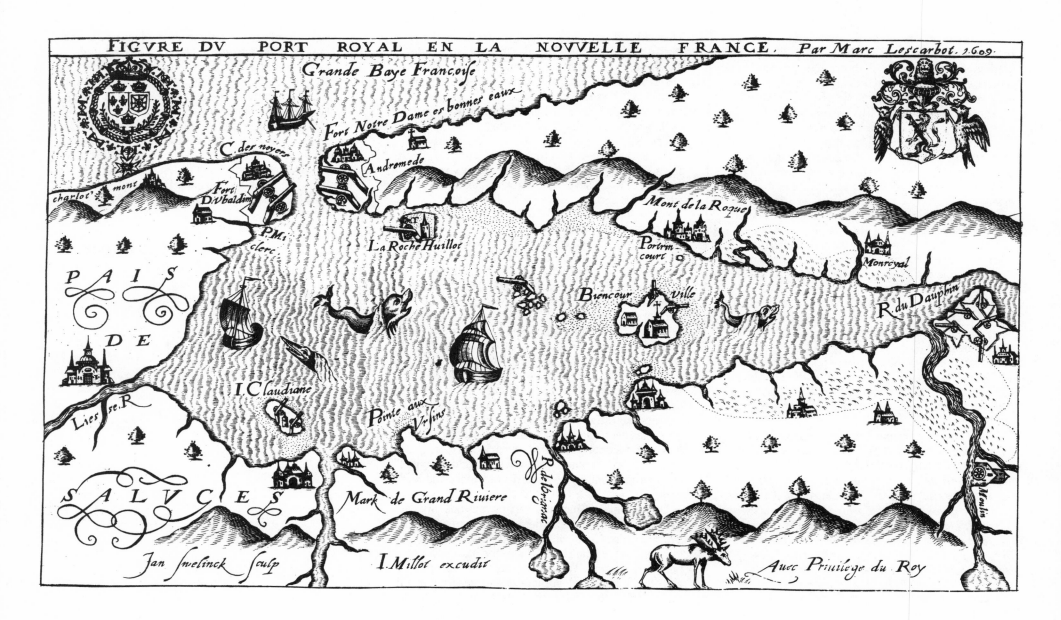

FIGVRE DV PORT ROYAL EN LA NOVVELLE FRANCE. *Par Marc Lescarbot. 1609.*

Grande Baye Francoise

Fort Notre Dame es bonnes eaux

C. der noyers

charlot' mont

Fort D. Vbaldin

Andromede

La Roche Huillot

Mont de la Roque

P.M. clerc

PAIS

DE

Portrin court

Monreyal

Briencour Ville

R. du Dauphin

I. Claudiane

Pointe aux Vrsins

Liesse R.

SALVCES

Mark de Grand Riuiere

R. de Voignac

Meulin

Jan Swelinck sculp

I. Millot excudit

Auec Priuilege du Roy

A dream of Port Royal

Marc Lescarbot's map of Port Royal was made as an illustration for his *History of New France*. The first edition of this book appeared two years after Lescarbot's return to France in 1607 after a year spent in Port Royal at the settlement established there by the Sieur de Monts. The account of his stay there, which forms part of the book, was the earliest first-hand description of the new colony to be published in France; Champlain, who returned at the same time, did not publish his *Voyages* until 1613.

Lescarbot's map covers much the same area as Champlain's *Port Royal* (Map 7:3, p. 101) and depicts much the same physical features. But while Champlain's map is a straightforward representation of the settlement as it was when both men left it in 1607, Lescarbot has produced what might be described as a prospectus for the settlement which his friend Jean de Poutrincourt was to try to establish there within a year or two of the publication of the map. In addition to the Habitation, which is shown as a magnificent establishment resembling one of the Loire *châteaux*, there are a number of other equally splendid and completely imaginary country houses scattered around the shores of the Annapolis Basin, along with churches, forts and batteries of cannon suitably distributed over the map.

In spite of the obvious exaggeration, for propaganda purposes, of the human elements in the map, there is an evident endeavour to convey to the public some idea of the country itself. In order to do this, Lescarbot included in his map not only the mountains, forests and marshes surrounding the Annapolis Basin, but also a sampling (albeit small) of the wildlife that he had observed and with which the average Frenchman would no doubt be unfamiliar.

Among the vessels illustrated in the Basin we see two dolphins playing. The great difference in their size suggests that, rather than being mere engravers' conventions, they represent real animals. Like the creatures in Champlain's map of Port Rossignol (Map 7:1), they may be inaccurate representations; the smaller one might be intended to record the presence in the area of porpoises rather than dolphins. The larger one may refer to Lescarbot's account of an interesting observation made by Poutrincourt and the crew of his vessel as they were about to leave on an expedition. "While they waited there for a space of three days in hope of a fair wind, every day a half grown whale. . .entered the harbour in the morning with the flood tide, sported at his ease, and went away at the ebb."[17] Champlain's map of Port Royal shows a creature swimming in the basin which Ganong suggests may represent this same animal.[18] Lescarbot also shows another rather sinister looking sea creature with an elongated head that may represent a swordfish.

More readily identifiable is the large mammal shown inland, with his feet firmly planted on the bottom margin of the map. His distinctive flat antlers and his stance proclaim him to be an adult moose. His location near the lake which is the source of one branch of the *R[iviere] de l'Orignac* (Moose River) confirms this identification. This large member of the deer family, more common in Acadia at the beginning of the seventeenth century than today, would have been unknown to Lescarbot's readers. He obviously thought that they would be impressed by his portrayal of the animal "which we have many times seen in our meadows there in troops of three or four, large and small. . . ."[19]

Lescarbot's map of Port Royal is romantic rather than scientific. While obviously unreliable in many respects, it conveys to his readers, some of whom he no doubt hoped might become settlers or financial supporters of Jean de Poutrincourt, some idea of the fascination which Lescarbot himself had felt in his visit to the New World.

Marc Lescarbot.

the second site of Port Royal

This map, one of a series based on Intendant Jacques Demeulle's tour of inspection of Acadia in 1686, is unsigned but is almost certainly by Jean-Baptiste-Louis Franquelin, the King's Hydrographer in Québec. It gives a large scale representation of the second settlement site at Port Royal, on the area originally considered but later rejected by de Monts and Champlain for their Habitation: "We had almost decided to build there, but considered that we should be too far within the harbour, and this made us change our minds."[20] Instead, the original French settlers had selected this area for farming, as shown on Champlain's map. When Samuel Argall and his followers raided and destroyed the Habitation in 1613,

Charles de Biencourt's companions were working in the fields here, and at the mill on the nearby river. Unable to rebuild the Habitation, they chose to remain on this site where they constructed a few poor houses for themselves and continued to trade with the natives for furs. This settlement remained the centre of French activity in Acadia, except for the short-lived colony set up by Isaac de Razilly at LaHave. When, between 1636 and 1640, Charles de Menou d'Aulnay transferred the LaHave settlers to Port Royal, it was to this site that they came.

Franquelin's map shows Port Royal about 50 years after that transfer. In the interim, the community had grown in spite of recurring hostilities between the

French and the English, and between rival French factions. According to the census taken at the time of Demeulle's visit in 1686, the population consisted of 592 persons, including some living farther up the river, and 30 soldiers.[21]

This map, unlike the previous two, illustrates not so much the geography of the region as a whole as it does the state of development of the settlement itself. The surrounding wooded hills, clearly decorative rather than indicative of actual relief, represent the forest that extended over most of Acadia except for this small, settled area. The outline of the shore and river bank is recognizably accurate, with Allain's River running into the mouth of the main river in a series of

Map 7:5 Jean-Baptiste-Louis Franquelin. "Plan
Tres Exact Du Terrain ou sont sçitüees les maisons du
Port Royal et ou lon peut faire une Ville considerable,"
1686. Manuscript.

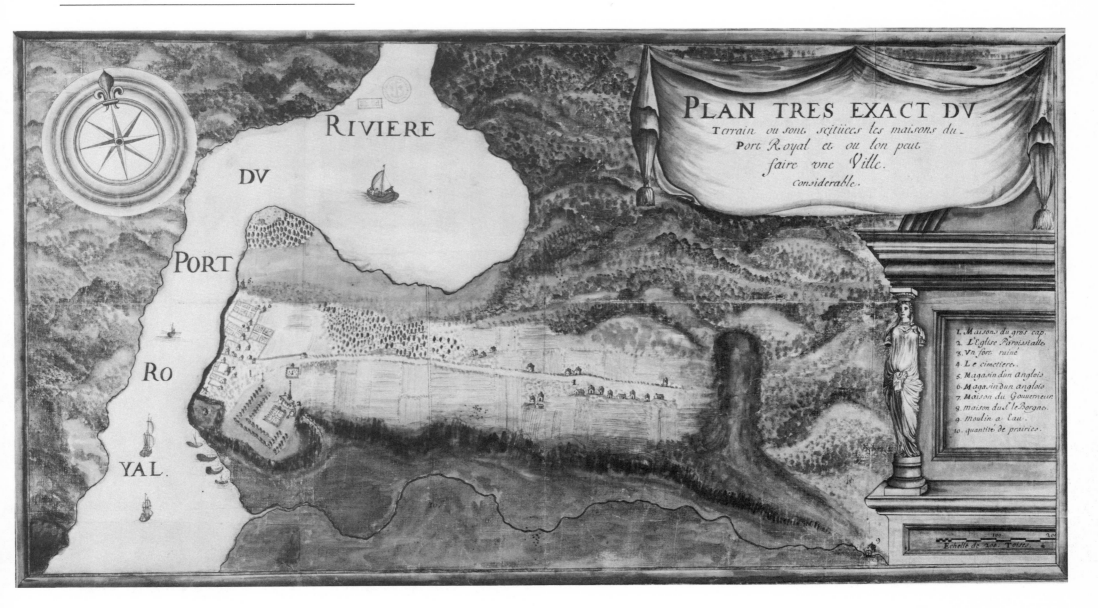

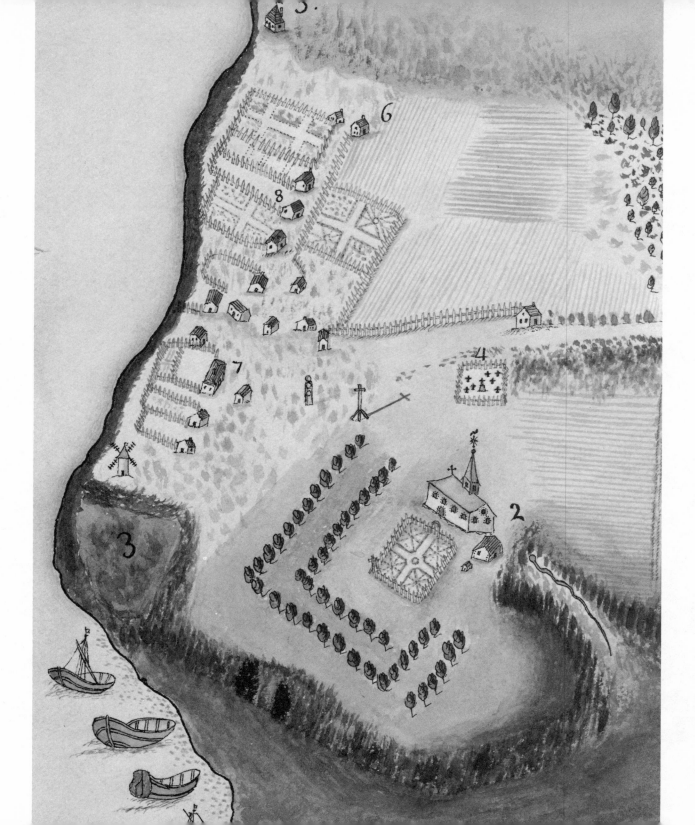

meanders through the marshes. Although dyking and draining had been carried on along the main river and basin since d'Aulnay's time, there is no evidence of its having been undertaken in the meadows close to the town.

From the evidence of this map, it is possible to reconstruct the community of Port Royal as it existed in 1686. The visitor would have arrived, as Demeulle did, by water, probably in one of the vessels shown in the river mouth. The ship would have passed the shallows where the smaller boats, used for fishing or local journeys, were moored at high tide or lay aground at low water, and rounded the point that was still dominated by the ruins of the fort (3). Passing below the windmill that stood beside the fort, the passengers probably came ashore, when the tide was high enough, near the centre of the village, where the single street intersected with the road leading to the houses of the Big Cape (1), a subsidiary settlement into which the population had by now expanded.

The street consisted of a row of houses with gardens running down to the water. To the right stood the Governor's house (7), an impressive building inhabited at that time by François-Marie Perrot, formerly Governor of Montréal, who had lost his previous post as a result of illegal fur trading, and was soon to lose the governorship of Acadia for illegally selling fishing licences to New Englanders. Along the street to the left was the house of Alexandre le Borgne de Belle-Isle (8), son of one of the early landholders in Acadia, and himself seigneur of Port Royal. At the end of the street stood a storehouse (6) belonging to an English merchant; another Englishman had his establishment (5) closer to the shore, apart from the rest of the community.

The newcomer to Port Royal might have been surprised to find two English merchants functioning in the area. Strange as it may seem in a period when France and England were bitter rivals for the control of North America, trade between New England and Acadia flourished. The reluctance of the French king to provide adequate supplies for his colonists meant that a lively commerce was assured between the merchants of Boston and the inhabitants of Port Royal, who were happy to buy all kinds of manufactured goods from them. For their part, the New Englanders bought furs at Port Royal, and fished in Acadian waters with or without having purchased a license from the governor.

These mutually satisfactory arrangements were in effect, regardless of the state of war or peace, throughout much of the period of French occupation of Acadia.

The settlement of Port Royal was dominated by the parish church (2). If the scale of this map is to be believed, the church, with its adjacent buildings, the formal garden surrounded on three sides by a double row of trees, and the cemetery (4) occupied almost as much space as all the other houses. The church itself is represented as an impressive building with a steeple and weathercock. It presumably served not only the nearby residents, but also the inhabitants of the Big Cape and those living higher up the Port Royal River (Annapolis River).

Between the two groups of houses in the main settlement were cultivated fields, some of which must have dated back to the time of Jean de Poutrincourt. The dwellings and the fields lay on a ridge of higher ground, separated by a tree-grown slope from the "quantity of meadows" (10) or marshes lying each side of the river, on which a mill stood somewhat above the settlement. This water mill was located close to— though apparently on the other side of the river from— the mill established by Poutrincourt 80 years earlier.

Fortification of the settlement sees at this time to have been virtually non-existent. The old fort that stood on the point overlooking the river mouth had apparently not been reconstructed since the reoccupation of Port Royal by the French in 1670. For 30 years before that, it had been subject to damage by attack and counterattack as its occupants fought off either French or English raiders. Its dilapidated state, like the presence of the English merchants, was symptomatic of the neglect of the French authorities for the well being and security of the Acadians.

The report sent to Louis XIV by Intendant Demeulle[22] following his visit drew the attention of the king to the way in which French indifference to the settlers in Port Royal was pushing them into closer ties with the New Englanders, and depriving France both of a market for its manufactured goods and of a supply of furs. This map, in which two of the principal buildings are English stores or trading posts, exemplifies this dependence on Boston rather than Paris for supplies. The Acadians, with an economy based on agriculture and the fur trade, could not exist in isolation. Nevertheless, as the map's title states, Port Royal could be made into "a town of considerable importance."

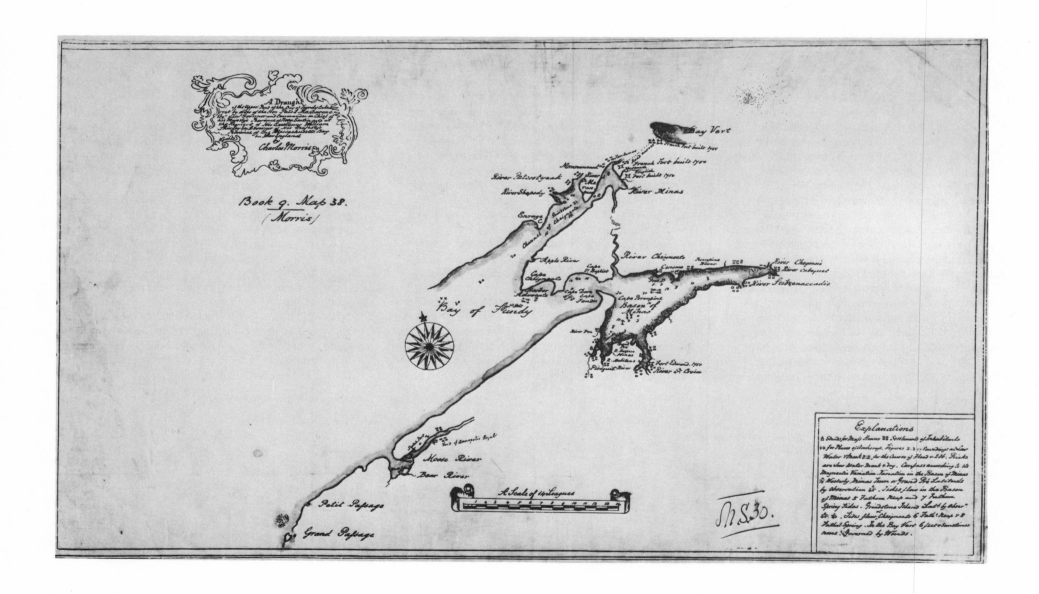

the spread of Acadian settlement

Map 7:6 is one of the early examples of the cartography of the first Charles Morris, a New Englander who spent most of his working life as Surveyor General for the Province of Nova Scotia. Always closely connected with the settlement of the province, he carried out a survey of this part of the Bay of Fundy in 1748, under the orders of both the Lieutenant Governor of Nova Scotia and the Governor of Massachusetts. Thirty-five years after the Treaty of Utrecht, the white population of Nova Scotia still consisted almost entirely of Acadians. Halifax would be founded the following year, but for the time being almost all of the inhabitants of the province were concentrated in the area shown on this map. At the time it was made, the authorities were seriously considering a scheme to settle groups of Protestants among the Catholic Acadians in an effort to counterbalance what was seen as a French threat to British sovereignty. In 1749, a series of plans for proposed settlements in the area, based on Morris's survey, was drawn up and sent to England.[23]

The settlements of the Acadians, who were, for the most part, farmers, lay close to the drained marshland where they had established their fields (Chapter 4). As some of the larger scale maps show, their homes were usually built on rising ground above the marshes, but never very far from the shore. Even the rather stylized representation of their villages ("Settlements of Inhabitants") on this map makes it clear that the chief concentration of population before the Expulsion lay around the Minas Basin; the settlements were clustered around the important farmlands of Grand Pré. Some Acadian names like Pero (Pereau), Canard and Habitant have survived in present-day rivers and villages, while the larger centres of population, established by the British

settlers who replaced the Acadians in the region, have English placenames, such as Windsor and Wolfville.

Another group of Acadian villages was established at the head of Cobequid Bay, and along its north shore. These, too, were later to be replaced by British settlements, most notably Truro at the mouth of the Cobequet (now Salmon) River. The name Cenome has survived as Economy, and the Shubenaccadie River has retained its name with only a slight change in spelling. A third group of settlements was in the Chignecto area, around the channel of Cheignecto (Chignecto Bay) and at Bay Vert (Baie Verte) on the Northumberland Strait. Most of these villages now lie on the New Brunswick side of the border, but up until the hostilities of the 1750s their inhabitants were considered an integral part of the Acadian population of Nova Scotia. Names such as Musquash (Missaguash), Tantamar (Tantramar), Memrooncook (Memramcook), Patcootyeak (Petitcodiac) and Shepody can still be found, alongside the English towns of Sackville and Amherst.

The remaining inhabited area shown on this map is the oldest permanent European settlement in Nova Scotia. Growing out of deMont's Habitation at Port Royal, it had expanded to the present site of Annapolis Royal, and upstream along both sides of the river. At the time this map was made, the Acadians of the Annapolis area existed alongside the British garrison and administration at Annapolis Royal. This was then the only area of Nova Scotia where there was a significant number of British residents.

The "Explanations" suggest that Morris had recorded not only the Acadians' villages, but also their "Mass Houses" or churches. Very few of these appear in this version of his survey; several more can be found on the other maps based on the same expedition (see above).

A number of features on this map were obviously added after the date of the original survey. We find not only the Scotch Fort, the remains of which dated from

the 1620s, and the Fort of Annapolis Royal, taken by the English in 1710, but also those forts built in the early 1750s. They include the three Chignecto area forts (see Map 6:4, p. 81), and also Fort Edward, built in 1750 to protect the Minas Basin area from attack.

Other details provided by this map include river mouths, capes, anchorages, soundings, and direction of tidal flow; the "Explanations" also offer navigational information.

Of greater interest, however, is the picture of the distribution of population in Nova Scotia immediately before the foundation of Halifax. The settlements shown here were to be almost entirely depopulated by the expulsion in 1755. Their scattered inhabitants would be gradually replaced by Planters, brought from New England in the 1760s, Loyalists and other settlers wishing to take advantage of the fertile farmlands originally worked by the Acadians. Despite the destruction of the original settlements, and the largely English nature of the communities which replaced them, the Acadian place names seen on this map have to a great extent survived and are a reminder of the early inhabitants of the area.

Map 7:6   Charles Morris. "A Draught of the Upper Part of the Bay of Fundy...," 1748. Manuscript.

A newcomers' impression of Halifax

This hand-drawn map was made by Moses Harris[24] shortly after the foundation of Halifax. Harris and his wife were among those who accompanied Cornwallis to Halifax in 1749. Harris' occupation is given on the printed version of the shipping list[25] as "sawyer," but it seems likely that this was a misreading for "surveyor" on the original list, which is now lost.[26] The present map is the source both for the "Porcupine Map" which follows, and for the central part of Jeffreys' composite (Map 2:5, p. 26). It appears to be the only surviving manuscript version of Harris' work.

The map shows the layout of Halifax, much as it appeared on Harris' separately published plan of the town (of which a reduced version also appears in Jefferys' composite map). The settlement is surrounded by dense mixed forest, with a cleared path leading back across the peninsula. The area depicted extends from the harbour mouth to the head of Bedford Basin, and some attempt is made to show the rivers running into the basin and harbour.

The features of the map are identified by an Explanation in the lower right corner. They are identified directly on the engraved versions, sometimes with a change of name: for example, at "Z", Rowses Island was to reappear as Cornwallis Island (now McNab's) and Hauks River, "I", was quickly renamed Sandwich River before settling down as the Northwest Arm. The original name for Bedford Basin, Torrington's Bay, "R", appears with the later Bedford Bay on the engraved maps. These changes were, undoubtedly, made for political reasons: apart from the obvious desire to recognize Cornwallis' service in the foundation of Halifax, the Lords Commissioners for Trade and Plantations would find it appropriate that the Earl of Sandwich, First Lord of the Admiralty, and his predecessor in the position and now Secretary of State, the Duke of Bedford, should be honoured in this way.

Harris' map, probably made on the spot, antedates such considerations, and records the names bestowed by the actual settlers. Many of them refer to obvious local characteristics (Red Island, Lobsters Hole, Stags Point) or to the officers involved in the settlement operation.

The vessels drawn in the harbour and basin represent both the new settlement's link with the outside world, and the naval defence on which it and the rest of Nova Scotia depended. They do not appear on the engraved maps. Another significant detail that was omitted from the later versions is a Micmac wigwam hidden away among the trees just above the scale cartouche. The palisades and forts that were to keep the natives from invading the town are evident, both in this and in printed versions of the map. We see, on a small scale, the layout of the town into blocks, with a central open space; all this is shown in very much more detail in Harris' Plan of Halifax in Map 2:5, p. 26.

Like Champlain's early maps, Map 7:7 conveys very clearly the sense of isolation of a new settlement set in the middle of unknown and possibly hostile territory. This feeling is emphasized, rather incongruously, by the decoration of the title cartouche, which, along with the familiar rocks, trees and plants of the surrounding area, shows a curious bear making his way round the corner, while a lion or perhaps, more appropriately, a lynx is crouched on the top of the cartouche as if ready to spring. This suggestion of predatory wild beasts is somewhat offset by the floral decorations of the scale cartouche.

The surveying of the entire area, and particularly of the rivers running into the harbour and basin, was obviously still at a very primitive stage. Harris would not have had time to conduct a very detailed investigation of the surroundings of the new settlement; it does not appear that he spent very long in Halifax, nor that he made any further surveys of the area. This example of his original work conveys, more vividly than the engravings that were based on it, Harris' impressions of the community which was being established. Cornwallis himself wrote on July 23, 1749: "As there was not one yard of clear ground, Your Grace will imagine our difficulty and what work we have to do. However they have already cleared above 12 acres."[27] Other map-makers were to record the early days of Halifax, but this picture of a town site planted in the wilderness emphasizes the difficulties that Cornwallis and his followers overcame in the initial period of settlement. This aspect of colonization, so apparent to a participant in the endeavour, was to be minimized in the versions of the map issued for public consumption.

Map 7:7 Moses Harris. "A Plan of Chebucto Harbour With the Town of Hallefax by Moses Harris Surveyor," 1749. Manuscript.

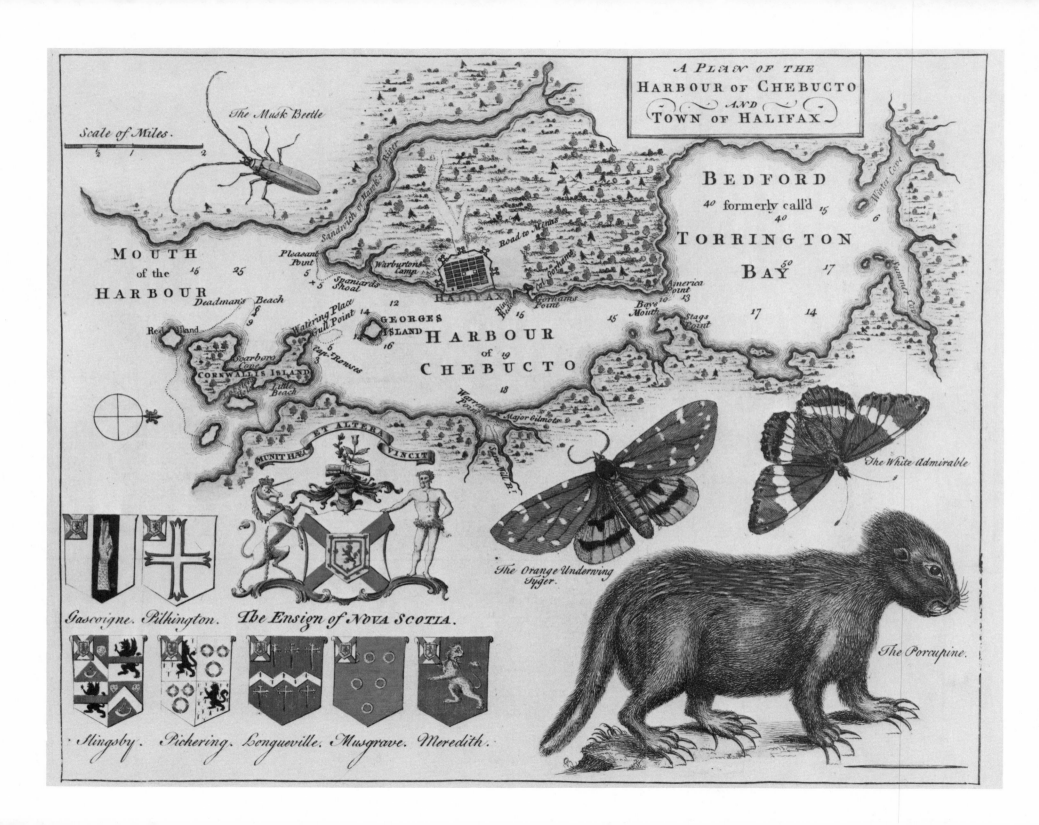

A PLAN OF THE HARBOUR OF CHEBUCTO AND TOWN OF HALIFAX

Scale of Miles.

The Musk Beetle

MOUTH of the HARBOUR

Sandwich or Hanks's River

Pleasant Point

Deadman's Beach

Watering Place

Red Island

Scarboro Cove

CORNWALLIS ISLAND

Little Beach

Cap. Rouses

Gull Point

Spaniards Shoal

Warburtons Camp

Road to Minas

HALIFAX

GEORGES ISLAND

Col Gorhams

Gorhams Point

HARBOUR of CHEBUCTO

BEDFORD formerly call'd TORRINGTON BAY

Winter Cove

Summer Cove

America Point

Bays Mouth

Stags Point

Warrens Point

Major Gilmots

MUNIT HÆC ET ALTERA VINCIT

Gascoigne. Pilkington. The Ensign of NOVA SCOTIA.

Slingsby. Pickering. Longueville. Musgrave. Meredith.

The Orange Underwing Tyger.

The White Admirable

The Porcupine.

The "Porcupine" Map

Although this map is topographically almost identical to the previous example (and to the central part of Map 2:5, p. 26), it gives a completely different impression of Halifax and its surroundings. In Harris' manuscript map, the town, laid out tidily with its palisade, occupied only a very small area compared with the surrounding forest. In this version only the peninsula and the land close to the shore are shown as forested, so that the apparently orderly settlement occupies a proportionately larger area. The rest of the space is taken up with information of a different kind: the coats of arms of seven of the baronets of Nova Scotia, some insects and the porcupine for which the map is best known.[28]

Harris was a naturalist as well as a surveyor, and had already published pictures of plants "Drawn from the Life at Halifax in Nova Scotia July 15 1749."[29] He did not stay in the province for very long; he may have returned to England before the publication of his first map of Halifax in October, 1749.[30] This decorated map illustrates some examples of the wildlife that captured his interest during his short stay.[31] It appears to reflect personal knowledge and observation, in contrast to the "official" version of his map put out by Jefferys in his capacity of Geographer to the Prince of Wales. By reducing the amount of wilderness depicted in the manuscript source and replacing much of it by general information, the map renders the wilderness less threatening.

The insects are notable for the accuracy with which they are portrayed. The "Musk Beetle," despite its unfamiliar name, is clearly a longhorn beetle which, living under tree bark, would have been quite familiar to the settlers as they cleared the town site and cut wood for houses and defences. The "Orange Underwing Tyger" is the name of an English moth,[32] undoubtedly known to Harris and similar in appearance to the moth depicted here, which is native to Nova Scotia.[33] The "White Admirable" butterfly, now known in both countries as the White Admiral, is immediately recognizable. The identification and depiction of these species suggests a serious interest in informing people in England about the wildlife to be found in the new colony.

Less satisfactory is the portrayal of the porcupine, an animal with which Harris was apparently not so familiar. Some degree of scientific accuracy has been achieved: it has the correct number of digits, four on the front feet and five on the back, and the presence of quills among the back fur is indicated. But, though Harris may very well have seen a live porcupine and had presumably been impressed by the animal, he did not attempt to draw it. The one shown here is a copy of the creature used to illustrate Henry Ellis' *A Voyage to Hudson's Bay* (London, 1748).[34] It adds nothing to the armchair traveller's knowledge of porcupines; instead it perpetuates misconceptions.

The inclusion of examples of wildlife in this map of the new settlement, apart from its decorative function, reflects both Harris' own interests and skills, and also the growing general interest in natural science in eighteenth century Europe. While the coats of arms flatter the individuals who were expected to contribute to the settlement of the province, the wildlife illustrations demonstrate that Harris' own contribution was to begin to record its natural history, and to replace the concept of an untamed wilderness with orderly scientific documentation. Even at this early stage of settlement, it was considered important that matters of intellectual interest should form part of the information being made available to the public, along with the practical record of colonization.

It is interesting to observe how, both in this map and in Jefferys' version, the device of filling up space, which would otherwise read as wilderness, with factual information reduces the impact of the wilderness. In addition to relieving the monotony of an endless expanse of trees, the illustrations give a positive indication of what is known about the new territory, where the manuscript map had represented much of it as essentially unknown. This reassurance, in maps intended for public consumption, probably increased popular support for the hazardous and expensive process of establishing the first major British settlement in Nova Scotia.

Map 7:8   Moses Harris. *A Plan of the Harbour of Chebucto and Town of Halifax*, 1750. Engraved. *Gentleman's Magazine*, London, July 1750.

"Foreign Protestants" come to Lunenburg

This copy of one of the early plans of Lunenburg shows the provisions made for the "Foreign Protestants" (German, French and Swiss immigrants) who were brought to Nova Scotia in the early 1750s and were settled in Lunenburg in 1753.[35] The original plan may have been made by Charles Morris, Surveyor General of Nova Scotia, whose task it had been to lay out the town of Lunenburg in the summer of 1753; it probably dates from about that time. The author of the copy, William S. Morris, Provincial Deputy Surveyor, was Charles Morris' great-grandson, one of several of his descendants who followed the same profession. He appears to have been active during the second quarter of the nineteenth century; he died in 1853. Dr. Frederick Morris (another great-grandson of the first Charles Morris), whose name appears on the southeastern part of the map, was practising medicine in Lunenburg at the same time. He applied for a grant of land there in 1827, soon after starting practice, and received 30 acres at Eel Pond, as shown on the map.[36]

Superimposed on the basic plan are the names of several people who were prominent figures in Lunenburg during the late 1800s and whose property is shown beyond the original blocks of the town. These land holdings, and the location of the ship yard and the "Supposed Railway," were obviously added to the plan at a later date. The ship yard, and the adjoining Lunenburg Marine Railway established for hauling ships up for repair, were part of the industrial development which, together with the fishery, brought prosperity to Lunenburg. They can still be seen today.

Although this map is undated, it has been possible to assign an approximate date to the original plan, and to establish broad periods within which the copy and the later annotations were made. For the purposes of studying the settlement of Lunenburg, which is described by W.P. Bell in his *Foreign Protestants* (Toronto, 1961) it is the contents of the original (of which this is "A True Copy") that chiefly concern us.

Charles Morris laid out the town of Lunenburg in the densely-built rectangular blocks that were typical of eighteenth century town plans in Nova Scotia. This method limited the amount of initial clearing necessary to house the population, and the number of streets that would eventually have to be maintained. It also provided a relatively small area to be defended against attacks by the natives; the town boundaries were initially protected on the west side by a palisade and what was known as the Star Fort, and, towards the peninsula, by the Eastern Blockhouse. These defences appear in other maps; the fort and the blockhouse appear to have stood on the shaded areas visible on each side of the town in this map.

Like the early maps of Halifax, this plan shows a street-pattern which survives today in the old part of the town. The street names remain unchanged, and are readily recognizable to a visitor, or by comparison with a modern street map. As in Halifax, they commemorate contemporary dignitaries: the names of the north-south streets include Cornwallis, Duke and Prince, all familiar to Haligonians, and the wide central thoroughfare was suitably designated King Street. His Excellency Peregrine Thomas Hopson Esq., under whose governorship the town of Lunenburg was established, was also honoured with a street perpendicular to the harbour, while the cross streets were named for other English notables.[37] Kaulbach Street, to the west of the town, is the one exception here, as it was named after one of the leading "Foreign Protestant" families; this name does not appear on other early plans, and was presumably added at a later date.

While Halifax was designed as a garrison town, with much of its economy based on the military and naval personnel and their activities, Lunenburg was intended to become the relatively self-sufficient centre of an agricultural community, acting as a balance to—and

Map 7:9   W.S. Morris. "A True Copy of A Plan of the Town of Lunenburg Garden Lotts and Commons adjoining Laid out by order of his Excellency Peregrine Thomas Hopson Esq. . . .," Undated. Manuscript.

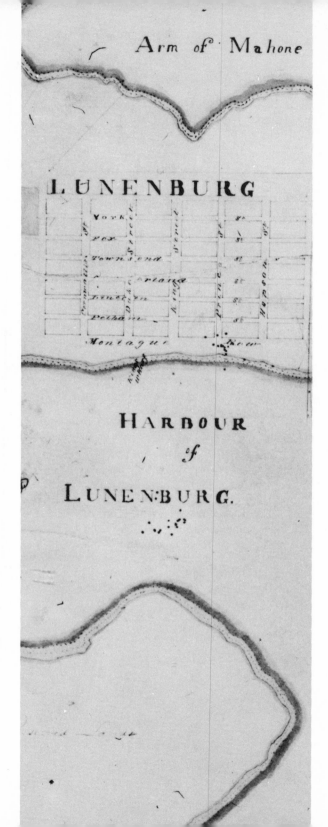

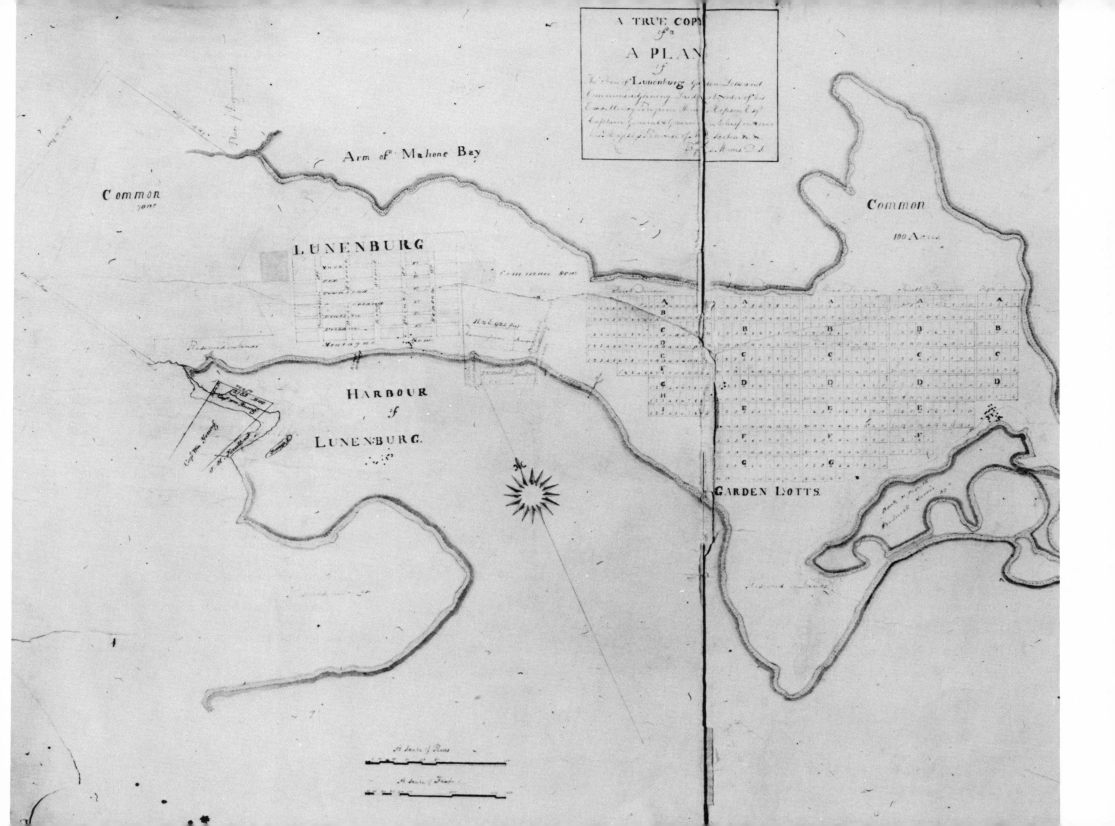

A TRUE COPY
of a
A PLAN
of
The Town of Lunenburg ...

Arm of Mahone Bay

Common

Common
100 Acres

LUNENBURG

HARBOUR
of
LUNENBURG

GARDEN LOTTS

possible substitute for—the Acadians on the other side of the province. Its location was chosen partly because some land had already been cleared there by the French, and because there was some relatively good soil in the area. Beyond the town, large farm lots were surveyed along the eastern side of the LaHave River and around part of Mahone Bay (see Map 4:4, p. 55), as well as in the immediate vicinity of Lunenburg. These were intended to be cleared and worked by the Lunenburg settlers, and it was hoped that they would eventually be able to supply produce to Halifax. But the more pressing need to provide subsistence for the settlers themselves is reflected in the laying out of a considerable area of land to the east of the town as the "Garden Lots" shown on this map. This was done by Morris in 1753; the name Garden Lots still survives in the area. The identification of the lots, like those of the town itself, was by numbered divisions, with blocks designated by letters, and numbered lots within each block. The orderly appearance of this system tends to conceal the fact that there was considerable variation in the enthusiasm and success with which different settlers tackled the clearing and cultivation of their gardens.[38]

A further provision for the self-sufficiency of the inhabitants of Lunenburg was the common land on the outskirts of the town. The West Common, marked here as 700 acres, but in an early plan of Lunenburg (reproduced by Bell, Fig. 6) as only 70, lay to one side of the town; other areas lay to the east and north of the garden lots. Families who had been allocated livestock in 1754 were required to assist in the clearing of the land, much of which was to be used for grazing, and regulations were laid down to ensure the smooth operation of the commons.[39] Although it is not clear how much of the designated common land had actually been cleared when the original map was made, it establishes the principle on which the economy of the town was to be run.

It will be noted that no roads appear on this map. Paths were no doubt soon worn between the town and the garden lots, and roughly cleared roads would eventually be constructed between the town and the farms, but communications between Lunenburg and the rest of the province continued for some time to be almost entirely by sea (See Chapter 8, p. 123). The King's Wharf, the only feature on the shoreline of the original plan, marked the point of arrival and departure of the vessels that formed the main link between Lunenburg and Halifax.

This map shows, in a neat and tidy fashion, the surveyor's provisions for the development of the town. But it cannot convey the discomforts and the frustrations of the settlers and the administrators as they struggled to bring some order into this "instant" community, composed of a miscellaneous assortment of Europeans, many of whom had neither the skills nor the experience to produce the kind of model agricultural settlement that British officialdom expected. W.P. Bell's *The Foreign Protestants*, an account of the settling of Lunenburg, adds a human dimension to the apparently orderly picture suggested by this map, as it examines contemporary descriptions of the establishment of the new community.

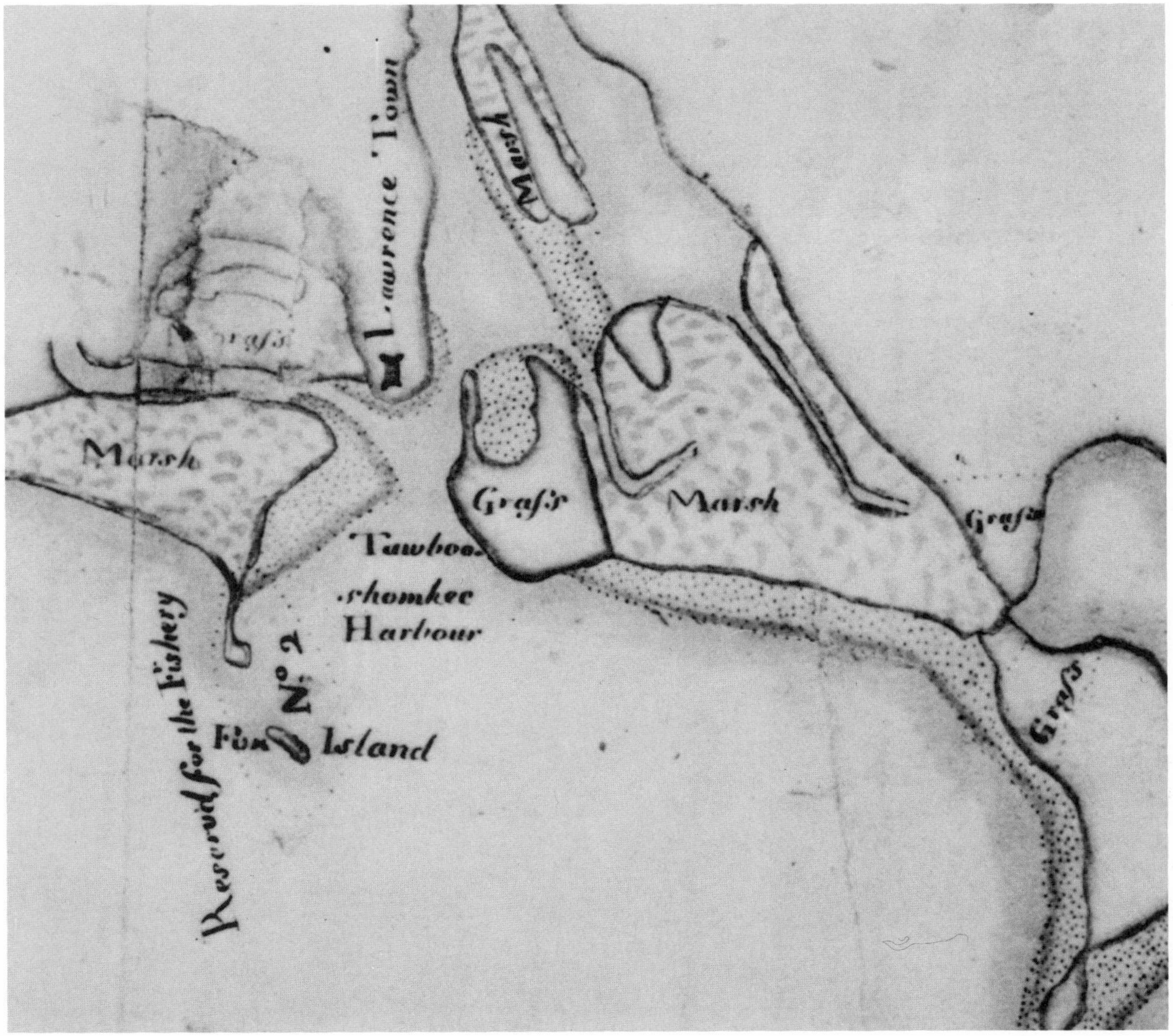

The attempted settlement of Lawrencetown

This somewhat confusing map records an early British attempt to settle and develop the Lawrencetown area east of Halifax. The site had been considered, and rejected, as the location for the Foreign Protestants who were eventually established at Lunenburg in 1753. The map represents an area originally surveyed by Charles Morris in 1752.[40] In 1754 the area was granted to a group of 20 people by Acting Governor Lawrence, after whom it was named.[41] The map includes a list of the grantees and a description of the land granted; it also shows something of its geography. The area represented extends from Cole Harbour to Chezzetcook Inlet. Only the coastal region is shown in detail; much of Lawrencetown Lake, and all of Porters Lake, along with other inland features, are omitted.

Comparison with a modern map will help the reader identify the places shown here, despite some confusing names and some obvious distortions. On the western part of the map lie the "Bay of Muscodoboit or Wampawk," and the "Inner Harbour of Muscodoboit, or Wampawk, by some called Cold Harbour." It was this final name which was to persist, as Cole Harbour; how this change came about is not at all certain. The actual outline of the shore and sandflats of the harbour differs somewhat from a modern map, but the area is clearly recognizable.

Lawrencetown itself lies just left of centre of the map. It is shown as a compact town, rather than the straggling community that eventually developed there. It was expected that the settlers would live initially within a protected compound, as they did at Halifax and Lunenburg, because of the still present threat of attacks by natives. A road, not shown on this map but visible on Map 8:3, p. 137, was to link the new settlement with Halifax Harbour. The townsite lay on a peninsula of higher land above the surrounding meadows and marshland. It overlooked the Tawtooshomkee

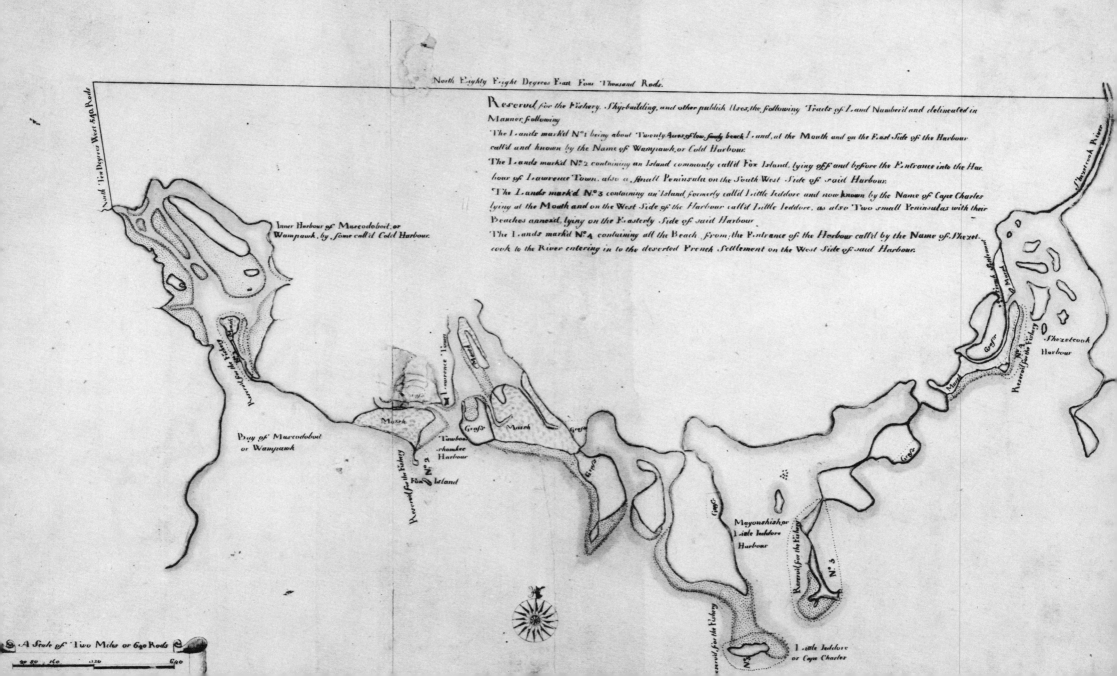

A Plan of a Tract of Land, granted by the Honourable Charles Lawrence Esquire Commander in Chief, for the Time being in and over his Majesty's Province of Nova Scotia, and President of his Majesty's Council, to John Bu...
William Drake Spike, John Hifsey, John Collier, Robert Ewer, Richard Bulkley, William Nesbitt, George Saul, Esquires; the Reverend John Breynton, Arthur Price, John Tuggart, William Magyee, Robert Grant, David Lloyd, Robert Walter, Richard Wenman, Matthew Barnard, Benjam...
...nier, John Baxter, and William Morris Gentlemen, Situate, lying, and being, to the Eastward of Dartmouth, and was Formerly called and known by the Names of Wampawk, Tawboothomkes, Mayonshish, and Shezetcook, and now to be called Lawrence Town: And is abutted and bounded, Weste...
...anted Lands, beginning at a small Brook on the Western Side of a Harbour called Wampawk, by some called Muscodoboit, by others Cold Harbour, and running thence North Ten Degrees West Five Hundred and Forty Rods, thence running North Eighty Eight Degrees East Fou...
...and Rods, be the same more or less to a River called and known by the Name of Shezetcook, and is bounded on the East by the said River Shezetcook, and on the South East and South West by the main Ocean; comprehending within the said Grant all the Islands at the Mouth of...
...iver and within the Harbour of Shezetcook, with all the other Islands and Headlands contained within the Limits aforesaid; Allowance being made for Lakes, waste Lands and such Roads as shall hereafter be thought necessary, for publick Use to pass through the same. Cont...
...e whole Twenty Thousand Acres.

North Eighty Eight Degrees East Four Thousand Rods.

Reserved for the Fishery, Ship-building, and other publick Uses, the following Tracts of Land Numbered and delineated in Manner following.

The Lands mark'd Nᵒ 1 being about Twenty Acres of low sandy beach Land, at the Mouth and on the East Side of the Harbour call'd and known by the Name of Wampawk, or Cold Harbour.

The Lands mark'd Nᵒ 2 containing an Island commonly call'd Fox Island, lying off and before the Entrance into the Harbour of Lawrence Town, also a small Peninsula on the South-West Side of said Harbour.

The Lands mark'd Nᵒ 3 containing an Island formerly call'd Little Jeddore and now known by the Name of Cape Charles lying at the Mouth and on the West Side of the Harbour call'd Little Jeddore, as also Two small Peninsulas with their Beaches annex'd, lying on the Easterly Side of said Harbour.

The Lands mark'd Nᵒ 4 containing all the Beach, from the Entrance of the Harbour call'd by the Name of Shezet-cook to the River entering into the deserted French Settlement on the West Side of said Harbour.

North Ten Degrees West 540 Rods.

Inner Harbour of Muscodoboit, or Wampawk, by some call'd Cold Harbour.

Shezetcook River.

French Settlement

Shezetcook Harbour

Reserved for the Fishery

Bay of Muscodoboit or Wampawk

Lawrence Town

Marsh

Reserved for the Fishery

Nᵒ 2 Fox Island

Tawboothomkee Harbour

Grafsy   Marsh   Grafsy

Marsh

Grafsy

Grafsy

Mayonshish, or Little Jeddore Harbour

Reserved for the Fishery

Reserved for the Fishery

Nᵒ 3

Little Jeddore or Cape Charles

Nᵒ 3

A Scale of Two Miles or 640 Rods.

20 80 160   320   640

Harbour, as the inlet was called then; Fox Island is now known as Egg Island, while the earlier name persists at Fox Point.

East of Lawrencetown, the coastal area consisted chiefly of marshes, grassland and sandy beaches. The shifting sands may account in part for the variations between this and a modern representation of the shoreline, but the main features can easily be identified. Lawrencetown Beach stretches along to what is now Half Island Point; the cove where Rocky Run drains out of Porters Lake is shown here as having two outlets to the ocean where there is in fact only one. Three Fathom Harbour is identified as Magonshish or Little Jeddore Harbour, with Little Jeddore or Cape Charles Island at the harbour mouth. Its size is greatly exaggerated by comparison with Cole Harbour and Chezzetcook Inlet.

The chain of islands and beaches on the east side of the harbour leads back to Shezetcook (Chezzetcook) Harbour, whose beaches, marshes and islands are all rather roughly drawn, though readily identifiable. The dog-leg to the east of the harbour presumably represents Fisherman's Beach. Shezetcook River formed the eastern boundary of the grant, so accuracy beyond that point was perhaps of minor importance.

The map explains in part why the area was originally considered as a location for the Foreign Protestants, and why it was later offered to the grantees named.

Map 7:10   Anonymous. "A Plan of a Tract of Land granted by the Honourable Charles Lawrence Esquire Commander in Cheif for the Time being in and over his Majesty's Province of Nova Scotia and President of His Majesty's Council, to John Barker [and nineteen others], Situate, lying and being, to the Eastward of Dartmouth,. . ., and now to be called Lawrence Town. . .," 1754. Manuscript.

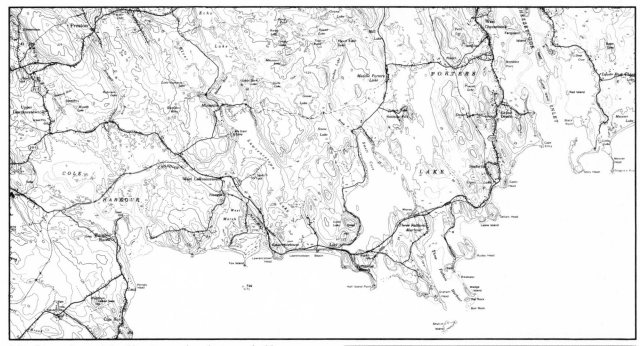

Map 7:10a   The Lawrencetown area today.

Like Lunenburg, it had been previously occupied by a small French population, whose presence demonstrated that it was possible to make a living here. According to Morris' 1752 survey, there were two French settlements in the area, one at the site selected for Lawrencetown, and another on the west side of Chezzetcook Inlet. The latter appears again in this map, though the notes describe it as deserted.

The areas of marsh and grass marked all along the coast suggest that the French had chosen this area because it appeared that these familiar attributes would enable them to support themselves by farming. The French population had never been very significant, and had survived partly by trading with the considerable Micmac population of the region.[42] The presence of the Micmac was, of course, a disadvantage rather than a benefit to the British. Nevertheless, the area appeared to have some potential for agriculture.

The other economic base of the projected community was, according to the map, expected to be fishing. Four areas were specifically reserved for "The Fishery,

Shipbuilding and other publick Uses." They are described in detail in the notes to the map, and consist of beaches, peninsulas and islands where fish-processing facilities could be established, and fishing vessels constructed.

Despite some apparent advantages of the area for settlement, the project foundered and was abandoned in 1757, largely because of the problems of providing adequate security for such a small group of people at a considerable distance from the garrison at Halifax.[43] The natives who had traded with the French were still overtly hostile to the British. Although the access road was cut and some attempt made to start farming, the community could not survive without military protection, and this was too costly to provide for an extended period of time. It would be some time before freedom from threat of attack, and a considerably expanded population, would make it possible to develop the Lawrencetown area.

the Loyalists come to Shelburne

This map dates from 1783, the year of the foundation of the town of Shelburne. Known to French fishermen during the seventeenth century as Port Razoir (Port Roseway), the area had been considered by the British authorities as a potential site for development since the early 1700s. The early 1760s saw the arrival of a group of Scots-Irish settlers, led by Alexander and Joseph McNutt, at Port Roseway, where the McNutts had received an extensive grant known as New Jerusalem. They were later joined by a further wave of immigrants from New England. As a result, when the Loyalists arrived in the spring of 1783, there was already an established, if sparse, population.[44]

In order to accommodate the new arrivals, of whom some 3,000 disembarked in May, 1783, a town was quickly laid out in the familiar grid pattern that has already been seen in Halifax and Lunenburg. The town was named Shelburne, as noted in this map. The principal street, as in so many other towns, was baptized King(s) Street. This roughly drawn map does not show all the details of the town itself; the original large scale plan drawn by Charles Morris (II), the Surveyor General, and approved by Governor Parr, shows a tidy, rectangular settlement with a spacious public square.[45] The surveying and laying out of the town and the surrounding area were carried out by William Morris, chief surveyor and son of the surveyor general, and by Benjamin Marston, who was appointed deputy surveyor.[46]

The division of the surrounding area is also represented on this map, which includes the region from Negro Harbour, identified as Cape Negro, to Ragged Islands, east of the Jordan River. The 50 acre farm lots to be allocated to the Loyalists lay on either side of Port Roseway (Shelburne Harbour), and on the peninsula jutting into it. There were also some areas marked "undivided" whose purpose was as yet undefined, as well as a number of "resarved" areas which were not to be included in the general distribution, but retained by the Government for various purposes. One of these areas, marked as "2½ acres across," was "said to be resarved for a Common"; the common was, in fact, established to the east of the town, and this area to the south appears in a later map as "Governor Parr's farm."[47]

A note on the peninsula at the centre of the map records that 34 lots of 50 acres each were "laid out by Mr. Marston at 12/6 (twelve shillings and sixpence) per lot ye men &c ware furnished by ye A[merican] Loyalists." The system of using Loyalist labour to help in the laying out, though sound in principle, was unreliable in practice. After an initial willingness to assist in clearing and marking out house lots in the town, the enthusiasm of many of the newcomers dropped off sharply. Perhaps the availability of labour for this project was because of the particular desirability of the farm lots close to the town.[48]

Other interesting features of the map include the Herring Fishery at the Upper Falls, also known as Herring Falls, and the Road to Annapolis Royal (see Map 8:4, pp. 140–141). Roseway Island is now known as McNutt's Island, after the family who were among the earliest English speaking settlers. Other "Inhabitants," the existing settlers in the area, were located on the western shore of the harbour, near the island. Next to their lands was the proposed site for a fort overlooking the harbour; to the north of it lies a boundary line bearing the name Durfee. Captain Joseph Durfee was the instigator of the original scheme to settle Loyalists in the area. He was one of the representatives of the Port Roseway Association who negotiated with Sir Guy Carleton and Governor Parr for their transfer to Nova Scotia, and for the granting of land to the newcomers.[49] His holding apparently extended southwards from the marked line to the present Gunning Cove.[50]

On the northwest shore of the harbour, which was marked for division into 50 acre lots, it is also noted that "Negroes landed here." This early group of Black immigrants consisted of freed slaves who had sought protection among the Loyalists. They were granted land for a settlement at this place, which became known as Birchtown, one of the earliest Black settlements in Nova Scotia. Subsequently, many of the group left for Sierra Leone.

Despite the rather sketchy nature of this map, it contains many interesting references to aspects of the early days after the Loyalists' arrival. The uncertainty of the hastily drawn up plans for their accommodation is reflected in the observations "Governor wants to Resarve" and "Said to be resarved. . . ." The problems faced by the Governor himself are eloquently described in Parr's own letter of September 30, 1783. *". . .whilst unexpected, and unprepared, great numbers have been landed in this Province, from the month of last November to the end of July upwards of 13000 Persons, men Women and Children, have arrived at Halifax, Annapolis Royal, Port Roseway and St Johns River, and*

Map 7:11 Anonymous. Map of the Shelburne area from Cape Negro to Ragged Islands, 1783. Manuscript.

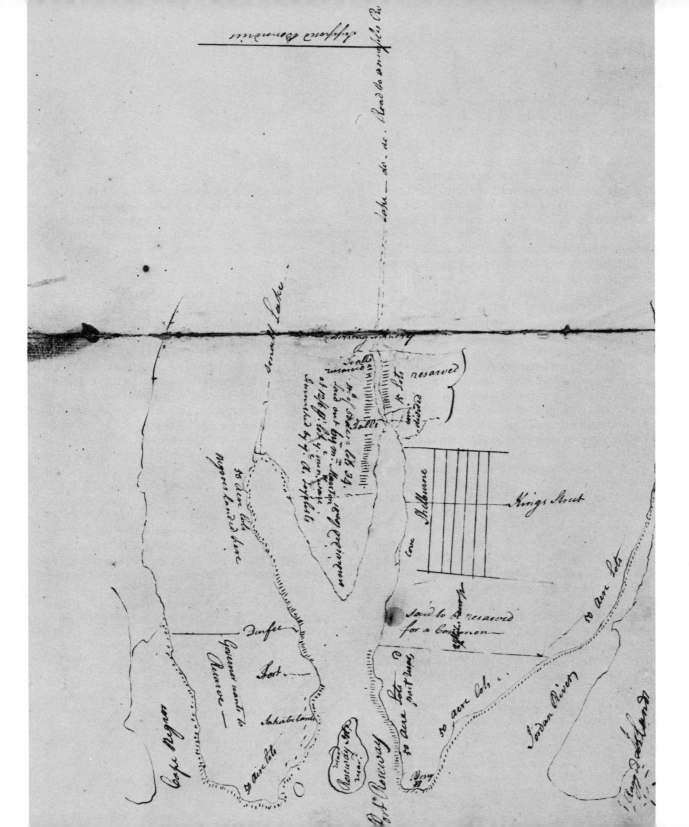

Cumberland, and, since that period great numbers have been Landed at those places and at Passamaquoddy, (between St Johns River and the River St Croix) the amount of whom I cannot yet ascertain for want of Exact returns, by Conjecture the whole already arriv'd may amount to upwards of 18,000 persons.

"But, being well assured of His Majesty's most gracious intentions towards these meritorious and Suffering people, I have exerted my Utmost Endeavours for their Accommodation, by Sending Surveyors to the different districts, where they had arriv'd, to Locate them on the lands. . .

"I visited Port Roseway, as soon as I could, after the arrival of the Refugees, the Number at that place are upwards of 5000 persons, and many more I expect will soon arrive there. I appointed Magistrates and Establish'd order amongst them, and I flatter mayself they will soon become a happy and flourishing Settlement." (Parr to Lord North. PAC, NSA CIII)[51]

As the following maps show, Parr and his officials were to be kept busy for several years with the task of establishing these "Refugees" in settlements scattered all over the province. These examples represent only a few of the many communities set up at this period to receive the Loyalists.

Scottish settlers in the Pictou area

Made by the second Charles Morris to become Surveyor General of Nova Scotia, this map is one of a number dating from the mid-1780s showing the lands granted in different parts of the province to the settlers who came to Nova Scotia at this time. Some of the immigrants, as the title reminds us, had fought in the American Revolutionary War, and others were Loyalists who preferred to remain under the jurisdiction of the British Crown. The map gives a physical description of the area, a record of its division into lots, and the names of the grantees to whom the lands were distributed. Oriented with north to the bottom, the complete map includes the area from the Harbours of Pictou and Merigomish to a considerable distance beyond the confluence of the two branches of the Pictou River. Only the lower part of the river is seen in this section.

By 1785, settlers had been established in the Pictou area for some 20 years. Alexander McNutt, the entrepreneur whose interests included an early attempt at developing Port Roseway, acquired land at Pictou in 1765, at the same time as the Philadelphia Company was given an extensive grant in the area.[52] In 1767, a group of settlers from Philadelphia arrived in Pictou, on board the *Hope*.[53] Among them were Robert Patterson, who by the time this map was made had a piece of land fronting on the West River, and James McCabe, whose grants on the lower West River and on the East River are shown here. A number of other private citizens received grants in the mid 1760s, including John Wentworth, later Lieutenant Governor of Nova Scotia, whose holding of 20,000 acres fronting on Merigomish Harbour is also visible.[54] Most of the land originally granted in the 1760s was subsequently escheated and redistributed to later groups of settlers.

Best known among the successive groups of immigrants to Pictou are the Scots, numbering close to 200, who came on the *Hector* in 1773. These pioneers were later joined by smaller groups of their countrymen. After some initial difficulties in acquiring title to land which had been granted earlier but never developed, in 1783 they received grants on the land which had originally been allotted to Alexander McNutt.[55] The names of the landholders recorded on this map, on the lots along the three rivers flowing into Pictou Harbour, leave no doubt as to their origins. They include Camerons, Frasers, McDonalds, McKays, McKenzies, McLeods, Rosses, a Stewart, a Sutherland and an Urquhart. These, and other familiar Highland names, reflect clearly the beginnings of Scottish settlement in this part of Nova Scotia. Among them was John Patterson, founder of the town of Pictou, whose name is on a lot fronting on the Middle River.

Two other large grants shown on this map were those set aside for the 82nd Regiment, disbanded in Halifax in 1783, after the American Revolution. The British Government favoured the settling of these soldiers in the province, and ordered that land should be made available for them. Not all those who were eligible took up the offer, and not all those who had received land actually settled on it. Those who did, however, were enough to establish a population along the whole eastern shore of the county.[56]

In the expectation of a considerable influx of settlers, a town was surveyed and laid out on the east side of Pictou Harbour, at what is now Pictou Landing. It was to be known as Walmesley, and like other "instant" towns of the period, was to consist of a rectangular townsite with a common close at hand. Unlike most of Morris' projected towns, this one came to nothing, and it was at a site on the opposite side of the harbour that the town of Pictou was established by John Patterson in 1787.

Among the lots granted to the Scottish settlers between the East and Middle Rivers, we find the School Lot and the Glebe. These tracts of land, set aside for the benefit of education and religion respectively, were features of a number of communities that were surveyed and laid out at this time.

On the west side of Middle River, a large tract of land is marked "Granted to Governor Patterson." Walter Patterson was the Lieutenant Governor of St. John's Island (Prince Edward Island) until 1787. He was a notorious land speculator,[57] and evidently turned his attention to property on the mainland as well as in his own province.

A final point of interest, which predates all the other dispositions of land recorded here, is the "Indian Burying Ground" at the mouth of the East River. Although the story goes that the local natives dispersed in haste on the arrival of the *Hector* and its passengers with their piper,[58] the existence here of their burial ground attests to their presence in the region long before the coming of the white man. It is interesting to note that the site was preserved when the surrounding area was being divided up among the settlers. Whether this gesture was made out of fear or out of respect, it allowed a token of the earlier history of the area to remain alongside the new settlement.

The Pictou area was to be linked to the rest of Nova Scotia by the road shown here, running from the point between the East and Middle Rivers along the height of land. A note on the upper portion of the map (not reproduced here) tells us that it was to join "the great Road leading to Halifax thro the County of Sydney" (Map 8:4, pp. 140–41). Highway 106 follows this line today.

The prospects for development of the area are summed up in the "Observations" of the surveyor, in the form of a note on the map:
The Lands about the Harbour of Pictou and Merigumish particularly on the Rivers that Empty into Pictou Harbour are Exceeding good Arable Lands. The Har-

Map 7:12 Charles Morris (II). Part of "A Plan of Surveys made and Lands Granted to Disbanded Soldiers Sailors and others, Loyal Emigrants at Merigumish & Pictou, done under the Orders of His Excellency Governor Parr by Chas. Morris," 1785. Manuscript.

bour of Pictou is Spacious & of sufficient depth to Admit Vessels of 400 Tons Burthen. The Country hereabouts Abounds with Timber Trees for Lumber, proper for the West India Market. And the Rivers with great Plenty of Fish such as Salmon, Bass, Mackrell, Alewives, Herring & Trout. And by proper Attention & Industry this district will become a Valuable Settlement.

The town of Pictou was established two years after Morris' map was made, on land not yet allocated according to this record. John Patterson chose the site on the opposite site of the harbour from Morris' Walmesley, and laid out a small town that was to survive as an administrative unit despite the more extensive commercial developments in the surrounding area. The lands originally granted to the Scottish settlers on the East and Middle Rivers have become part of the New Glasgow industrial area. Many of the names found on this map were associated with its development, among them Thomas Fraser and Alexander Mackay, two of the earliest residents. This map is an interesting record of settlement by a group of people whose enterprise and "proper Attention and Industry" were instrumental in turning the district into a valuable community.

Sydney becomes established

This "Plan of Sydney River" (Sydney Harbour), incorporating a large scale "Plan of the Town of Sydney" was sent to Lord Sydney, the Colonial Secretary after whom the area was named, in September 1788. After the destruction of Louisbourg in 1760, nothing had been done for many years to develop Cape Breton Island. The British Government had even shown itself reluctant to allow the mining of coal deposits there, for fear that the coal might support industries that would compete with domestic production (see Chapter 5). For 20 years, settlement was officially discouraged. Then in 1784, with the expectation of more settlers as a result of the influx of Loyalists to the Maritime Provinces, Cape Breton became a separate province, and J.F.W. DesBarres became its first lieutenant governor. Early in 1785, he arrived at Spanish Harbour, as the Sydney area was originally named, and set about planning his new capital. But the elaborate town plan that DesBarres drew up was not, in fact, completed. He was recalled from his post after less than two years, and only a partial and very modified version of his project was carried out.[59]

DesBarres had selected, as the site of the town of Sydney, a peninsula jutting out into the South West Branch of the Sydney River. This location can be seen on the upper plan, which is oriented with north to the upper right. His original plan[60] had included the entire peninsula, and unlike most town designs of the 1780s, it took into account the curve of the land. DesBarres' street plan included a large central open space, and gracious circles among the streets. The street lines on the western side of the peninsula were to break at the central plaza, so that the two halves of the Esplanade formed a gentle angle along the waterfront. The angle was to widen with successive streets, until the central street, Great George Street, ran straight from north to south. This elegant but costly scheme was only partially fulfilled.

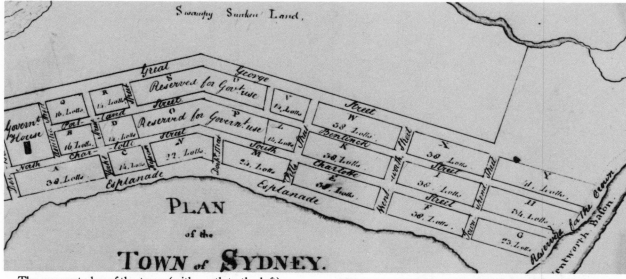

The present plan of the town (with north to the left) shows the modified version that was actually constructed, and which survives in the street plan of modern downtown Sydney. The waterfront Esplanade still breaks at an angle following the shoreline, and the streets behind it lie parallel, breaking at the same angle. By 1788 only the streets between the waterfront and Great George Street were laid out, and they were intersected by short, simple streets dividing the town into blocks of between 14 and 41 lots each. The developed part of the town was bounded on the southern end by the Crown lands along Wentworth Basin (now Wentworth Park) and at the northern tip of the peninsula by the Military Ground. This area incorporated the barracks and other military buildings; the Department of National Defence still owns land there. One reason for the failure to develop the eastern side of the town at this time is made clear by the reference on the map to "Swampy, Sunken Land."

Map 7:13 Anonymous. "Plan of Sydney River" with "Plan of the Town of Sydney," 1788. Manuscript.

The small scale upper map shows that provision was made for further suburban growth of Sydney and that, as with other towns, common land was provided. Along the shore of the South West Branch, on both sides of the town and across from it, small farm lots had been laid out, and some already granted. Among those grants on the west side of the river we find two in the name of J.F.W. DesBarres, and one belonging to A. DesBarres; this was Amelia, the daughter of the former governor. Probably one of the DesBarres lots in fact belonged to his son, William, who had also received property as a gift from his father.[61]

Another interesting property owner with a large lot not far from the DesBarres grants was A(braham) Cuyler, who had come to Cape Breton from Albany,

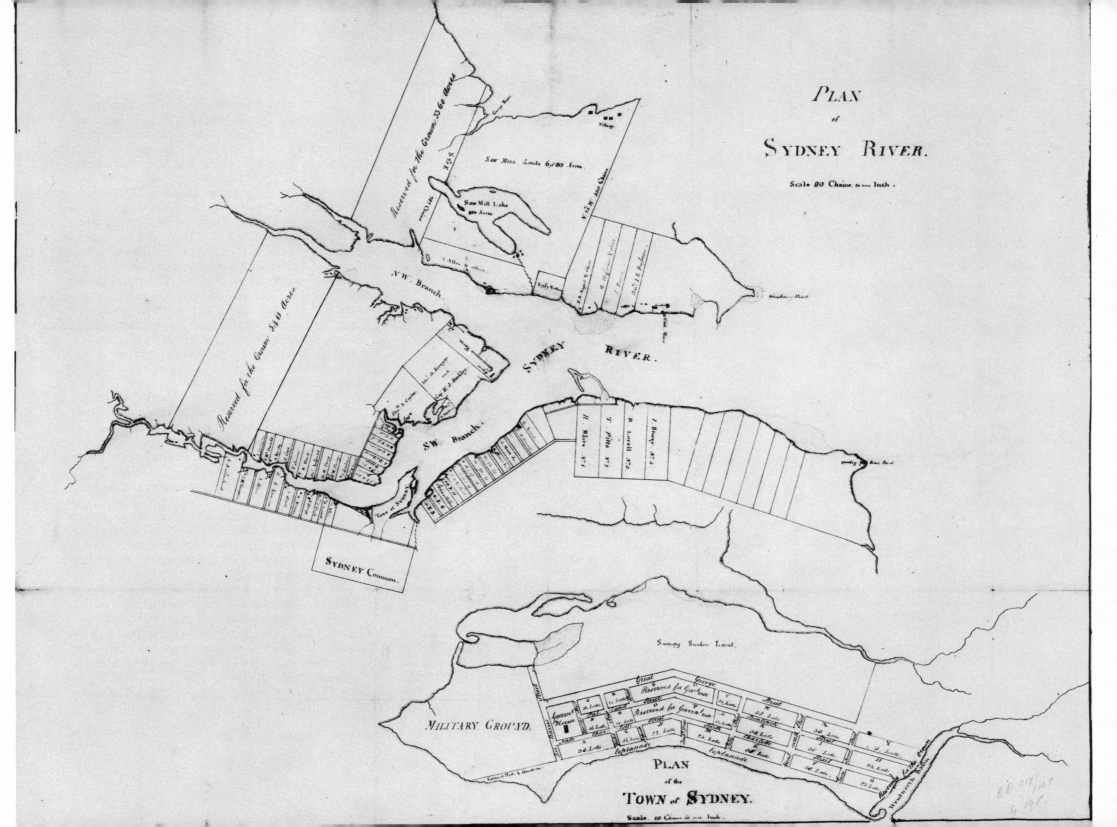

PLAN
of
SYDNEY RIVER.

Scale 80 Chains to one Inch.

PLAN
of the
TOWN of SYDNEY.

Scale 40 Chains to one Inch.

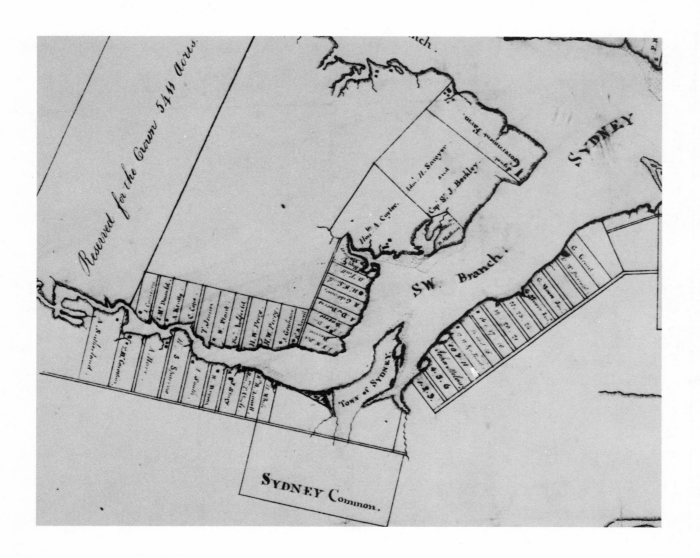

New York, at the head of several hundred Loyalists.[62] His neighbour, D(avid) Mathews, formerly Mayor of New York, was another influential Loyalist.[63] R(ichard) Gibbons, a friend of DesBarres with whom his son had boarded while at school in Halifax,[64] also owned property across the river from Sydney, while farther upstream a lot bears the name of T(homas) Ashfield, DesBarres' secretary[65] and later Chief Justice.

Government property included the "Government Farm," at what is now Point Edward, and two large lots "Reserved for the Crown" which form the western limits of the Sydney River settlement. Towards the harbour mouth, several large lots of land had been laid out, and some granted to individuals. One very large tract of land extending across to Little Bras d'Or is identified as the Saw Mill Lands, consisting of 6,580 acres. It included most of the Saw Mill Lake, now Pottle Lake, which fed the mills that were part of the earliest industrial developments of Cape Breton Island (see Chapter 5).

The resource on which the settlement of Sydney was to come to depend was, of course, coal. The only mine shown as functioning at this time—at what was to become the community of Sydney Mines—appears here, with its wharf for loading coal onto ships. Other early indications of the industrial base of this area of Cape Breton Island appear on a number of maps in Chapter 5.

A final detail of this map is the series of signal masts that stood at the harbour mouth, at the mine area and at Point Edward. These would transmit information to the residents of the town, and the military in particular, about incoming vessels.

In all, despite the hardships that accompanied the early days of settlement, the Sydney area is shown here as a potentially viable community. With coal, lumber, and at least an initial attempt at farming, it had attracted a sufficient number of settlers to found what was to become, in later years, the centre of an important industrial region.

Chapter 8 *Inland Transportation:*
Roads, Rivers and Portages

The early French explorers of Acadia crossed the Atlantic by ship, and they used those same vessels to move from place to place along the coast of the New World. Champlain's harbour maps, while giving soundings to enable navigators to enter port, show only stylized trees and hills extending back from the shoreline, which is often shown as peopled with natives. To new arrivals, the apparently impenetrable nature of the forested interior, where Micmac inhabitants travelled with ease, must have presented a formidable barrier. Knowledge of the region was inevitably restricted for some time to accessible parts of the coast and to the lower reaches of the rivers. The French penetrated inland only slowly, and with the help of native guides.

The earliest inland routes to appear on seventeenth century maps such as Franquelin's "Carte Général. . ." (Map 8:1) are the traditional native river and portage trails. Travel over them was by canoe and on foot in summer, and on snowshoes and by toboggan in winter.[1] These means were no doubt difficult for the newcomers, even with the assistance of the natives, but those who seriously intended to stay in Acadia soon learned the necessary skills.

Later maps in this chapter illustrate paths and roads between settlements that supplemented the river routes, but to a great extent they followed the same courses. Many of the major routes across the province were established at a fairly early date, and have remained relatively intact into modern times. The tendency of roads to follow the canoe and portage trails is partly a matter of familiarity and habit, but it also reflects the greater ease of movement along the relatively gentle gradients of the river valleys, and over established portage routes. Only in recent times has technology made it possible to build roads through natural obstacles, but even now gradients and surface water influence the choice of route. Another consideration was the problem of constructing bridges. A wide body of water presents a considerable obstacle even today, and suitable crossing places had to be found before a road could be planned over a route interrupted by rivers. For this reason, although a trail had been broken between Halifax and Lunenburg as early as 1755 (see Map 8:3), travel between the two settlements was primarily by sea for many years to come.

What are referred to on eighteenth century maps as "roads" would hardly be recognizable as such today. Although they are distinguished on some maps from lesser paths and trails (by a double rather than a single dotted line), A.H. Clark conjectures that the " 'roads', eight feet wide, must have been the roughest sort of cart-tracks through the stumps, rocks and swamps."[2] Even so, they represent the beginnings of the network of inland transportation routes in use today.

Demeulle takes the portage trail

This large map, of which only a section is reproduced here, is one of the earliest to show details of the interior of the province. It was made by Franquelin, the king's official hydrographer in Québec, as a record of the tour of inspection carried out in Acadia by Jacques Demeulle, the Intendant, in 1685–86.[3] It is a carefully drawn and beautifully decorated map, with cartouches displaying the title, dedication and scale. Latitudes are shown on the margins, and a compass rose provides orientation. Sea routes are illustrated with large and small sailing vessels, including canoes along the coast, while a whale appears in the Gulf of St. Lawrence.

As well as giving a recognizable outline of the coast and offshore islands, Franquelin identifies a large number of rivers, some in considerable detail. Among the most interesting features of the map are the portage routes, one of which appears in this section. Marked as the *Portage de Monsieur l'Intendant*, the route crosses the province between *Port Royal* (Annapolis Royal) and *P[ort] Rossignol* (Liverpool). This series of rivers and lakes can be identified without much difficulty on a modern map, from Lequille on Allain's River, via Grand Lake and Fisher Lake to the head of the Mersey, and through Lakes Kejimkujik and Rossignol to its mouth.

The route across the peninsula was one known to the Micmac as a link between the Bay of Fundy and the South Shore. We know from Demeulle's report that the party consisted of six Frenchmen and two native guides, travelling in three canoes. They can, indeed, be seen on the map: three men carrying canoes head the procession along the portage route, followed by the other five on foot. Demeulle's narrative fills in the details of their journey:

I was told that I could go across country by canoe to Port Rossignol or LaHaive by a route thirty leagues long. I was reluctant to undertake this trip, for some of the inhabitants said it was very difficult and others that it

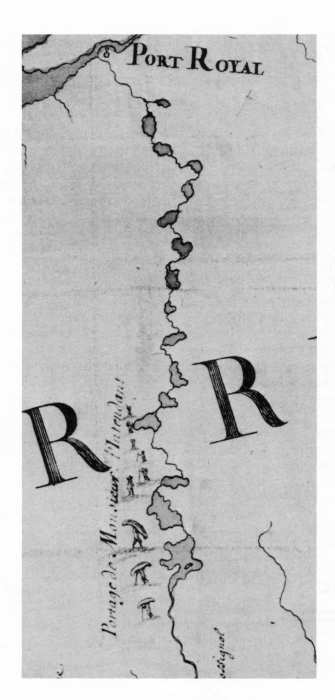

was impossible. . . . There were eight of us in the three canoes, that is, the members of the party and the Indians who were acting as my guides. The latter were very skilful in carrying the canoes through the woods, while one of my men was no less skilful than they. We followed our boatmen in all of the portages, of which there were twenty-four along the route. Three men carried the canoes, and each one of us others carried a package of belongings or of food, which we put down at the point where we were to re-embark. Then the three men who had carried the canoes and the four others of my party went back to get the rest of our food and belongings. . . . This trip may be considered as one of the hardest one could make in a lifetime, for in addition to all the difficulty we had in carrying all our food and belongings through the woods where there were no trails, and when we were often obliged to go up and down mountains with heavy loads, we also found some very dangerous rapids, full of great boulders and rocks, and of extraordinary length. (From the Account of the Voyage of Monsieur de Meulles to Acadie. 1686. W.I. Morse, *Acadiensia Nova*, Vol. I, pp. 110–111.)

The party arrived at Port Rossignol on the fifth day, no doubt to the immense relief of its French members. For the Indians who were accustomed to such travel, the journey over open lakes and rivers provided a safer and more pleasant alternative to travelling through the almost impenetrable forest. It also represented a much shorter route than sailing round the end of the peninsula, though the time saved would depend on the weather encountered on the coastal route, and on the degree of experience of the travellers.

Map 8:1 Jean-Baptiste-Louis Franquelin. Part of "Carte Gé[né]ralle du Voyage que Mons. De Meulles Intendant. . .a fait par ordre du Roy, et commencé le 2e Novembre & finy le 6e Juillet 1868 ensuivant, comprenant Toutes les Terres de l'Acadie, Isle du Cap Breton, [etc.]", 1686. Manuscript.

ECHELLE DE VINGT LIEUES

1686.

The cross-country route following the waterways is similar to that taken today by Highway 8 from Annapolis to the centre of the province. From there southward, the main highway diverges to bypass the lakes; a minor road still connects it with the north shore of Lake Rossignol at Low Landing. From Indian Gardens on the lake's south shore, a road follows the Mersey to join the highway again just above Milton. Although Franquelin's map does not show relief, the very existence of the waterways suggests the possibility of a relatively easy land route, with—despite Demeulle's "mountains"—fewer difficult gradients than elsewhere.

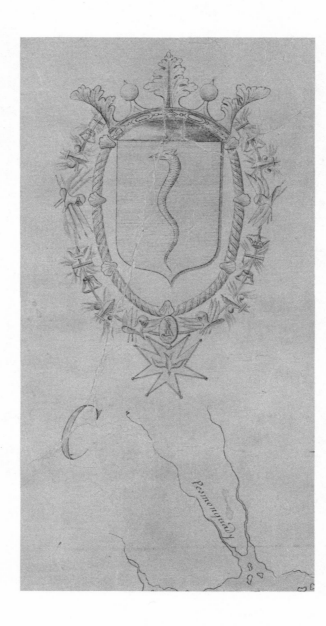

It is interesting to note that the canoes were also used to travel between Port Rossignol and LaHave, the intendant's next destination. The Micmac obviously found travelling on water easier than travelling on foot along the rugged and indented shore.

The value of this map, apart from its stated objective of recording Demeulle's journey, is its clear indication of the routes taken and its illustration of the means of transport used. It demonstrates how the Micmac's experience in travelling through an environment that seemed hostile and uninviting to Europeans was to be invaluable to the settlers who shared their territory.

The French legacy

This French map was made some time after 1738 (the year in which Abbé Le Loutre began his missionary work in Acadia) but before the foundation of Halifax. Although the outline of the coast is very crudely executed, and the rivers grossly exaggerated and in some cases poorly oriented, it shows with great clarity the chief river and portage routes used during the eighteenth century prior to the expulsion of the Acadians.

By this time, Nova Scotia was in English hands, but the Acadians and the Micmac still constituted almost the entire population, the exception being the English garrison at *Port Royal* (Annapolis). Along the Annapolis Valley from Port Royal to *Les Mines* (Minas) and around the Minas Basin to *Gobequit*, more usually spelled Cobequid (now Truro), Acadian settlement was well established, as we can see from the map. Missions had been set up among the natives, including Le Loutre's mission at *Chebenacady* (Shubenacadie), and another at *Artigoniche* (Antigonish), both of which appear here. Beside the main settlement, small communities of French inhabitants were scattered around the region from *Beaubassin* (Cumberland Basin) to *Pobomcoup* (Pubnico) at the western end of the province and *Ched-abouctou* (Guysborough) at the eastern end. Neighbouring *Isle Royale* (Cape Breton Island) was entirely in French hands, with the population mostly concentrated at Louisbourg.

The map indicates very clearly the network of communications that connected the various settlements. The centre of Acadian population had shifted eastward from Port Royal, and the Minas Basin had become the hub of a fairly elaborate system of waterways and overland trails that radiated from it in all directions.

Between the Annapolis and Minas Basins, the *R[iv- ière] du Port Royal* (Annapolis River) links the town of

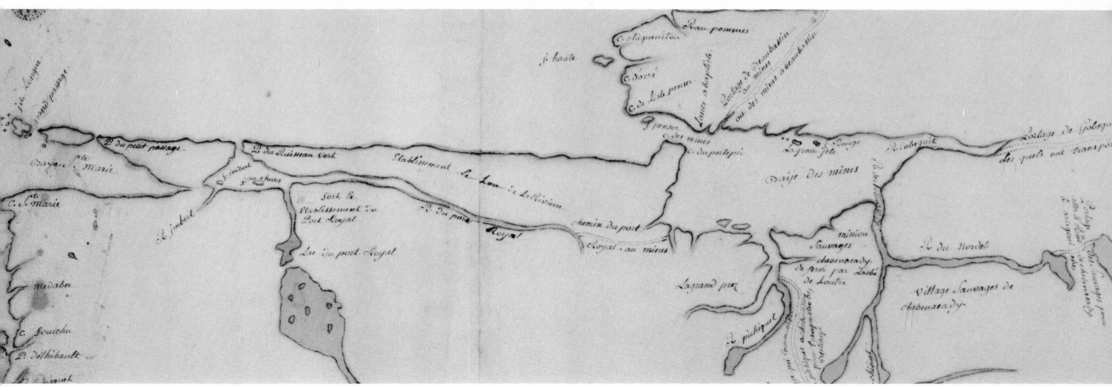

Map 8:2 Anonymous. Map of Acadia, Undated [1738–48]. Manuscript.

Port Royal and the settlements (*établissements*) along the river to an overland route marked *"chemin du Port Royal au[x] mines"* (road from Annapolis to Minas). Having made this journey, the traveller had a wide choice of destinations. *Grand Pré, Pichiquit* (usually Pisiquid, now Windsor) and *Gobequit* all lay along the Minas Basin shore or a short distance inland. The routes radiating from the Basin gave access to many other parts of the province.

By taking the land route southwards from the mouth of the Avon River at *Pichiquit*, it was possible to reach *Chibouctou* (Halifax) harbour through the head of the Bedford Basin. This route, the map tells us, was a drove road, used to move cattle from *Pichiquit* to *Chibouctou*. These cattle were intended for shipment to the French settlers on Cape Breton Island, where pastureland was scarce.[4]

The *Pichiquit* (possibly St-Croix) River is shown as forming a potential link with a vaguely suggested river running into St. Margarets Bay. In fact, this route is probably the one which appears on the following map as going through Panuke or Ponhook Lake to Mahone Bay by way of East River. The unnamed (Avon) river, shown here to the south of Grand Pré, seems to have served only the settlements along its lower course at that time. It was only with later population growth along the South Shore that these routes became significant.

A second route from Minas Basin to Halifax was by way of the *Chebenacady* (Shubenacadie) River. This traditional Micmac trail follows the river to its source in Shubenacadie (or Grand) Lake, and joins the Dartmouth lake system by a short portage. This route was to be the basis of the Shubenacadie Canal proposal at the end of the century (see Map 8:5).

Another branch of the Shubenacadie system leads to a portage, suggested but not marked on the map, to the *R[ivière] de Mouchoudaboit* (Musquodoboit), and a third follows the *Rivière du Nordet* (Stewiacke River) to join the St Mary's River system at an unidentified *Lac Ste Marie*. The overland trail between these two systems is marked *"Portage des Sauvages pour aller [de] la Riv[ière] de Chebenacady à Artigoniche"*—a native portage linking the Shubenacadie River with Antigonish. This somewhat unlikely sounding description begins to make sense as we see the trail following the West St Mary's River, then turning north (upstream) towards what is probably today's Lochaber Lake. From there another portage connects with more lakes and a river which, despite its orientation, seems to represent the South River. South River does lead to Antigonish. There is in addition, of course, the southward route down St Mary's River that forms a link with the Atlantic Coast.

East of St Mary's River, and parallel to it, is an overland route between Chedabucto Bay and the Atlantic. Named *Portage de Tarbé*, it links the present Cook's Cove to Tor Bay by a portage from the head of the inlet to a lake, and by way of Larry's River. This relatively short portage route was valuable in that it avoided the necessity of taking small craft around the rocks and islands off Canso and took many miles off the coastal route.

Returning to Minas Basin, we find another important route leading from the head of Cobequid Bay overland to *"Tatamigouche."* Although described as a "portage" between these points, the route is also identified as the one by which cattle "destined for *l'Isle Royale*" were driven to Tatamagouche to be loaded onto ships. Once again, the orientation is faulty, but the route is quite clear.

The final route from the Minas Basin runs northeast across the Chignecto Peninsula towards Beaubassin; in fact this probably represents the north-south route which reaches the Cumberland Basin at River Hebert, but the representation of the coast is too imprecise for certain identification. From *Beaubassin*, the portage to *Baie Verte* became a relatively simple matter, as shown on the map.

The last major route on the map consists of the waterways and portages between *Port Royal* and *Port Rossignol*. Although not specifically identified on this map, the rivers and lakes are clearly those used in the previous century by Demeulle and his party, and presumably by the Micmac for many years before that. With the majority of Acadians living on the Fundy side of the province, this trail was probably still used almost exclusively by the Micmac.

The network of communications shown on this map was, except for the two drove roads used for cattle, based on travel by water in summer and on snowshoes over the ice in winter. By those means, the settlers' initial dependence on coastal navigation was reduced considerably. But there were still many places that could be reached only by sea, including many of the fishing ports. It is probably for this reason that the other features of this map include the marking, with a conventional anchor symbol, of safe harbours around the coast, and the notation of soundings off the South and Eastern Shores.

The map indicates, above all, the presence of a population which, with the help of the Micmac, had become familiar with the interior of their territory, and had learned how to travel within it by the traditional native routes. The patterns of transportation that they established supported both their commercial endeavours (e.g. cattle export routes) and the need for internal communication among different settlements. Rough though the map is, it is a valuable record of a transitional stage in the development of inland transportation.

Routes from Halifax & Lunenburg

This map, made in 1755 or soon afterwards, differs in many respects from the previous one. Drawn to a larger scale, it shows evidence of a detailed survey of parts of the coast, particularly the Lunenburg–Mahone Bay, St. Margarets Bay and Halifax Harbour areas. The compass rose and rhumbs, and the soundings of the harbour entrances, make it a more serviceable aid to navigation than Map 8:2. Despite its title, it is not merely a navigational chart: some inland features also appear. Although no attempt is made to indicate relief, a number of lakes and rivers are shown in some detail, and overland routes are clearly marked. A fair degree of accuracy has been achieved, even though the courses of some of the rivers and the shape of many of the lakes are apparently conjectured rather than surveyed.

The area covered by the map reflects a major shift in the centres of population from the Fundy to the Atlantic shores since the making of the previous map. The foundation of Halifax in 1749 as a garrison town and administrative centre for the colony was followed by the settlement of the "foreign protestants" in Lunenburg in 1753, to counterbalance the Acadian Catholic population around the Minas Basin. The English place names on the map, and the anglicization of earlier French and Indian names, illustrate this new phase of settlement. With the establishment of two distinct centres of population in the area came the need to provide for communication between them, and from each to small neighbouring settlements, as well as with the rest of the province. In this map we see how such communications began to develop.

Looking first at the western side of the map, we find that Lunenburg is the focal point of a small group of roads. The most obvious of these is the road leading to the Block House, an outer defensive position near which a settlement of the same name has grown up. The road itself follows the route of the present Highway 3

from Lunenburg to Maders Cove, but then takes the more protected route later occupied by the Canadian National railroad track running behind Mahone Bay.

The other routes from Lunenburg involve a combination of land and water travel. From the earliest days of French settlement two well established portage trails had been known between the LaHave River and an arm of Merliguash (Lunenburg) Bay and Rose Bay respectively. When this map was made, the routes were utilized for roads linking Lunenburg with the older LaHave settlement. These roads still exist, one running through Indian Path, whose name testifies to the antiquity of the route, and the other between Rose Bay and Riverport.

At the time when this map was made, Halifax had been established for about six years. It appears as a major settlement, with Dartmouth occupying a small point of land on the opposite shore. At the eastern extremity of the map stands Lawrencetown. This planned community did not thrive, and was abandoned in 1757 (see Map 7:10, p. 120); by this time, however, a road shown on this map as the Lawrence Town Road had been cleared from Dartmouth to the town site,

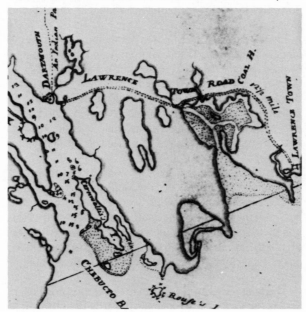

Map 8:3 Anonymous. "A Chart of the Coast of Nova Scotia from Port Maltois to Lawrence Town," *ca* 1755. Manuscript.

following, roughly, the route of the present Cole Harbour Road (Highway 207).

Northwards from Dartmouth, the old Shubenacadie trail is shown as "an Indian path to the lakes by which and the River Shebenacadie they go to Cobequid." This route does not appear to have changed or been improved since Map 8:2 was made. The other link with the Minas Basin, the overland "Pisiquid Road," was vital for bringing agricultural produce to Halifax, and represents an upgrading of the Acadian drove road of the previous decade. Following approximately the route of Highway 1, it was linked with Halifax by a road constructed in 1749 along the peninsula and around the Bedford Basin. From Fort Sackville, where the two roads meet, yet another road leads eastwards towards lakes giving access to the Shubenacadie portage system (see Map 8:5). Slightly farther north, a dotted line marks the route of "Capt. Floyer's March to the Bason of Mines," skirting the western shore of Grand Lake. This route was apparently unsatisfactory, as no permanent road was constructed on this side of the lake.

There was still at this time no established road linking Halifax with Lunenburg. A potential route, not very different from that now followed by Highway 103 but rather more inland, is shown here by the single dotted line identifying "Capt. Lieut. Lewis's March with a party of Rangers to Lunenburg in Feb. 1755 and from thence." It runs from the neck of the Halifax peninsula through Hammonds Plains and the Head of St. Margarets Bay to pick up the road to Lunenburg at Blockhouse. Since the journey was made in winter, the fact that the trail leads straight across lakes and rivers indicates travel over the ice, which was easier than clearing

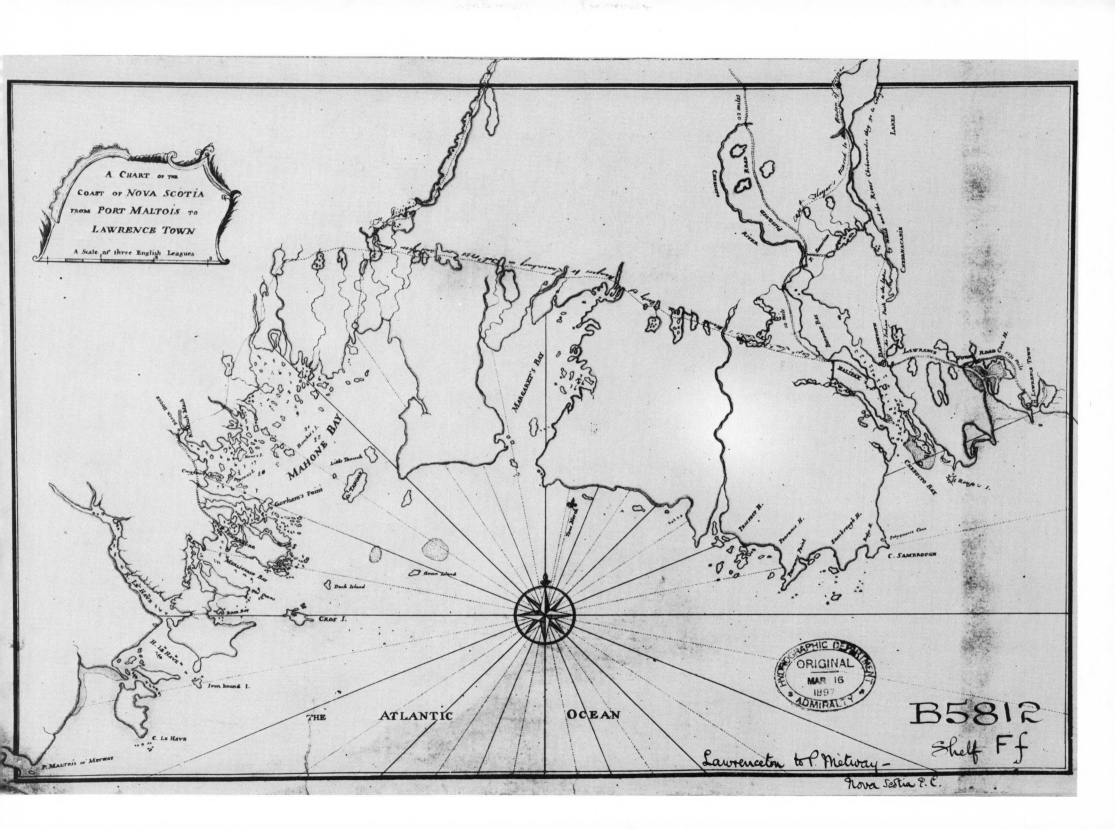

A CHART OF THE COAST OF NOVA SCOTIA FROM PORT MALTOIS TO LAWRENCE TOWN

A Scale of three English Leagues

MAHONE BAY

MARGARET'S BAY

THE ATLANTIC OCEAN

a path through the forest. Nevertheless, the going must have been difficult, and normal travel between Halifax and Lunenburg continued to be by sea.

Cutting across this route is a trail marked "To Pisiquid," from the shore of Mahone Bay near the present town of Chester. This is clearly a canoe and portage route, utilizing the long Panuke or Ponhook Lake from which the St. Croix River runs north to Windsor. Until the construction of a parallel land route (Highway 14), this route provided the only link between the Minas Basin and Mahone Bay.

Despite the appearance of "roads" on the map, contemporary accounts remind us that travel was still by no means easy. Ten years or more later, Governor Francklin was to write from Halifax to the Lords Commissioners for Trade and Plantations:

For at present although several Paths have been cut to some of the settlements; yet none but that to Windsor have been so far compleated, as to admit of carriages, which is yet in an imperfect state, nor is any passable for horses without great Difficulty, (that to Annapolis excepted) on account of the swamps and Rivers over which there are no Bridges; so that they may be deemed a Direction to foot travellers only; and although many settlements are forming for the fishery on the coast between this and Canso, they have no communication but by water only, and all the settlements to the westward of Lunenburg are in the same state. (from 20 Sept. 1766. PAC, NSA, LXXVIII, 115–118)[5]

Map 8:4 confirms the construction of a road from Halifax to Lunenburg, following Lewis's route. All but the hardy, however, continued for many years to prefer to make the journey by sea.

Despite the enormous problems involved, a network of roads was beginning to develop between Halifax and the rest of the province. With some modifications, the routes used in the 1750s formed the basis for the province's modern highway system.

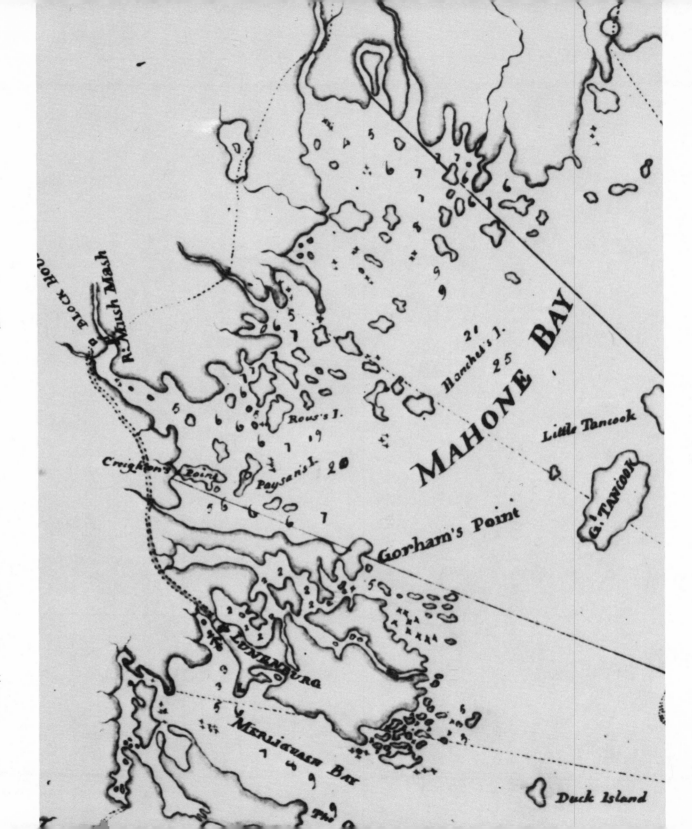

Roads & Post House

This map indicates that by the end of the eighteenth century, overland communications were becoming established in parts of central, northern and western Nova Scotia. The eastern end of the province was still accessible only by sea, or, for the adventurous, by the old portage routes, but roads now linked Halifax to many other settlements. The routes that had appeared in earlier maps were now supplemented by others, constructed or projected, to serve the communities established as a result of loyalist and other immigration in the 1780s. A number of these new settlements are shown on the map, as well as the boundaries of the counties as they existed then.

While the quality of all the roads shown in the map was undoubtedly poor, some of them were by this time well established. Among these was the official "Post Road" from Halifax to Annapolis Royal, with post houses at Windsor and Horton. Following the route of the present Highway 1 for much of the way, it ran along the north bank of the Annapolis River to Granville. Travellers to Annapolis crossed the river by ferry — Hick's Ferry, as the settlement there became known until the building of a bridge gave rise to the new name of Bridgetown — and came to the head of the Basin by road along the south side. From the post house at Annapolis the road gave way to a water route over the Annapolis Basin to Digby, where there was another post house, and thence across the Bay of Fundy to Saint John. The post houses, with the distances between them, are shown on the map; a legend in one corner also names their proprietors. The houses were staging points where rest, refreshment and probably a change of horses were available for official messengers and other travellers; their existence testifies to the importance of this route within the province itself, and as a link with New Brunswick and Canada.

The other route to New Brunswick ran along the southeastern side of the Shubenacadie River to Truro (see Map 8:3), round the head of Cobequid Bay to Onslow, and northwest to the border. The northern section does not appear on maps of the 1750s, but in the title of a map made in 1774 by Charles Morris, Chief Surveyor,[6] it is described as "the road leading from Cumberland to Fort Belcher in the Township of Onslow at the Head of Cobequid Bay, This Road will be the Grand Road of Communication thro' the County of Cumberland and Halifax. . . ." Now superseded by the Trans-Canada Highway, this "Grand Road of Communication" appears to correspond, at least in part, with the older Route 204.

From Onslow, a road that also serves as the boundary between Halifax and Cumberland Counties crosses the province to Tatamagouche, probably joining the old Acadian drove road seen in Map 8:2, and following the North River. Farther south, another road leads across to Pictou. We know something of the origins of this road from a note on a 1785 map of the Pictou area (Map 7:11, p. 123). The map shows a road running parallel with the East River from the south side of the harbour, where a number of lots had been granted. It is described as "A Road marked out nearly in this direction which will fall into the great Road leading to Halifax thro the County of Sydney, from the Settlements forming at Chedabuctou (now called New Manchester) Antigonish and all the Eastern Coast, which Main Road passes within about 4 Miles of the 2,000 acres Tract." Clearly the eastern section of this "main road" was not sufficiently advanced two years later to be included in the present map, but the section from Pictou to Truro was in place. This same road, now represented by Route 4 and the Trans-Canada Highway, remains the chief route to eastern Nova Scotia.

Across the Minas Basin, the old portage route crossing the Chignecto Peninsula (see Maps 5:2, p. 63 and 8:2, p. 134) appears in this map as the Chignecto Road, which still runs between Parrsboro and River Hebert.

The route taken by Captain Lewis from Halifax to Lunenburg in 1755 (see Map 8:3) appears on this map as an accepted road, as does the old portage trail between Windsor and Chester. Branching off from the Lunenburg road at the county boundary is a "road marked out by Gov' Parr's order in 1784," providing a second link between Halifax and Annapolis. Although this road does not exist as a major route today, there is evidence that parts of it were cleared and passable by 1785, when a note on a map of Lunenburg County (Map 4:4, p. 55) describes it as "a Proposed Road from Annapolis to Halifax marked out by order of the Governor on many parts of which Loyal Emigrants & Soldiers are settling." Where the road crosses the upper part of the LaHave River, it is stated that "Captain Miller and other Loyalists are settling on this part of the Road." On the modern map, parts of the western section of the road appear to survive between Annapolis and Albany Cross, and between Dalhousie and New Ross. As for Captain Lewis' route, it was to be replaced, first by the shore route taken by Highway 3, and then by the more direct 103. The road marked between Windsor and Chester still appears to represent the old Panuke Lake and East River route; it has been replaced by today's Highway 14, following the Avon River.

The remaining road across the province is that shown as running between Shelburne and Annapolis. This road is also referred to on a 1783 map of Shelburne (Map 7:11, p. 123) and probably represents the existing road through Lower, Middle and Upper Ohio. No trace of the rest of its length can be located on a modern map. The road from Shelburne to Argyle also peters out today after a few miles, superseded by the coastal route by way of Barrington.

The early road between Shelburne and Barrington followed approximately the route of Highways 3 and 103. The link to Liverpool is shown as lying rather

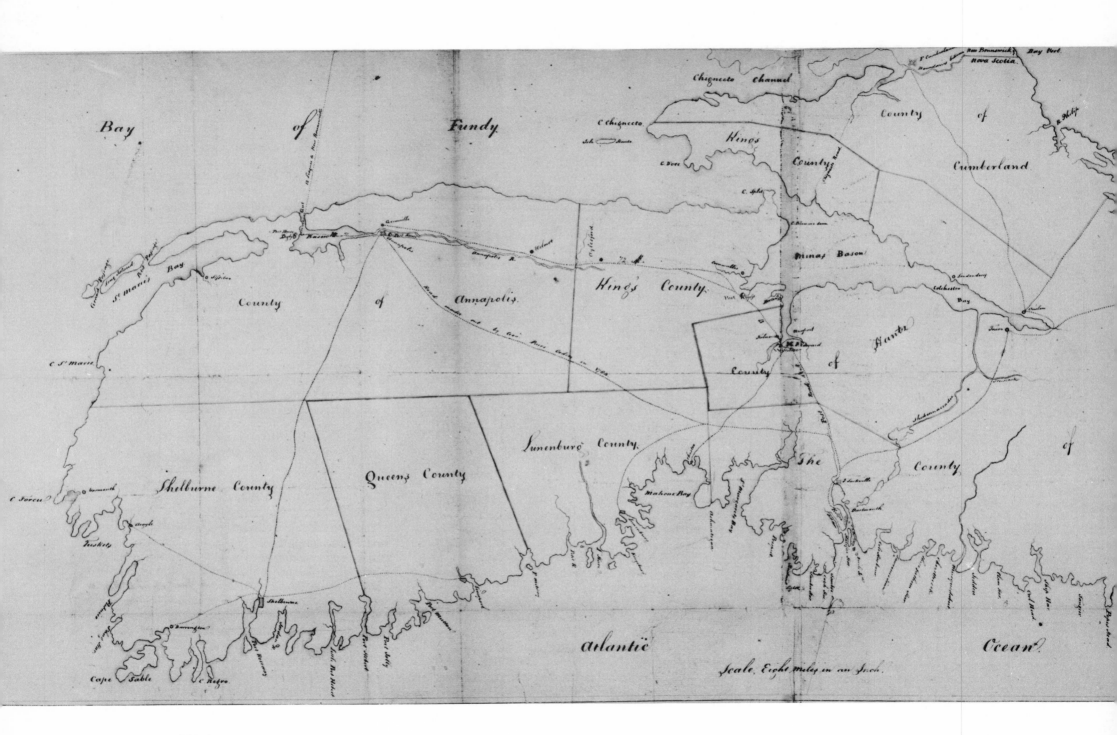

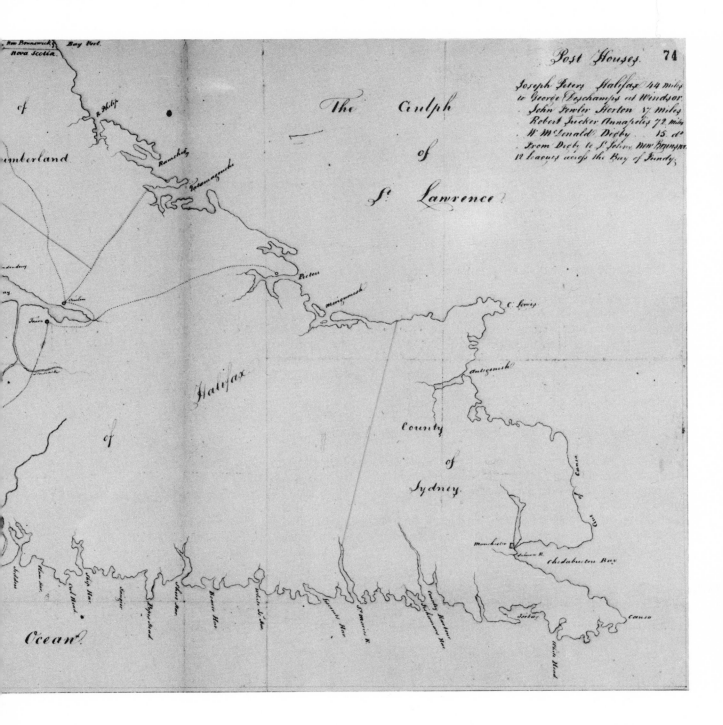

Post Houses. 74

Joseph Peters Halifax 44 miles
to George Deschamps at Windsor.
John Fowler Horton 17 miles
Robert Tucker Annapolis 72 miles
W. McDonald Digby 15 do
From Digby to St John, New Brunswick
12 Leagues across the Bay of Fundy.

Map 8:4 Anonymous. Map of Nova Scotia showing Post Houses, "Enclosed in letter of 25th Nov. 1787 Parr to Nepean." Manuscript.

more inland, but parallel to the modern highway. The new loyalist settlements had created a need for over-land communication as an alternative to sea travel along this rugged coast and southwest Nova Scotia's high-ways system began to take shape as a result.

Not all the roads planned, or even cleared, in the eighteenth century survived to become modern high-ways. Most of those shown on this map were undoubt-edly primitive and unpleasant to travel on for much of the year, and in unpopulated areas their maintenance must have proved almost impossible. The idea of driv-ing direct trails through the wilderness succumbed to the reality of the harsh prevailing conditions.

The absence today even of tracks marking the loca-tion of roads such as that planned between Upper Ohio and Annapolis can be attributed to a preference for safer, more congenial routes through the more popu-lated coastal areas. Travellers, whether on foot, on horseback or in horse drawn vehicles, would, given a choice, willingly take a longer route in order to be assured of shelter, assistance in emergencies, and relative safety from attack by human or animal pred-ators. Regardless of Governor Parr's designs, security must have been a strong motivation factor in the even-tual development of the coastal road system of Nova Scotia. Moreover, the low-lying coastal areas offered more level sites where road construction could be carried on more easily. Technology has only recently enabled travellers to drive securely across the tracts of uninhabited wilderness that are still found in parts of inland Nova Scotia. Today's inland roads correspond more closely to the natural routeways used by the Mic-macs and the Acadians than to those which the British colonists tried to impose on its uninhabited and inhos-pitable interior. In the late eighteenth century, the "Post Road" was the only reasonably reliable highway in the region and it is still in use today.

The Shubenacadie Canal

The late eighteenth century was a period of enthusiastic canal building in Britain, and it is not surprising that the English settlers in Nova Scotia recognized the possibilities for similar development of the ancient water route between Dartmouth and Cobequid. This fairly large scale map, oriented with north to the right, analyzes the streams and lakes between Halifax Harbour and the navigable tidewater of the Shubenacadie River. It describes, by means of a legend, the physical obstacles that the builders of the Shubenacadie Canal would have to overcome in order to create a continuous navigable waterway to the Minas Basin from the Atlantic coast. Despite the falls, rapids, currents and a portage which he notes, the cartographer is optimistic: "The whole distance where there is not now Navigable Water is but 3 Miles & ½."

Residents of Dartmouth will be familiar with the remains (now partially restored) of the canal, which was eventually begun in 1826. The canal was probably the most ambitious engineering project undertaken in Nova Scotia up to that time; it was described in some detail by T.C. Haliburton in his *History of Nova Scotia*, published in 1829, three years after the formation of the Shubenacadie Canal Company:
The artificial communication is confined to a few places, advantage being taken, when practicable, of navigating the lakes and channels of the river; when completed, small stream boats, of 12 or 14 horse power, will be employed for towing; each boat performing the passage from Halifax harbour to the mouth of the Shubenacadie in 15 hours, and carrying each four trade boats of 30 tons burden. (Vol. 2, p. 28)

Unfortunately, the technology employed for the initial construction proved inadequate for the severe ice conditions produced by a Nova Scotia winter. Physical setbacks and recurring financial problems delayed the opening of the canal until the 1860s, when for a few years it provided the long dreamed of water link between the two sides of the province.

In spite of the problems encountered, the project as outlined in this map was not unreasonable. Although relief is not indicated in a conventional way, the legend gives details of the differences in level between the different sections of the route. Once the steep rise at the Dartmouth end of the system, where the watershed lies close to the Atlantic coast, had been overcome by a series of locks, relatively few obstacles would have to be negotiated on the more gentle northerly descent. The already navigable waters included the Dartmouth Lakes (Banook and Micmac), "D", on the ascent, and the first, second, third and fourth Shubenacadie Lakes (Charles, William, Thomas and Fletcher's) leading to Great Lake (Shubenacadie Grand Lake) and the Shubenacadie River. The long distances over which uninterrupted navigation was already possible, as the Micmac had realized long ago, made this a very advantageous route.

As well as the survey for the proposed canal, we find in this map evidence of the further development of land communications which had taken place over the previous 40 years. Except for the details of the project itself, the map is fairly roughly drawn, but it gives some idea of the routes leading from Halifax at the end of the eighteenth century.

A second road out of the town had been constructed on the peninsula, parallel to the earlier one, to join the road to Sackville near the present Fairview Cove. The road beside Bedford Basin now had a distinctive landmark, the Lodge. This edifice was at the time of the making of the map the residence of Prince Edward, Duke of Kent. The round building that served as a music room is all that remains of the estate, and is visible from the present Bedford Highway; the name Prince's Lodge has also survived here.

The old road from Sackville across the province was now known as the Windsor Road, this name having supplanted Pisiquid. The road branching off at (Lower) Sackville to meet the Shubenacadie system at Fletcher's, or No. 4 Lake, had been extended to form an alternative land route, the "Road from Halifax to Cobequid." It ran along the eastern side of the Shubenacadie River, thus avoiding bridging the river below Grand Lake. The easier crossing at the head of Fletcher's Lake is identified as "McNabb's Bridge." The section of the road near Lower Sackville is still known as the Old Cobequid Road. It has been superseded for practical purposes by Highways 2 and 102, which run from Enfield to Shubenacadie on the western side of the river where the ground is less marshy. Part of the old road, through Keys (Gays River), is still in use.

The map also shows the existence, by this time, of the road from Dartmouth to Preston, now part of Highway 7. The unidentified lakes near which it passes are clearly Topsail and Loon Lakes. Although this first section of what was to become the main highway along the Eastern Shore is not very impressive, it shows how the expansion of the population outside of Halifax brought with it a growing network of communications.

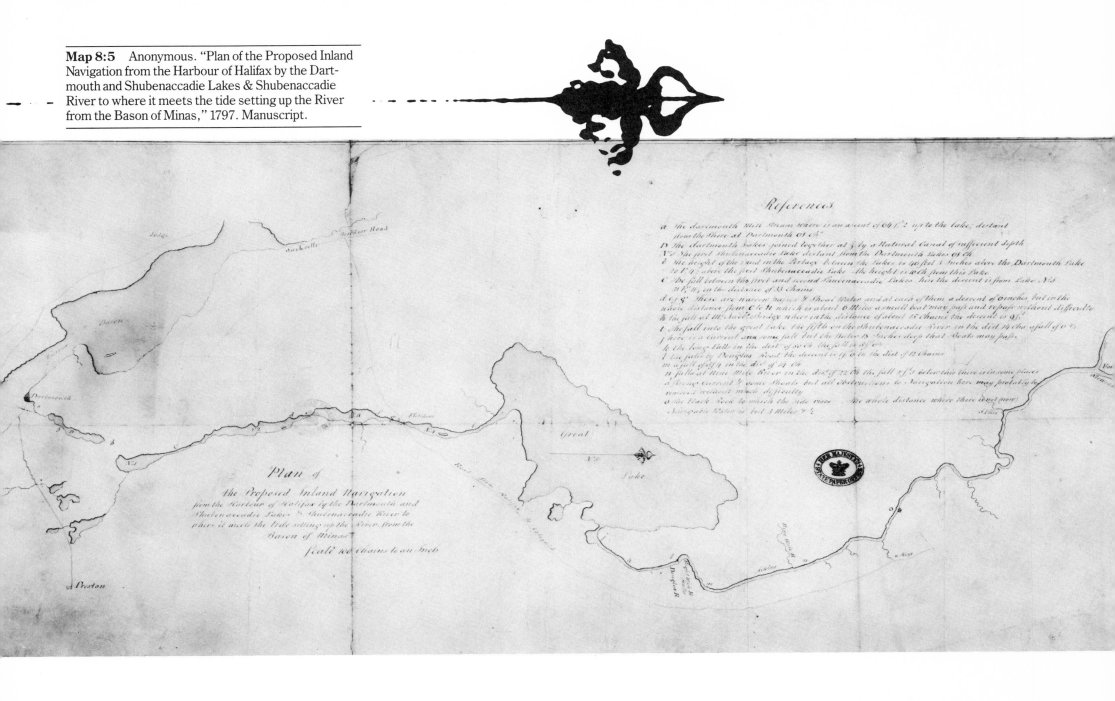

Map 8:5 Anonymous. "Plan of the Proposed Inland Navigation from the Harbour of Halifax by the Dartmouth and Shubenaccadie Lakes & Shubenaccadie River to where it meets the tide setting up the River from the Bason of Minas," 1797. Manuscript.

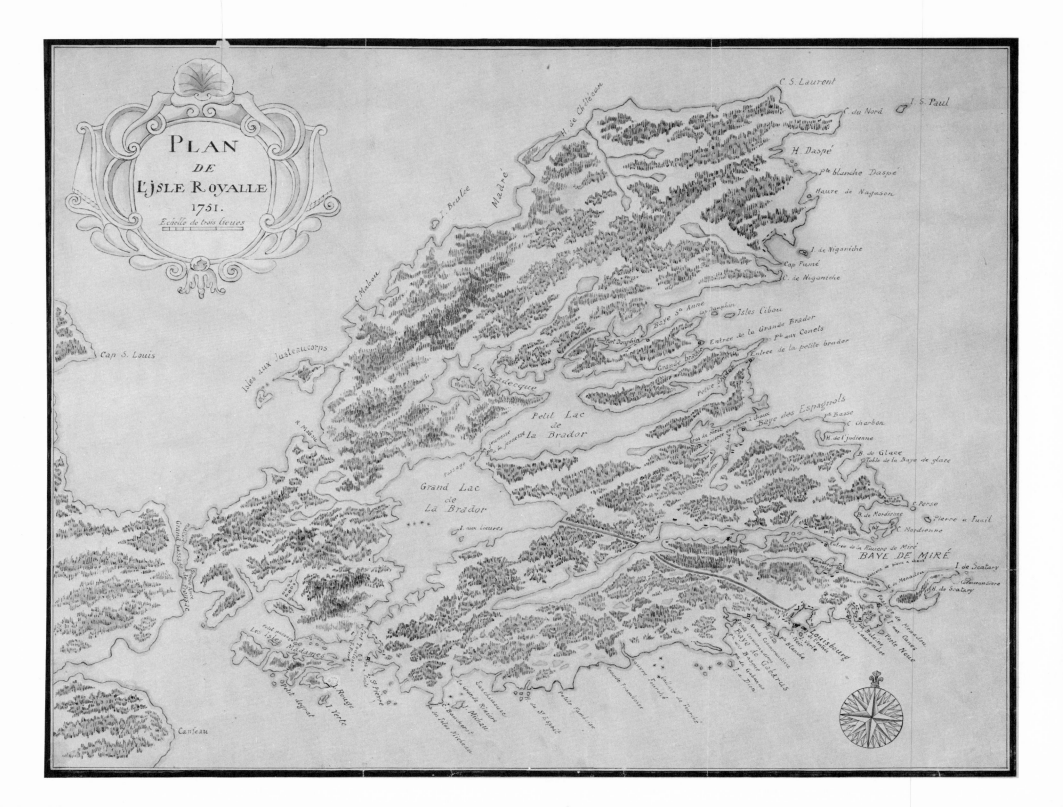

PLAN
DE
L'ISLE ROYALLE
1751.
Echelle de trois lieues

C. S. Laurent
C. du Nord
I. S. Paul
H. Daspé
Pte blanche Daspé
Havre de Nagason
H. de Château
Madré
I. Brulée
I. de Niganiche
Cap Fumé
C. de Niganiche
C Mabou
Baye Ste Anne
Isles Cibou
Cap Dauphin
Port Dauphin
Entrée de la Grande Brador
Pte aux Conets
Cap S. Louis
Isles aux Justeaucorps
La Badecque
Grande brador
Entrée de la petite brador
Petite Brador
R. Mabou
Petit Lac de La Brador
pte Basse
Baye des Espagnols
Bras de nord est de pierre à fusil
C charbon
H. de l'Indienne
B. de Glace
Table de la Baye de glace
jeunesse
Passage de la jeunesse
Grand Lac de La Brador
C Perse
B. de Mordienne
Pierre à Fusil
C. Mordienne
I aux Lieures
Entrée de la Riviere de Miré
BAYE DE MIRÉ
Grand passage de Fouchie
I. de Scatary
Passage de Menadou
Commandiere
H. de Scatary
Louisbourg
Petite Noue
Baye de Gabarus
Les Isles Madames
Petit passage
I. St Pierre
I Rouge
I Verte
Petit Degrat
Grand Degrat
I. Michau
Canseau

Travel on Cape Breton Island

T his map of *Isle Royale* (Cape Breton Island) dates from the final period of French occupation of the island, between the first and second sieges of Louisbourg. Conventionally oriented with north at the top, it is a fairly accurate representation, particularly of the coastal areas, although like so many maps of the period it provides only conjectural details of the upper reaches of many rivers. The most immediately striking feature of the map is the representation of the dense forest which covers the whole of the interior; the settlements, here as in mainland Nova Scotia, cling precariously to the shore or to the deep inlets of the east coast.

Since 1713, except for a short period after the first siege, Cape Breton Island had been the chief French outpost on the Atlantic coast. The population, apart from the garrison at Louisbourg, consisted of small groups established in fishing ports along the coast, and a scattered agricultural community along the *Rivière de Miré* (Mira). Their numbers had been increased by the addition of some Acadians from the mainland, particularly in the *Baye des Espagnols* (Spanish Bay, now Sydney) area. Settlement was confined almost entirely to the southeast half of the island, with a small group also at *Nigoniche* (Ingonish).

It is clear from the map that the Bras d'Or lake system, consisting of *Grand Lac de La Brador, Petit Lac de La Brador* and *La Badecque*, formed the basis for inland transportation between different parts of the island. Smaller inlets gave access from the coast to settlements such as *Port Dauphin* (Englishtown) on *Baye Ste Anne*, and what is now Sydney on the *Baye des Espagnols*. The Mira River provided access to the settlements scattered along its shores.

These water routes were supplemented, as on the mainland, by land routes that were still essentially portages. Of these, probably the earliest used by Europeans was the portage route between the Atlantic Ocean and the Bras d'Or lakes, at *St. Pierre* (St. Peter's), which appears on this map. This road dates back to the 1650s, when Nicolas Denys operated a fishery there. In his *Description de l'Amérique Septentrionale* (1672) Denys writes of the narrow neck of land that separates the lake from the ocean: "I had a road built in this space, to manhandle shallops from one sea to the other, and to avoid the circuit which would be necessary by sea."[7] This route would, of course, have already been familiar to the natives. It is the route followed today by the St. Peter's Canal, which was constructed to avoid the portage and to provide continuous navigation, by means of locks, between the two bodies of water.

A second land route, from *La Badecque* (Baddeck Bay) to St. Ann's Harbour, provides another short cut from the lake system to the settlement near *Port Dauphin*. The third, and longest, overland route is that leading from the eastern part of the *Grand Lac de La Brador*, by way of the *Miré*, to Louisbourg. This vital "back door" link between the fortress and other parts of the island was used for carrying agricultural produce from the Mira farms to the garrison. It also provided a protected route for supplies brought in from Acadia, which could be carried by way of St. Peter's and the lakes rather than along the coast.

The concentration of the population in the south and east parts of the island, and the rugged nature of the rest of the terrain, account for the absence of land routes in the north and west. Undoubtedly the rivers and lakes shown on the map were used by the native inhabitants, but there must have been little incentive for the French to penetrate the heavily wooded highland area. And, as on the mainland, there were still many places that remained inaccessible except by coastal navigation.

Map 8:6 Anonymous. "Plan de L'Isle Royale," 1751. Manuscript.

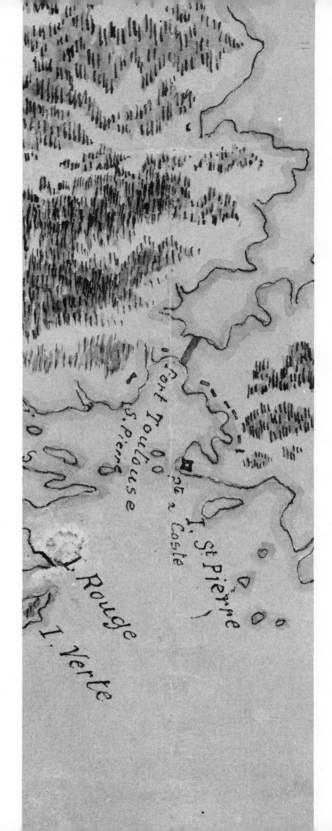

Conclusion

The examples we have looked at are intended as a representative selection, rather than an exhaustive collection, of the maps of Nova Scotia made during the seventeenth and eighteenth centuries. Some are purely descriptive of what their authors observed. Others reflect the possibilities that the cartographers saw for further settlement, for community fortification, for the economic development of fishing, agriculture, industry or trade, and for communications. The maps were made by a wide variety of people, and reflect their different interests, concerns and responsibilities.

Initially, mapmaking and exploration went hand in hand, the one being the record of the other. By surveying an area and committing the topographical details to paper, the pioneers provided a visual image that would permanently identify the features they had observed. Later surveys with more sophisticated instruments would refine and increase awareness of the area depicted, but even a crude map established shapes, names and spatial relationships that are the beginnings of scientific knowledge.

With knowledge came an increased sense of power and control over an environment that had been reduced, on one level, to a series of lines on a piece of paper. These impressions of power and control could be transferred from the mapmaker, who had actually seen the area represented, to colonial bureaucrats and politicians in Paris or London. Printed maps were then made available to the European public who derived from them an awareness of distant lands in which they now had a vested interest. While in some cases the transition from the manuscript to the printed version of a map involved a degree of "sanitization," knowledge was nevertheless increased by its publication.

Manuscript maps themselves were not always free from a certain amount of editing on the part of their authors. Each cartographer brought to the task his own background knowledge, his personal interests and often those of his employers, which might well be reflected in his maps. Because of this, it is usually helpful to have some idea of the circumstances under which a map was made when studying it as an historical document.

Not all maps show a very clear distinction between existing and proposed elements. A degree of caution should therefore be used in interpreting a map in isolation from other contemporary records, unless its author has made his position clear in the title or in annotations. A map, even one bearing a date, may not always provide an accurate picture of an area at that particular moment. While natural physical features are likely to be shown as they appeared to the cartographer, some man-made features may be suspect. For example, a map may indicate the existence of buildings, defences, roads, etc., which were indeed there at the time it was made. But they may have only been planned, and not yet constructed; or they might have been constructed differently, or never constructed at all. There are great differences, to take an early example, between Champlain's and Lescarbot's maps of Port Royal (Map 7:3, p. 101, and 7:4, p. 104). Both were published as illustrations of accounts of Acadia, but while Champlain's plan is confirmed by both those accounts, Lescarbot's is clearly in the realm of fantasy and romantic speculation.

In later maps, too, the potential for propaganda should be kept in mind. Colonial officials were often at pains to put their achievements and intentions in the best possible light when reporting to their superiors.

When accompanying a request for further funding, the plan for an orderly, well laid out town need not dwell too heavily on the chaos evident during the construction period. Roads drawn across maps may have been impassable by European standards, but they represented potential routes linking one community with another that were to the credit of the administration. This is not to detract from the overall value of most of the maps sent back to authorities in Paris and London; but while a modern map may show a road under construction which has, in fact, been completed by the time the map is published, early maps often show completed roads where they are only projected.

Maps indicating land holdings may bear the date when they were drawn up, but the record of ownership may have been added to as further grants were made. This is often made clear by annotations and additional dating, but in doubtful cases it may be necessary to seek confirmation from other sources. Conversely, an undated map may be pinpointed, at least within a certain period, by referring to other records of features, place names, grantees, etc., found on it.

We have observed in these examples from over two centuries of the mapping of Nova Scotia a general progression from a sketchy awareness of the coastline to a detailed knowledge of much of the interior. The transition from the relatively primitive maps of the early period to the more sophisticated late eighteenth century surveys is based on the development of sounder geographical knowledge and greater technical skills. But the progression was not necessarily a smooth one, and it was marked both by some outstandingly good cartography and some notably inadequate surveys. This is due in part to differences in skill and experience on the part of the map-makers, and to some extent reflects the time available during which they could become familiar with the area depicted. Jean Delabat's remarkable 1708 manuscript map of Port Royal (Map 2:3, p. 20) is the work of a trained military engineer of considerable seniority and experience who had spent a number of years in the settlement. On the other hand, Thomas Jefferys' 1750 printed map of Halifax Harbour (Map 2:5, p. 26) is based on the work of surveyor Moses Harris, who seems to have spent no more than a few months in Halifax and may have been as young as 18 years. Taken from Harris' not very accurate original (Map 7:7, p. 113), by the time the map had been through the hands of the compiler and engraver, it is perhaps not surprising that the result is full of distortions.

Provided that we keep in mind the circumstances of their making, maps can serve either as a valuable adjunct or as a starting point for research into local and provincial history and historical geography. Many early maps bring together and present in a clear, visual form a variety of facts that may be less apparent from a verbal description. A map may confirm or clarify at a glance information gleaned from other documents; it may also suggest lines of inquiry not yet explored. Maps can serve as useful guides in archaeological exploration, and help in historical reconstruction.

Whether they initiate or supplement research, maps form an important part of the documentation both of Nova Scotia's impact on Europeans and of the European response to the challenge of the New World. Even the comparatively primitive maps of the earliest days have something to tell us, though they may be harder to interpret than the more sophisticated surveys of the end of the period. It is hoped that the illustrations presented here will encourage readers to look for further examples in their own areas of interest.

References

Chapter 1
Prologue: First Impressions

1   See W.F. Ganong, *Crucial Maps in the Early Cartography and Place-nomenclature of the Atlantic Coast of Canada* (Toronto, 1964) for a detailed examination of this period of mapping.
2   Ganong, *Crucial Maps*, p. 8.
3   See Gastaldi's *Tierra Nueva*, reproduced by Ganong, *Crucial Maps*, p. 126.
4   Ganong, *Crucial Maps*, pp. 111–112.
5   For a more recent discussion of the history of the name Acadia, see Alan Rayburn, "Acadia: the Origin of the Name and its Geographic and Historical Utilization," *The Canadian Cartographer*, 10, 1 (1973) pp. 26–43.
6   For a more legible version of this map see Ganong's tracing, *Crucial Maps*, Fig. 122.

Chapter 2:
The Maps and the Mapmakers

1   See C.E. Heidenreich, *Explorations and Mapping of Samuel de Champlain, 1603–1632, Cartographica* Monograph No. 17 (Toronto, 1976), pp. 42 ff.
2   H.P. Biggar, ed. *The Works of Samuel de Champlain*, 6 vols. (Toronto: Champlain Society, 1922–36, facs. ed. 1971), Vol. 6, pp. 253–346.
3   *The Voyages*, Book 1, 1604–1607, ed. and transl. W.F. Ganong, forms part of Vol. 1 of the Champlain Society edition: pp. 191–469. Hereafter referred to as Champlain, *Voyages*, 1.
4   Champlain, *Voyages*, 1, notes to plate LXIV, facing p. 237.
5   N. Denys, *The Description and Natural History of the Coasts of North America (Acadia)*. Transl. and ed. W.F. Ganong (Toronto, 1908) p. 405.
6   W.I. Morse, *Acadiensia Nova* (London, 1935) Vol. 2, pp,. 55–56.

7   Cartographic Journal of the Coast of Acadia, 1684. Acadian Manuscript Collection, Special Collections, Dalhousie University Library. See J. Dawson, "Voyage from LaHave: a Journal of Summer, 1684" in *Nova Scotia Historial Review* (hereafter *N.S.H.R.*) Vol. 4, no. 1 (1984), pp. 85–98.
8   National Archives of Canada (hereafter NAC) AC, C11D, Vol. 3 (1696) f. 227.
9   Public Archives of Nova Scotia (hereafter P.A.N.S.) RG1, Vol. 2, doc. 28.
10 Morse, *Acadiensia Nova*, Vol. 2, p. 46.
11 A.J.E. Lunn, "Denys de Bonaventure, Simon-Pierre", *Dictionary of Canadian Biography* (Toronto, 1966–) (hereafter *D.C.B.*), Vol. 2, p. 177.
12 B. Pothier, "Gannes de Falaise (Falaize), Louis de" *D.C.B.*, Vol. 2, p. 236.
13 B. Pothier, "Goutin, Mathieu de", *D.C.B.*, Vol. 2, p. 257.
14 J. Dawson, LaHave in the Late Seventeenth Century: A Comparison of the 1686 and 1693 Census Returns", *N.S.H.R.* Vol. 2, no. 2 (1982), p. 86.
15 J. Grégoire, "Etudes sur les familles de Labat et Labatt, leurs origines françaises," *Mémoires de la Société Généalogique Canadienne-Française*, Vol. 20, no. 2 (1969), p. 85.
16 P. Beaudry, "Guyon, Louise", *D.C.B.*, Vol. 3, p. 681.
17 J.S. Pritchard, "French Charting of the East Coast of Canada" in D. Howse, ed., *Five Hundred Years of Nautical Science, 100–1900* (Greenwich, 1981), pp. 121–125.
18 Harris and his work are discussed in more detail in Chapter 7.
19 Notice drawn to my attention by Scott Robson.
20 H. Piers, *The Evolution of the Halifax Fortress 1749–1928* Halifax, 1947), p. 2.
21 Cornwallis to the Duke of Bedford, July 23, 1749. T.B. Akins, ed., *Selections from the Public Documents of the Province of Nova Scotia* (Halifax, 1869), p. 563.
22 See D.W. Thomson, *Men and Meridians: The History of Surveying and Mapping in Canada* (Ottawa, 1966), Vol. 1, p. 121 for an account of this remarkable family.

23 Two copies of Durrell's map, one unsigned, are in the Public Record Office, London.
24 H.C. Hart, *History of the County of Guysborough* (Bellville, 1975).
25 For a commentary on DesBarres' work, and an index to his oddly-named charts, see W.K. Morrison, "The 'Modern' Mapping of Nova Scotia", *The Map Collector*, no. 18, (March 1982), pp. 31–33.
26 DesBarres returned to England in 1773 to supervise the publication of his atlas, so information recorded is from before that date. See L.K. Kernaghan, "'A most eccentric genius': The Private Life of J.F.W. DesBarres", *N.S.H.R.* Vol. 5, No. 2 (1985), p. 46.
27 M.G. Smith, *The King's Yard: An Illustrated History of the Halifax Dockyard* (Halifax, 1985), p. 5.
28 Smith, *The King's Yard*, p. 6.
29 Smith, *The King's Yard*, p. 7.
30 Piers, *The Halifax Fortress*, p. 7.
31 Piers, *The Halifax Fortress*, p. 9.
32 I.W. Wilson, *A Geography and History of the County of Digby, Nova Scotia* (Halifax, 1900) p. 48.
33 Wilson, *County of Digby*, p. 49.

Chapter 3:
Fishing: The Ports and the Banks

1   Originally published in 1672. Transl. and ed. William F. Ganong (Toronto, 1908), See ch. 1, note 4. Hereafter Denys, *Description*.
2   Denys, *Description*, pp. 258 ff.
3   Denys, *Description*, pp. 269 ff.
4   Denys, *Description*, pp. 341 ff.
5   Marc Lescarbot, *History of New France*. Transl. and ed. W.L. Grant (Toronto, 1907–14), vol. 2, p. 362.
6   Denys, *Description*, pp. 305–307; 310–314.
7   Denys, *Description*, pp. 324–326.
8   Denys, *Description*, p. 166.
9   Southack to Doucet, Boston, 9 Jan. 1717/18. (PRO, CO 217/2, fols 188–9) Quoted by D.B. Flemming, *The Canso Islands, an Eighteenth Century Fishing Station*. (Ottawa, 1977) p. 12.

10 Flemming, *The Canso Islands*, p. 27.

11 Armstrong to Lords of Trade, Annapolis Royal, no date. (PANS, RG1, vol. 18, no. 2) Quoted by Flemming, *The Canso Islands*, p. 11.

12 Southack to Doucet, 9 Jan. 1717/18.

13 Quoted by H.A. Innis, *Select Documents in Canadian Economic History, 1497–1783.* (Toronto, 1929), p. 153.

14 Quoted by Innis, *Select Documents*, p. 64.

15 J. Green (unsigned). *Explanation for the New Map of Nova Scotia. . .* (London, 1755) p. 5.

16 Unsigned; Versailles, 25 Feb. 1715. Original quoted by Innis, *Select Documents*, pp. 74–75.

Chapter 4:
Farming and Food Production:
The Acadians and their Successors

1 Denys, *Description*, p. 318.

2 Champlain, *Voyages*, 1, p. 368.

3 Champlain, *Voyages*, 1, p. 390.

4 Morse, *Acadiensia Nova*, Vol. 2, p. 8.

5 A.H. Clark, *Acadia: The Geography of Early Nova Scotia to 1760* (Madison, 1968) pp. 163–166.

6 Clark, *Acadia*, pp. 166–175.

7 Quoted by Clark, *Acadia*, p. 340.

8 Clark, *Acadia*, p. 297.

9 Clark, *Acadia*, p. 292.

10 Innis, *Select Documents*, p. 237.

11 Innis, *Select Documents*, p. 188.

12 Innis, *Select Documents*, pp. 194–5.

13 Clark, *Acadia*, p. 334.

14 Morse, *Acadiensia Nova*, Vol. 1, p. 104.

15 Census of 1686. P.A.N.S., RG1 Vol. 2, doc. 28.

16 Morse, *Acadiensia Nova*, Vol. 1, p. 182.

17 Clark, *Acadia*, p. 236.

18 W.P. Bell, *The "Foreign Protestants" and the Settlement of Nova Scotia. . .*(Toronto, 1961), p. 403.

19 Innis, *Select Documents*, p. 190.

20 Bell, *The Foreign Protestants*, pp. 486 ff.

21 See Petition from M. McCleod, 17 Nov. 1761, P.A.N.S. RG1, Vol. 204, p. 23.

22 See map in Clark, *Acadia*, p. 353.

23 Bell, *The Foreign Protestants*, p. 429.

24 M.B. DesBrisay, *History of the County of Lunenburg*, 2nd ed. (Toronto, 1895), p. 35.

25 Clark, *Acadia*, p. 283.

26 Clark, *Acadia*, p. 284.

27 Clark, *Acadia*, p. 284.

28 Clark, *Acadia*, p. 298.

Chapter 5:
Minerals, Wood and Water;
Industrial Beginnings

1 Innis, *Select Documents*, p. 212.

2 Innis, *Select Documents*, p. 237.

3 Clark, *Acadia*, p. 328.

4 Denys, *Description*, p. 182.

5 Clark, *Acadia*, p. 327.

6 Clark, *Acadia*, p. 286.

7 Innis, *Select Documents*, p. 213.

8 Clark, *Acadia*, p. 281.

9 Clark, *Acadia*, p. 290–291.

Chapter 6
Forts and Harbours: Military and Naval Strength

1 Champlain, *Voyages*, 1, facing p. 273.

2 W.I. Morse, *Acadiensia Nova*, Vol. 1, pp. 216–217.

3 C.P. Stacey, "Phips, Sir William," *D.C.B.*, Vol. 1, p. 544 quotes Phips' journal for 22 May 1690.

4 Parks Canada, *Fort Beauséjour, National Historic Park* (Ottawa, n.d.) p. [7].

5 Parks Canada, *Fort Beauséjour*, p. 5.

6 Piers, *The Halifax Fortress*, pp. 2–3.

7 Akins, *Selections from the Public Documents*, pp. 565, 575. Drawn to my attention by Scott Robson.

8 Piers, pp. 4–7.

9 Boscawen to Cleveland, Nov. 15, 1755. National Archives of Canada, Cartographic and Architectural Archives Division, Catalogue.

10 Piers, p. 8.

11 The "23" on the Grand Parade is an error. The "Presbyterian Church", 23 on the key, stood southeast of the Parade.

12 Such as St. George's Tavern, top centre.

13 Piers, pp. 13–14.

14 Piers (p. 21) gives an account of the buildings seen on this map.

15 Piers, p. 9.

16 Piers, p. 18.

17 Piers, p. 19.

18 Piers, p. 8.

19 Piers, p. 15–16.

20 Piers, p. 17.

21 Piers, p. 9.

22 Piers, p. 16.

23 Piers, p. 19–20.

24 For details, see Piers, pp. 22 ff.

25 F.K.J. Thorpe, *Remparts lointains: la politique française des travaux publiques à Terre-Neuve et à l'Ile Royale, 1695–1758* (Ottawa, 1980) p. 12.

26 J.S. McLennan, *Louisbourg from its Foundations to its Fall, 1713–1758* (London, 1918) pp. 2–4.

27 McLennan, *Louisbourg*, pp. 157–158.

28 Thorpe, *Remparts lointains*, p. 12. Unless otherwise stated, the dates of construction in this section are based on Thorpe's Chronology.

29 McLennan, *Louisbourg*, p. 85. Thorpe considers that the work was still incomplete in 1738.

30 Richard Gridley. "A Plan of the City and Fortifications of Louisbourg. . .1745" P.A.C.: "Lithographed to accompany the Report on Canadian Archives for 1886, by Douglas Brymner, Archivist."

Chapter 7
Habitation and Settlement: Community Growth

1 Denys, *Description*, p. 142.

2 Champlain, *Voyages*, 1, note to Plate LXV, facing p. 237.

3 Champlain, *Voyages*, 1, p. 237.

4 Champlain, *Voyages*, 1, p. 237.

5 Champlain, *Voyages*, 1, note to Plate LXVI, facing p. 251.

6   Lescarbot, *History of New France*, 2, p. 230.

7   Lescarbot, *History of New France*, 2, p. 311.

8   Lescarbot, *History of New France*, 2, p. 311.

9   Champlain, *Voyages*, 1, p. 368.

10   Champlain, *Voyages*, 1, facing p. 373.

11   Champlain, *Voyages*, 1, p. 371.

12   Champlain, *Voyages*, 1, p. 372, n. 1.

13   Clark, *Acadia*, pp. 232–233.

14   Champlain, *Voyages*, 1, p. 439.

15   Champlain, *Voyages*, 1, p. 441.

16   Champlain, *Voyages*, 1, note to Plate LXVII, facing p. 259.

17   Lescarbot, *History of New France*, 2, p. 318.

18   Champlain, *Voyages*, 1, note to Plate LXVII, facing p. 218.

19   Lescarbot, *History of New France*, 2, p. 321.

20   Champlain, *Voyages*, 1, p. 368.

21   P.A.N.S. RG1, Vol. 2, Doc. 28, Demeulles 1686.

22   France. Archives des Colonies. Série C11D, Vol. 2, ff. 33–33v.

23   "A Plan of settlements proposed to be made at Annapolis, Menis and Schegnecto", Public Record Office, London.

24   A Moses Harris is identified in the *Dictionary of National Biography* (London, 1891–) Vol. 25, p. 20, as an "entomologist and engraver." He may also have been the "surveyor" who made maps of Halifax and drew some of its plants, but his identification is not clearly established.

25   T.B. Akins, ed., *Selections from the Public Documents of the Province of Nova Scotia* (Halifax, 1869) p. 513.

26   Walter K. Morrison, "The Porcupine Map", A.C.M.L. Bulletin no. 62, March 1987, p. 18.

27   Akins, *Selections*, p. 563, Cornwallis to the Duke of Bedford.

28   See Morrison, "The Porcupine Map", for a full discussion of the illustrations.

29   *Gentleman's Magazine,* London, Feb. 1750, p. 72. See M. Sparling, *Great Expectations: The European Vision in Nova Scotia 1749–1848* (Halifax, 1980) p. 12.

30   *Gentleman's Magazine,* Oct. 1749, p. 440.

31   Sparling, *Great Expectations*, p. 10.

32   *Brephos parthenia* (Linn.) E.B. Ford, *Moths,* 2nd ed., (London, 1967) p. 143.

33   *Parasemia parthenos* (Harr.) D.C. Ferguson, *The Lepidoptera of Nova Scotia* (Halifax, 1955) Pt. 1, p. 216.

34   Morrison, "The Porcupine Map", p. 18.

35   For a full account of this operation, see W.P. Bell, *The Foreign Protestants* (Toronto, 1961) which has been of great value in interpreting this map.

36   T.H. Lodge's notes on the Morris family: P.A.N.S., Family Papers, Lodge collection, MG1, Vol. 544.

37   Identified by Bell, pp. 246–7, n.

38   Bell, p. 475–6.

39   Bell, p. 479.

40   A number of maps record this survey. This present map may be Morris' work, or a copy.

41   Clark, *Acadia*, p. 344, gives a brief account of the attempted settlement of Lawrencetown.

42   Clark, *Acadia*, pp. 224–255.

43   Clark, *Acadia*, p. 344.

44   M. Robertson, *King's Bounty; A History of Early Shelburne, Nova Scotia. . .*(Halifax, 1983) pp. 8ff., gives an account of the early settlers.

45   Robertson reproduces this plan: p. 46.

46   Robertson, *King's Bounty*, p. 42

47   Robertson reproduces this map: p. 54.

48   Robertson, *King's Bounty*, p. 67.

49   Robertson, *King's Bounty*, p. 32.

50   Robertson, *King's Bounty*, p. 135.

51   Innis, *Select Documents*, p. 185.

52   J.M. Cameron, *Pictou County's History* (Pictou, 1972) p. 5.

53   Cameron, *Pictou County*, p. 7.

54   Cameron, *Pictou County*, p. 5.

55   Cameron, *Pictou County*, p. 11.

56   Cameron, *Pictou County*, p. 11.

57   H. Baglole, "Patterson, Walter", *D.C.B.* Vol. 4, pp. 605–611.

58   Cameron, *Pictou County*, p. 9.

59   D.B. Foster, "DesBarres the Town Planner", *N.S.H.R.*, Vol. 5, no. 2, Dec 1985, p. [29]–37, gives account of DesBarres' designs for Sydney.

60   Foster, p. 33.

61   L.K. Kernaghan, "'A most eccentric genius': The Private Life of J.F.W. Desbarres", *N.S.H.R.* Vol. 5, no. 2, Dec. 1985, p. 52.

62   R.J. Morgan, "Cuyler, Abraham", *D.C.B.* Vol. 5, p. 222.

63   R.J. Morgan, "Mathews, David", *D.C.B.* Vol. 4, p. 522.

64   Kernaghan, "'A most eccentric genius'", p. 48.

65   Kernaghan, p. 50.

Chapter 8
Inland Transportation: Roads, Rivers and Portages

1   Clark, *Acadia*, p. 253.

2   Clark, *Acadia*, p. 356.

3   Demeulles' account of this journey is printed in Morse, *Acadiensia Nova*, Vol. 1, pp. [91]–126.

4   Clark, *Acadia*, pp.. 252–253 describes the cattle export routes. This map confirms the use of the Pisiquid–Chebucto route for this purpose.

5   Innis, *Select Documents*, pp. 214–215.

6   C. Morris, "A Plan of Lotts surveyed & laid out between the Township of Amhurst and Londonderry. . ." 1774. Public Record Office.

7   Denys, Description, p. 179.

Bibliography

Cartobibliography

The maps are arranged in chronological order.

1:1 Giocomo Gastaldi. *La Nuova Francia*. [1556] State 1. In Giovanni Battista Ramusio, *Delle Navigationi e Viaggi*. Venice, 1556. National Archives of Canada (hereafter NAC), Cartographic and Architectural Division (hereafter CAAD), NMC 52408.

1:2 Bolognino Zaltieri. *Il Disegno del discoperto della nova Franza*. . . . [Venice] 1566. NAC, CAAD, NMC 6577

1:3 Guillaume Levasseur. [Atlantic Ocean] "Fait a dieppe Par Guillaume Levasseur le 12 de juillet." 1601. Bibliothèque Nationale, Département de Cartes et Plans, Paris (hereafter BN), SHM Archives No 5, Catalogue Fonçin No. 138.

7:4 Marc Lescarbot. *Figure du Port Royal en la Nouvelle France*. 1609. State 1. In Lescarbot, *Histoire de la Nouvelle France*, Paris, 1609. NAC, CAAD, NMC 97968.

Cover map — *Figure de la Terre-Neuve, Grande Riviere de Canada, et Côtes de l'Ocean en la Nouvelle France*. 1609. In Lescarbot, *Histoire de la Nouvelle France*, Paris, 1609. NAC, CAAD, NMC 97952.

2:1 Samuel de Champlain. *Port de la heve*. 1613. In Champlain, *Les Voyages*, Paris, 1613. National Library of Canada (hereafter NLC) NL 15315.

5:1 — *Port des mines*. In Champlain, *Les Voyages*, Paris, 1613. NL C130981.

7:2 — *port au mouton*. 1613. In Champlain, *Les Voyages*, Paris, 1613. NLC NL 12423.

7:1 — *Por du Rossÿnol*. 1613. In Champlain, *Les Voyages*, Paris, 1613. NLC NL 15313.

7:3 — *port Royal*. 1613. In Champlain, *Les Voyages*, Paris, 1613. NLC NL15325.

3:1 Paul Ollivier. [North Atlantic] "Faite, à Grace, Par, Paul, ollivier, année, 1624." 1624. BN, Ge. BB. 246 (1–30, 31) Catalogue Foncin, No. 132 bis.

2:2 Lalanne. "Carte des Costes de l'acadie 1684. BN, SH, 132:4:13.

3:1 Jean-Baptiste-Louis Franquelin. "Carte ge'ralle du voyage que Monsr. De Meulles. . .a fait. . .comprenant toutes les terres de l'Acadie. . . ." 1686. BN, SH, 132:2:2.

3:2 [Jean-Baptiste-Louis Franquelin] "Baye de Che'dabouctou avec les passages de Canceaux et de Fronsac . . . ." 1686. BN, SH, 133:2:2D.

2:4a — "Le Port de La Haive. . . ." 1686. BN, SH, 133:6:1D.

7:5 — "Plan Tres Exact Du Terrain ou sont sçìtüees les maisons du Port Royal. . . ." 1686. BN, SH, 133:8:2.

6:1 Pasquine. "Plan pour la reparation du fort du port Royal en l'Acadie." 1688. Archives Nationales, Dépôt des Archives d'Outre-mer, Aix-en-Provence (hereafter AN), DFC, Am. Sept. 50c.

6:2 Vincent de Saccardy. "Port Royal d'Acadie." 1690. AN, DFC, Am. Sept. 54c.

2:3 Jean Delabat. "Plan de la Banlieue du Fort Royal de l'Acadie." 1708. Newberry Library, Chicago, Cartes Marines, 90 Ayer MS map #78.

6:3 Anonymous. "Plan of Annapolis Royal Ffort the principall place of Strenght (sic) in Nova Scotia. . . ." 1710. Public Record Office, London (hereafter PRO), MPG 274.

2:4b Anonymous. "Cate (sic) du Port de La Heve." 1715. BN, SH, 133:6:3.

3:5 [Jacques L'hermitte] "Veue du Port de Louis-bourg dans l'Isle Royale." 1717. Newberry Library, Chicago (Cartes Marines, 95) Ayer MS map #118.

3:3 Cyprian Southack. *The Harbour and Islands of Canso*. . . . Boston: Dewing, 1720. PRO, C.O. 700 Nova Scotia no. 6.

6:8 Jean François de Verville. "Plan de Louisbourg Avec les Ouvrages Faits et les Projets." 1720. Archives Nationales, Paris, Colonies C11B 39 p. 120. (Transcript NAC, CAAD, NMC 487.)

4:1 Anonymous. "A Draught of Part of the British River and of the Fort of Annapolis Royal. . . ." 1725. British Library (hereafter BL), King's Maps, CXIX, 80.

3:4 Cyprian Southack. South Western Nova Scotia n.d. In *The New England Coasting Pilot*, London, Boston, 1729–34? Bodleian Library, Oxford, F6:2a:1. Sheet 7.

5:2 George Mitchell and Edward Amhurst. "A Map of a Peninsula Situate in yᵉ Bay of Fundy. . . ." 1735. PRO, MPG 972.

8:2 Anonymous. [Nova Scotia] (ms) n.d. [1738–48] National Maritime Museum, Greenwich, DUF 246: 4/8 NS.

2:4c [Dépôt de la Marine]. "Carte du Port de la Heve" n.d. [*ca*. 1740?] BN, SH, 133:6:4.

2:4d [Dépôt de la Marine]. "Carte du Port de la Heve, a la Coste de La Cadie." n.d. *ca*. 1740?] BN, SH, 133:6:2.

4:5 Boucher. "Plan de L'Entree et d'une Partie de la Petite Brasdor." 1742. BN, SH, 124:4:3.

2:4e Jacques-Nicolas Bellin. "Plan du Port de La Heve." n.d. [*ca*. 1744?] BN, SH, 133:6:5.

2:4 — *Plan du port de la Haive Situé à la Côte d'Accadie*. In F.-X. Charlevoix, *Histoire et Description général de la Nouvelle France*, Paris, 1744. NAC, CAAD, NMC 15074.

6:9 Verrier, fils. "Plan de Louisbourg dans l'Isle Royale." 1745. AN, DFC, 219A.

7:6 Charles Morris. "A Draught of the Upper Part of the Bay of Fundy. . . ." 1748. PRO, C.O. 700 Nova Scotia no. 17. (Transcript NAC, CAAD, NMC 218.)

6:5 John Brewse. "Project for Fortifying the Town of Hallifax in Nova Scotia." 1749. PRO, MPG 803.

7:7 Moses Harris. "A Plan of Chebucto Harbour with the Town of Halifax." 1749. BL, King's Maps CXIX, 73.

7:8 [Moses Harris]. *A Plan of the Harbour of Chebucto and Town of Halifax*. In *Gentleman's Magazine*, London: E. Cave, July, 1750. NSM coll. 80.11, copy neg. N-14, 638.

2:5 Thomas Jefferys. [Halifax and environs]. State 2. London: T. Jefferys, 1750. NAC, CAAD, NMC 1012.

5:3 Anonymous. "a Chart of the South East Part of l'Isle Royal, or Cape Bretton. . . ." n.d. [*ca*. 1750]. BL, King's Maps CXIX, 86.

5:6 [Louis Franquet]. "Plan de l'Isle Royalle." 1751. BN GEF 5909. (Transcript NAC, CAAD, NMC 148.)

6:4 — "Carte Particuliére de l'Ishme de l'Acadie ou sont situés les Forts de Beauseiour Gaspareaux et Fort Laurent Anglois." 1751. AN, DFC 42C.

7:9 William Shephard Morris. "A True Copy of a Plan of the town of Lunenburg Garden Lotts and Commons adjoining. . . ." [original *ca*. 1753; copy pre-1853.] Nova Scotia Provincial Crown Record Centre. Lunenburg Co. Portfolio, plan no. 29.

4:2 John Hamilton. "A General Plan of Annapolis Royal. . . ." 1753. NAC, CAAD, NMC 18312.

7:10 [Charles Morris]. "Plan of a Tract of Land granted by the Honourable Charles Lawrence Esquire. . .now to be called Lawrence Town. . . ." 1754. PRO, C.O. 700 Nova Scotia no. 27.

6:6 [Philippe de Rigaud de Vaudreuil]. ["A Plan of Halifax with a scheme of attacking it from Canaday. . . ."] 1755. PRO, S.P. 42/38 p. 224.

(Frontispiece) Charles Morris. "A Chart of the Peninsula of Nova Scotia. . . ." 1755. BL, King's Maps CXIX, 57.

4:3 Anonymous. [Fort Cumberland and Fort Lawrence]. (ms) (*ca.* 1755). NMC 18151.

8:3 Anonymous. "A Chart of thee Coast of Nova Scotia from Port Maltois to Lawrence Town." [1755] Ministry of Defence, Hydrographic Dept., Taunton. Admiralty B5812 Shelf Ff.

2:6 Charles Morris. "A Draught of the Harbour of Canso with the Islands Circumjacent. . . ." 1764. PRO, C.O. 700 Nova Scotia no. 39.

5:4 Samuel Holland and John George Goldfrap. "A plan of the Sea Coast from Gage Point to Cumberland Cape. . . with the coal mines in that extent." 1767. William Clements Library, University of Michigan.

2:7 Joseph Frederick Wallert DesBarres. *The Harbour of Halifax.* London, 1777. NAC, CAAD, NMC 18358.

7:11 Anonymous. [Port Roseway. 1783] (ms). PRO 30/55199. Document 10423.

6:7 Charles Blaskowitz and Henry Castleman. "A Plan of a Peninsula upon which the Town of Halifax is Situated . . . ." 1784. PRO, C.O. 700 Nova Scotia no. 49B.

7:12 Charles Morris II. "A Plan of Surveys made & Lands Granted to Disbanded Soldiers Sailors and others, Loyal Emigrants at Merigumish & Pictou. . . ." 1785. PRO, C.O. 700 Nova Scotia no. 54.

4:4 [Charles Morris II]. "A plan of part of the County of Lunenburg including the townships of Chester and New Dublin. . . ." [1784] PRO, C.O. 700 Nova Scotia no. 51.

2:8 Charles Morris II. "Plan of the Township of Digby with the Alotments of Land Laid out and granted Loyal Emigrants and disbanded Corps. . . ." 1786. PRO, C.O. 700 Nova Scotia no. 17.

8:4 Anonymous. "Post Houses" [1787]. PRO, Colonial Correspondence N.S. Vol 18 p. 5.

7:13 [Patrick R. Nugent]. "Plan of Sydney River" with an inset plan of the town. 1788. PRO MPG 195.

5:6 Anonymous. "Chart of Spanish or Sydney River in the Island of Cape Breton With a View to represent the Situation and Circumstances of the Coal Ground." 1794. PRO, Colonial Correspondence C.B. Vol. 69 p. 547.

5:5 Jas. Miller. "Cape Breton." 1794. PRO, Colonial Correspondence C.B. Vol. 70 p. 479.

8:5 Anonymous. "Plan of the Proposed Inland Navigation from the Harbour of Halifax by the Dartmouth and Shubenacadie Lakes & Shubenacadie River to where it meets the tide setting up the River from the Bay of Minas." 1797. PRO, MFQ 128.

Modern Maps and Atlases

Bujak, J.P. and Donahoe, H.V., Jr. *Geological Highway Map of Nova Scotia.* Atlantic Geoscience Society. Special Publication No. 1, 1980.

[Canada 1:250,000] Surveys and Mapping Branch, Department of Energy, Mines and Resources. 1:250,000. Ottawa: Dept. of EMR. 11D: Halifax. Ed. 2, 1972.

— *11E: Truro.* 1955.

— *11F and 11C: Canso.* Ed. 2, 1976.

— *11K: Sydney.* Ed. 2, 1972.

— *20O and 20P: Shelburne.* Ed. 2, 1976.

— *21A: Annapolis Royal.* Ed. 2, 1977.

— *21H: Amherst.* Ed. 3, 1972.

[Canada 1:500,000] Surveys and Mapping Branch, Department of Energy, Mines and Resources. 1:50,000. Ottawa: Dept. of EMR.

— *11D/11: West Chezzetcook.* Ed. 4, 1982.

— *11D/12: Halifax.* Ed. 5, 1980.

— *11D/13: Mount Uniacke.* Ed. 5, 1982.

— *11G/13: Louisbourg.* Ed. 4, 1975.

— *11J4: Glace Bay.* Ed. 4, 1979.

— *11K1: Sydney.* Ed. 4, 1980.

— *21/A1: LaHave Islands.* Ed. 2, 1976.

— *21/A8: Lunenburg.* Ed. 2, 1977.

— *21/A12: Digby.* Ed. 3, 1976.

Nova Scotia Department of Development. *Nova Scotia Resource Atlas.* Halifax, 1986.

Nova Scotia Department of Lands and Forests, Department of Government Services. *A Map of the Province of Nova Scotia.* Rev. ed. with index of geographic names. Halifax, 1985.

[Nova Scotia Department of Transportation] *Official Nova Scotia Highways Map, 1985.* (Cover Title: Nova Scotia: there's so much to sea). Halifax, 1985.

Books and Articles

Akins, Thomas B., ed. *Selections from the Public Documents of the Province of Nova Scotia.* Halifax: Charles Annand, 1869.

Bell, Winthrop P. *The 'Foreign Protestants' and the Settlement of Nova Scotia: The History of a Piece of Arrested British Colonial Policy in the Eighteenth Century.* Toronto: University of Toronto Press, 1961.

Biggar, H.P., ed. *The Works of Samuel de Champlain.* 6 vols. Toronto: Champlain Society, 1922–36. Reprinted Toronto, University of Toronto Press, 1971.

Blakemore, M.J. and J.B. Harley. *Concepts in the History of Cartography: A Review and Perspective (Cartographica* Monograph 26). Toronto: University of Toronto Press, 1980.

Cameron, James M. *Pictou County's History.* New Glasgow: Pictou Historical Society, 1972.

Clark, Andrew Hill. *Acadia: The Geography of Early Nova Scotia to 1760.* Madison: The University of Wisconsin Press, 1968.

Dawson, Joan. "LaHave in the Late Seventeenth Century: A Comparison of the 1686 and 1693 Census Returns" in *Nova Scotia Historical Review,* II, 2 (1982), pp. 83–95.

Dawson, Joan. "Voyage from LaHave: A Journal of Summer, 1684" in *Nova Scotia Historical Review,* IV, 1 (1984) pp. 85–98.

Denys, Nicolas. *The Description and Natural History of the Coasts of North America (Acadia).* Trans. and ed. William F. Ganong. Toronto: The Champlain Society, 1908.

Desbrisay, Mather Byles. *The History of the County of Lunenburg.* 2nd ed. Toronto: William Briggs, 1895.

Deveau, J. Alphonse. *Two Beginnings: A Brief Acadian History.* Yarmouth: Lescarbot, 1980.

Dictionary of Canadian Biography. Gen. ed. George W. Brown *et al.* Toronto: University of Toronto Press, 1966–.

Dictionary of National Biography. Vol. XXV, ed. Leslie Stephen and Sidney Lee. London: Smith, Elder & Co., 1891.

Dièreville, Sieur de. *Relation of the Voyage to Port Royal in Acadia or New France.* Trans. Alice Webster, ed. with notes J.C. Webster. Toronto: Champlain Society, 1933.

Ferguson, D.C. *The Lepidoptera of Nova Scotia.* Pt. 1 (Macro-lepidoptera). Halifax: Nova Scotia Museum of Science, 1955.

Fergusson, Charles Bruce. *Place-Names and Places of Nova Scotia.* Halifax: Public Archives of Nova Scotia, 1967.

Flemming, David B. *The Canso Islands: An Eighteenth Century Fishing Station.* (Parks Canada MS Report) Ottawa: Parks Canada, 1977.

Ford, E.B. *Moths.* 2nd ed. London: Collins, 1967.

Foster, D.B. "DesBarres the Town Planner" in *Nova Scotia Historical Review,* V, 2 (1985) pp. 29–37.

Ganong, W.F. *Crucial Maps in the Early Cartography and Place-nomenclature of the Atlantic Coast of Canada.* Toronto: University of Toronto Press, 1964.

The Gentleman's Magazine, or, Monthly Intelligencer. ed. Edward Cave. London. Oct., Dec., 1749; Feb., 1750.

[Green, John]. *Explanation for the New Map of Nova Scotia and Cape Britain. . . .* London: Thomas Jefferys, 1755.

Grégoire, Jeanne, "Étude sur les familles de Labat et Labatt, leurs origines françaises" in *Mémoires de la Société Généalogique Canadienne-Française,* XX, 2, 1969. pp. 80–95.

Haliburton, Thomas C. *An Historical and Statistical History of Nova Scotia.* Halifax: J. Howe, 1892. Reprinted with preface by C. Bruce Fergusson. Belleville: Mika, 1973.

Hart, Harriet Cunningham. *History of the County of Guysborough.* Akins Historical Prize Essay, 1877. Belleville: Mika, 1975.

Heidenreich, Conrad E. *Explorations and Mapping of Samuel de Champlain 1603–1632. (Cartographica* Monograph 17). Toronto: B.V. Gutsell, 1976.

Heidenreich, Conrad E. and Edward H. Dahl. *The French Mapping of North America 1600–1760.* Originally published as "The French Mapping of North America in the Seventeenth Century" in *The Map Collector,* 13, Dec. 1980, pp. 2–11, and "The French Mapping of North America 1700–1760" in *The Map Collector,* 19, June 1982, pp. 2–7. Reprinted with additions. Berkhampstead: The Map Collector, 1982.

Innis, Harold Adams, ed. *Select Documents in Canadian Economic History 1794–1783.* Toronto: University of Toronto Press, 1929.

Kernaghan, Lois K. "'A most eccentric genius': The Private Life of J.F.W. DesBarres" in *Nova Scotia Historical Review,* V, 2, 1985, pp. 41–59.

Lescarbot, Marc. *History of New France.* Trans. and ed. W.L. Grant. Toronto: Champlain Society, 1907–14.

McLennan, J.S. *Louisbourg, from its Foundation to its Fall, 1713–1758.* London: McMillan, 1918.

Morrison, Walter K. "The 'Modern' Mapping of Nova Scotia" in *The Map Collector,* 18, March 1982, pp. 28–34.

Morrison, Walter K. "The Porcupine Map" in *ACML Bulletin,* 62, March 1987, p. 18.

Morse, William I. *Acadiensia Nova.* 2 vols. London: Quaritch, 1935.

Parks Canada. *Fort Beauséjour: National Historic Park.* Ottawa: Dept. of Indian and Northern Affairs, n.d.

Piers, Harry. *The Evolution of the Halifax Fortress, 1749–1928.* Revised, edited and completed by E.M. Self and P. Blakeley. Halifax: Public Archives of Nova Scotia, 1947.

Pritchard, J.S. "French Charting of the East Coast of Canada" in *Five Hundred Years of Nautical Science, 1400–1900,* ed. D. Howse. Greenwich: National Maritime Museum, 1981, pp. 119–128.

Rayburn, Alan. "Acadia: The Origin of the Name and its Geographic and Historical Utilization" in *The Canadian Cartographer,* X, 1 (1973) pp. 26–43.

Robertson, Barbara R. *Sawpower: Making Lumber in the Sawmills of Nova Scotia.* Halifax: Nimbus, Nova Scotia Museum, 1986.

Robertson, Marion. *King's Bounty: A History of Early Shelburne, Nova Scotia, Founded in 1783 by the Port Roseway Associates Loyalists of the American Revolution.* Halifax: Nova Scotia Museum, 1983.

Smith, Marion Gurney. *The King's Yard: An Illustrated History of the Halifax Dockyard.* Halifax: Nimbus, 1985.

Sparling, Mary C. *Great Expectations: The European Vision in Nova Scotia 1749–1848.* Halifax: Mount Saint Vincent University, 1980.

Thomson, Don W. *Men and Meridians,* Vol. I. Ottawa: Queen's Printer, 1966.

Thorpe, F.K.J. *Remparts lointains: la politique française des travaux publiques à Terre-Neuve et à l'Ile Royale, 1695–1758*. Ottawa: Université d'Ottawa, 1980.

Webster, J.C. *Acadia at the End of the Seventeenth Century: Letters, Journals and Memoires of Joseph Robineau de Villebon, Commandant in Acadia, 1690–1700 and Other Contemporary Documents*. Saint John: The New Brunswick Museum, 1934, reprinted 1979.

Wilson, Isaiah W. *A Geography and History of the County of Digby, Nova Scotia*. Halifax: I.W. Wilson, 1900.

Manuscript Material

Dalhousie University, Halifax. Acadian Manuscript Collection, Special Collections. Cartographic Journal of the Coast of Acadia, 1684.

National Archives of Canada. AC C11D vol. 2, ff. 33–33v. DeMeulles 1686. (Original in Archives Nationales, Paris).

National Archives of Canada. AC C11D vol. 3 ff. 227–230. Remarques faites par le Sr. de Lalanne. . .(1684). (Original in Archives Nationales, Paris).

Public Archives of Nova Scotia. MG1 vol. 544. Family Papers, Lodge Collection. T.H. Lodge. Notes on the Morris Family.

Public Archives of Nova Scotia. RG1 vol. 2, doc. 28. Recensement fait par Monsieur De Meulles Intendant. . .1686. (Original in Archives Nationales, Paris).

Public Archives of Nova Scotia. RG1 vol. 204 p. 23. Petition from M. McCleod.

Index